B. Traven:
A Vision
of Mexico

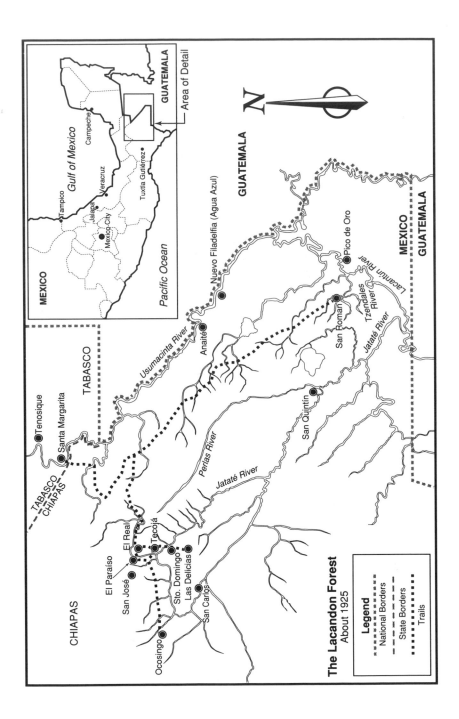

The Lacandon Forest
About 1925

Legend
National Borders
State Borders
Trails

B. Traven:
A Vision
of Mexico

Heidi Zogbaum

A Scholarly Resources Inc. Imprint
Wilmington, Delaware

The paper used in this publication meets the minimum requirements of the American National Standard for permanence of
paper for printed library materials, Z39.48, 1984.

© 1992 by Scholarly Resources Inc.
All rights reserved
First published 1992
Printed and bound in the United States of America

Scholarly Resources Inc.
104 Greenhill Avenue
Wilmington, DE 19805-1897

Library of Congress Cataloging-in-Publication Data

Zogbaum, Heidi, 1944–
    B. Traven : a vision of Mexico / Heidi Zogbaum.
        p.   cm. — (Latin American silhouettes)
    Includes bibliographical references and index.
    ISBN 0-8420-2392-5
        1. Traven, B.—Contemporary Mexico. 2. Authors,
Mexican—20th century—Biography. 3. Mexico—History—
20th century. I. Title. II. Series.
PT3919.T7Z97 1992
813'.52—dc20
[B]   91-28235
                                                             CIP

Contents

Acknowledgments

My thanks go first and foremost to Barry Carr, who kept my nose to the grindstone, criticizing, correcting, revising, and in the process shaping this study to what it is now. The debt I have to Barry for the time and care he invested in this work I can never repay.

I am also indebted to Steve Niblo for his valuable criticism, and to Alan Knight for his generosity and his unstinting support. I owe gratitude to Michael Burton, who taught me the intricacies of a computer, but most of all I must thank my husband, who had to live with Traven for five years and only rarely complained.

La Trobe University, Melbourne, gave me a generous travel grant for a trip to Mexico in 1984, and the staff of La Trobe University Library was reliably helpful and resourceful. In Mexico, I enjoyed the hospitality and friendship of many who generously shared their knowledge with me; chief among them are Traven's widow Rosa Elena Luján, Pedro Vega, José Toriello Bulnes, Juan Celorio Hernández, Professor Moscoso Pastrana, and many others who helped make my stay in Mexico a memorable one. The chapter on Traven in Tampico was only possible through the help of Lief Adleson and Juany Olivo Maldonado. I only hope that I have met their expectations.

I would like to add that all translations in this study, those of Traven's first editions as well as of German- and Spanish-language secondary sources, are mine.

Foreword

When German actor, journalist, and anarchist Ret Marut (later B. Traven) landed in the Mexican port city of Tampico in 1924, he was only one of hundreds of left-wing writers and intellectuals attracted to Mexico by the epic qualities of its revolution. Most of the visitors were from the United States—journalists such as John Reed and John Kenneth Turner, antiwar socialists, Wobblies, and pacifists (pejoratively labeled "slackers" after they fled across the Rio Grande) including Carleton Beals and the Communist novelist Mike Gold, and pioneer Communist organizers such as Bertram Wolfe. The history of some of these sojourns has been recounted in several recent studies.[1] The experiences of the smaller number of European radical visitors to Mexico, however, are much less well known.

Of the many individuals who came searching for evidence of worker and peasant power and a new communitarian and anticapitalist culture, B. Traven was among the most enthusiastic. Between 1925 and 1940 his literary output was immense. His novels and short stories offered first German-speaking and then English-speaking readers a stream of proletarian adventure narratives. Moreover, although Traven was interested in universal questions of personal and group liberation, he was careful to locate all of these writings within the boundaries of revolutionary Mexico.

The popularity of his works notwithstanding, when I began using Traven's *March to the Montería* in a course on agrarian societies and peasant movements, I was astonished at how many gaps there were in the literature dealing with its author. To be sure, there was no shortage of books and newspaper articles on the man himself. Most of them, however, were either literary

[1] Some notable examples include Paco Ignacio Taibo, *Bajando la Frontera* (Mexico City: Ediciones LEEGA/JUCAR, 1985); and John A. Britton, *Carleton Beals: A Radical Journalist in Latin America* (Albuquerque: University of New Mexico Press, 1987).

studies or part of the huge industry generated by those seeking after Traven's identity. At various times, Traven had been identified as the illegitimate son of the German Kaiser Wilhelm II, a U.S. Wobbly, and even Mexican President Adolfo López Mateos.

Given that, with the exception of *Das Totenschiff*, virtually all of Traven's writings were set in Mexico, I have always been surprised that no one has systematically explored the German writer's relationship to the great revolutionary episodes with which he was so obsessed. Traven was not only interested in the drama of individual struggles by the poor and oppressed against injustice but also was clearly fascinated by many particular developments in the 1920s and 1930s, including agrarian reform and the history of struggles waged by workers and indigenous peoples. Finally, it was the survival well into the revolutionary era of coerced and semicoerced labor systems in the southern states of Chiapas and Tabasco that most fired his imagination.

Heidi Zogbaum's exploration of these concerns makes her study unique. Rather than mining Traven's books to find scraps of information to enliven a biography of the German writer, Zogbaum sets out to show how Mexican history, especially the country's politics from 1924 to 1940, shaped the direction and tenor of Traven's writings.

The book breaks new ground in three areas. Zogbaum is the first writer to demonstrate how the radical shifts in Traven's stand toward the Mexican Revolution are related to the particular circumstances he encountered in his journeys. In his earliest novels (*Der Wobbly*, and especially the still-untranslated documentary study *Land des Frühlings*), Traven developed an uncritical position toward the Mexican governments of the 1920s. *Land des Frühlings* is in fact a piece of barely disguised propaganda presenting President Plutarco Elías Calles (1924–1928) as the architect of working-class power and the progenitor of a new nationalist synthesis of indigenous and proletarian culture. Traven did not take long to realize how mistaken his conclusions were, and he refused to allow *Land des Frühlings* to be republished or translated into Spanish or English.

Traven did not pluck his vision of proletarian Mexico out of thin air; a series of real-world experiences gave plausibility to his arguments. Traven's first experience of Mexico was in the oil town of Tampico at a time when anarcho-syndicalist-influenced unions exercised enormous authority for a brief period. Even though the authority of the state and private capital was quickly reestablished, Traven allowed his experiences in "red" Tampico to color his overall judgment of Mexican politics, persisting until at earliest 1929.

By the time Traven embarked on his Jungle Novels, his writing had undergone a major shift in emphasis. He now began a lengthy exploration and condemnation of the cruelty and injustices toward workers in the timber industry of Chiapas and Tabasco. In part, as Zogbaum notes, Traven's crusade against ethnic and class oppression in southern Mexico was a reaction to the slowdown in social and economic reform during the governments of the *maximato* (1929–1934), when a series of puppet presidents held back land reform and launched a major persecution of agrarian and labor militants.

Traven's writing and his understanding of Mexico during this period also were shaped by local circumstances. The Epic Revolution (1910–1920) and its emancipatory action took a long time to reach the Mexican south. The power of the logging companies, coffee *finqueros*, and the agrarian elite in Tabasco and Chiapas was maintained nearly intact through the teens and 1920s. This circumstance helps to explain why Traven made contradictory statements about the period in which his Jungle Novels were set. At times, Traven seemed—and claimed—to be describing social conditions as they had existed during the pre-revolutionary dictatorship of Porfirio Díaz (1876–1910); on other occasions, he appeared to be signaling his preoccupation with the uneven balance sheet of the revolution itself. Traven was undoubtedly cautious about the political implications of his writings, for he feared being expelled from Mexico as a pernicious foreigner. But Zogbaum more than any other Traven scholar has realized that Traven's caution and natural prudence were over-shadowed by his discovery of a region in which the economic and social structures of the Porfirian order had barely been modified.

Even the massive shift to the left in Mexican politics during the presidency of Lázaro Cárdenas (1934–1940) failed to modify the pessimism of Traven's writings, which became more and more pronounced in his last important novel, *Ein General kommt aus dem Dschungel*. The Cárdenas *sexenio* witnessed worker and peasant mobilizations on a scale never before seen in Latin America, and the Cardenista years saw a massive expansion of agrarian reform, the expropriation of foreign-owned petroleum companies, and experiments with worker and peasant self-management. Although Traven sympathized with the radicalism and anti-imperialism of this period, his old anarchist beliefs were offended by Cárdenas's policies, which greatly strengthened the authority of the state and its control over mass organizations of workers and peasants.

Traven's writings are not informed solely by responses to the Mexican political scene. A second achievement of Zogbaum's book is to show how developments in Germany crucially shaped Traven's reading of Mexican events. Traven wrote not only to entertain (something he did brilliantly) but also to further the political education of his first and most important audience—the German-speaking, working-class readers of Central Europe. His writing is full of pointed remarks about the origins and impact of the Hitler dictatorship. Moreover, even when Traven was ostensibly writing about the oppressed population of southern Mexico, he was addressing key events in the recent memory of the German working class. Traven's attacks on the iron discipline exercised by political parties, for example, were also attacks on the German Socialist party, whose role in the suppression of the 1919 Bavarian Revolution Traven could never forgive.

Finally, Zogbaum's study makes an important contribution to our knowledge of the economic history of Chiapas and Tabasco and, in particular, the history of the labor process in the *monterías* (mahogany-logging camps) of those states. Although most of the *monterías* had ceased operation by the time he began his crusade, Traven was an indefatigable researcher and a good listener, and there was certainly no shortage of tales to be heard and transcribed; storytelling was ever present in the world of timber fellers and itinerant peddlers. Traven was in fact the first person to research the mahogany-logging trade and to publish his findings, albeit in fictional form.

While Traven's Jungle Novels have sometimes been recommended as good sources for understanding the social and economic history of the Mexican south, *B. Traven: A Vision of Mexico* is the first study that systematically examines the accuracy of Traven's claim that his writings were "documentaries" based on real events and processes. Zogbaum's work builds on the limited secondary research published on the *montería* system, but she also has scoured Traven's archives (in particular his notebooks) and, like Traven, has drawn on the stories and memories of local informants. For someone whose future-centered vision was impatient with history as a field of study, Traven's descriptions of labor and social conditions were remarkably accurate and nuanced. Nowhere is this seen more clearly than in the care Traven took to distinguish between other labor systems and *montería* management styles.

In an era in which the victory of the free market is being triumphantly proclaimed everywhere, Traven's anticapitalism and anti-imperialism may no longer be fashionable. But the contemporary struggle for democracy in Mexico, where governments enthusiastically embrace economic liberalization while denying autonomy to peasant and worker organizations, lends pertinence to some of Traven's warnings. His advice to workers to "put a good fire under [your trade union] officials' bums each year" must raise a wry smile among Mexican workers today as they fight against both corrupt labor bosses and huge declines in the standard of living.

Barry Carr
La Trobe University

Introduction

Between 1925 and 1940, B. Traven published in rapid succession nine novels, one substantial travelogue, and two volumes of short stories.[1] Each of his books was a success: the works were translated into fifteen languages and sold millions of copies, and their author came to be ranked close to Jack London in popularity. What captivated Traven's audience was his understanding of the plight of the exploited, particularly the Indians of Mexico, and his deep commitment to improving their lot. "Traven wrote ... with the blood of his heart," one admirer has rightly noted.[2]

The source of Traven's popularity, however, is strangely at odds with what we know about the person. A telling incident of his egocentricity occurred during the making of the now-classic film *The Treasure of the Sierra Madre* (starring Humphrey Bogart as Fred C. Dobbs), which was fashioned after one of Traven's best-known novels. By the end of World War II, the internationally famous author had created an effective smoke screen around his identity. All that was known was that he lived in Mexico and that he was accessible only through post office boxes. All other biographical data—his real name, nationality, country, and place of birth—had been supplied by Traven under pressure and were contradictory or blatantly false.

In 1947, when the young Hollywood director, John Huston, attempted to approach the mysterious author in Mexico City to discuss the *Sierra Madre* project, Traven believed that Huston was overstepping the boundaries. He let Huston stew in his hotel room for an entire week. Then, one morning at dawn a gray-haired man of small stature came to Huston's room, identifying himself as "Hal Croves," Traven's translator and agent. He handed over a letter signed by B. Traven that recommended Croves to Huston as a connoisseur of Traven's work. Huston engaged Croves to act as a consultant for his film for $150 per week—this despite the fact that the director found the screenplay, which Traven had produced from his novel, so wanting that he rewrote it himself.

Shooting of the movie began in Tampico and then moved to a small village near San Juan Purua in Michoacán. Here, Croves joined the crew and soon annoyed everybody on the set by giving instructions to all and sundry. Although his advice was rarely sought, he always stressed that he was interpreting the special wishes of Traven. Walter Huston, John Huston's father, had been assigned the role of the gold prospector Howard. Croves thought Walter Huston too young for the part. Needless to say, Croves's advice was not heeded.

Croves was particularly adamant about cameras: He did not wish to be photographed. However, someone on the set managed to take a picture of the cranky consultant dressed in a white singlet and a Panama hat. A few years later, Bogart was shown a photograph of B. Traven after the author's identity had been discovered by a Mexican journalist. Bogart immediately recognized the querulous man who had called himself Hal Croves on the set of *The Treasure of the Sierra Madre.*

The film became an instant success and catapulted John Huston to fame. The U.S. press, especially *Time* and *Life*, reported extensively on the making of the movie and the strange role of the "Consultant Hal Croves," who was suspected from the first of being Traven himself. The publicity only fed Traven's mystery mongering and concentrated the public's view on the question of the famous author's identity. This issue became so crucial that for decades Traven's work was used only as a pool from which biographical information could be drawn. The author, always well informed about the progress of the Traven legend, fed the rumors until it was whispered that he was the illegitimate offspring of the last German Kaiser.

When John Huston came to Mexico in 1947 to gather important information from the author of *Der Schatz der Sierra Madre,* he was confronted with the Croves farce. In 1979, Huston, a connoisseur of Traven's work and an admirer of his compassion and political convictions, refused to cooperate in a BBC program about Traven's identity. He hinted that he was far from convinced that the Hal Croves who had tried to play hide-and-seek with him could possibly be the same man who wrote *Der Schatz der Sierra Madre* and other outstanding novels about Mexico.[3]

It is indeed difficult to believe that such a cantankerous and self-important person as Croves had the emotional depth to produce such a gem as *Die Brücke im Dschungel* or such a tale of wisdom as *Der Schatz der Sierra Madre*. If there is a Traven mystery, Huston put his finger on it: What happened to the man who began his literary career by stirring millions with his tales of exploitation and cruelty only to end it playing games with people who had a genuine interest and admiration for his work? The challenge, then, is to find a way of discovering how to reconcile the conflicting pictures we have of the committed and compassionate novelist and the cantankerous consultant Hal Croves.

One shortcoming of existing Traven studies is that they tend to use the available biographical information about Traven that emerged after World War II and superimpose it on the biographical vacuum of Traven's life in the 1920s and 1930s, without considering that the circumstances of his life and the political climate in which he wrote had changed beyond recognition. We know very little about Traven's life during the years of his literary activity, beginning with his landing at the Mexican Gulf port of Tampico in 1924 and concluding with the publication in 1940 of his last significant novel, *Ein General kommt aus dem Dschungel*. But we do have detailed knowledge of the political circumstances that his novels addressed. This aspect of his life has not been explored in any depth, yet it exposes more about him than he ever wished to see revealed.

Traven dedicated his last two decades to creating a long and ingenious array of impediments and false leads for prospective biographers. He loathed biographers and "literary critics, that class of people for whom a special hell would have to be created."[4] His considered opinion was that "the biography of any creative person is quite irrelevant. If that man is not recognizable in his work, then he is either worthless as a human being or his work is worthless."[5] Consequently, biographers trying to explore the years of Traven's literary career raked his books searching for information about the author's life. Thus, the adventures of Gerard Gale, Traven's narrator in his first novels, were taken to be autobiographical. This approach was facilitated by Traven's own efforts to present himself as a swaggering hero and swashbuckler. When editing his work for republication, he removed all passages that could shed light on his early years in Mexico but left undisturbed those passages that marked him as astute, courageous, adventurous, and at times even heroic. The resulting "biographies" were truly impressive; they portrayed

Traven's life as "the stuff legends are made of."[6] Using his writings as a source of autobiographical information means walking into a trap of Traven's making.

Other writers have tried to find an answer in Traven's own archives to the question: Who was B. Traven? But a closer look at the archives, which fill several rooms of his house in Mexico City, reveals that Traven, in his frenzied attempts to brush over his tracks, also edited his private papers in such a way that many remain incomprehensible unless given a historical context that it seems only Traven could provide. At the time, it must have looked like an effective way of keeping out prying eyes without having to destroy his entire archives. Working from Traven's personal records, without recourse to sources that allow us to place his papers in the context from which they sprang, poses the danger of using his records according to Traven's directions. The latest study to emerge from the most thorough investigation yet made of his archives has concluded that Traven was really the illegitimate son of a German baroness,[7] rather than the son of working-class parents from a small town in present-day Poland.[8]

Other solutions to the problem of researching Traven's life and literary career in Mexico have been proposed. Developing the theory of the *Erlebnisträger* (literally "the carrier of the experience"), Michael Baumann has argued, for example, that Traven could not possibly have experienced all the adventures retold in his first novels in the short period he had spent in Mexico before their publication in Germany. Baumann concludes that a more experienced resident of Mexico, perhaps a Wobbly, a member of the outlawed Industrial Workers of the World, told Traven stories of his adventures, which Traven then incorporated into his novels.[9] Such a theory could explain the discrepancy between the personalities of the author B. Traven and Hal Croves, but, in light of the evidence of the present study, the *Erlebnisträger* theory proves too farfetched.

Breakthroughs in Traven studies have always come from sources other than his own statements. It took until 1963 to refute, by demonstrating that his mother tongue was German, Traven's claim to be an American by birth.[10] The most important finding yet came from the German scholar, Rolf Recknagel, who demonstrated through textual analysis that Ret Marut, editor of the small anarchist newspaper *Der Ziegelbrenner*, and Traven were one and the same person.[11] With the help of documents made available under the U.S. Freedom of Information Act and the examination of birth registers, Will Wyatt, a BBC journalist, traced Traven's origin to a small town in Poland. But without Traven's confirmation, no theory of his origin can ever be proven beyond a doubt.

Although access to a writer must come first and foremost through his work, nothing Traven could tinker with can be regarded as beyond suspicion. Only the first German editions of his books, published at a time when his obsession with the secret of his identity had not yet taken complete hold of his mind, can be regarded as credible sources. Furthermore, not all of his work has been translated. His 1928 travelogue *Land des Frühlings*, and *Die Troza*, published in 1936, both of which contain crucial information about the writer, are inaccessible to non-German-speaking scholars.

Another body of Traven literature attempts to locate the author either among so-called proletarian writers of the 1930s,[12] or among contemporary literati who traveled in and commented on Mexico, such as Graham Greene and D. H. Lawrence.[13] Traven, however, sits uneasily with each group. His particular political ideology is almost impossible to categorize adequately in terms of his fellow proletarian writers. Comparing him to Greene or Lawrence is misleading as well, because both Englishmen responded with loathing and near hysterical fear to what they witnessed in Mexico and neither made a serious attempt to understand his experiences,[14] whereas Traven's work documents continually his struggle to come to terms with what he saw and experienced there.

Although Traven's writing career only spanned fifteen years, there is a profound change midway in his outlook on Mexico that defies easy definition. His work falls into two distinct parts. He first produced a series of books exalting the progress ushered in by the Mexican Revolution of 1910 and then wrote the so-called Jungle Cycle, in which he publicized the labor exploitation that continued to dominate southern Mexico long after radical change had transformed most other areas of the country. This shift in Traven's outlook has never been explored; in fact, it has not even been acknowledged. But it is this abrupt change that gives us the clue to the riddle of B. Traven and Hal Croves.

Traven always insisted that his novels are not fiction but are documentaries, and that is how he wished them to be read. Few contemporary readers, however, regarded his Mexican settings as more than an exotic framework. Only those familiar with the political events in Mexico during the 1920s and 1930s can see that Traven for once spoke the truth: The course of Mexican politics from the early years of the presidency of Plutarco Elías Calles (1924–1928) until the rise of Lázaro Cárdenas in 1934 is faithfully reflected. Therefore, Traven must be seen as a political writer, passionately involved in the politics of his adopted homeland. Only then can we identify what fascinated, and ultimately disillusioned, him to the point where, disgusted by the political developments in Mexico, he began to devote himself to feeding the rumors of the Traven legend.

By examining the events of the period of reconstruction initiated by President Calles in 1924 and Traven's reaction to them, we are able to gauge his changing emotions and growing understanding of Mexico. By tracing the interaction between Traven and Mexican politics, the deeply compassionate and committed author of the Traven novels comes to life. We are able to understand what moved Traven so profoundly that he not only adopted Mexico as his new homeland but also became a propagandist for its social and political innovations. Furthermore, we can see what so disappointed and embittered the author that he decided to abandon his literary career. But most important the existing historical record of the years between 1924 and 1940 has been beyond Traven's tinkering.

The historical approach, in conjunction with the scant biographical information we possess of Traven's early years in Mexico, enables us to reconstruct the settings in which he lived and which influenced his work. Such an approach allows us to see a man shaped by the world around him and not as a disembodied enigma whose actions bear no relation to his times. The historical approach also can throw light on the vexed question of why the author of the Jungle Novels insisted on the secret of his identity, although it cannot clarify why as an old man Traven elevated it to his raison d'être at a time when the circumstances that had prompted his caution had all but disappeared.

More importantly, however, the historical approach allows a reevaluation of Traven's work as a valuable and highly individual contribution to Mexican historiography. His writings reflect faithfully the struggle of a European anarchist confronted with the Mexican Revolution and struggling to understand the profound upheaval in his new homeland. When the forty-two-year-old Traven arrived in Tampico in mid-1924, he was destined to begin a new and exciting life. He was probably close to destitute; perhaps the only luggage he brought with him was his political ideology, as it was shaped during his Munich days as the editor of *Der Ziegelbrenner*.

Although Traven held on to his political beliefs throughout his life, they were neither monolithic nor inflexible. The beliefs of Ret Marut can be traced throughout Traven's work; however, the ideological stance of the German anarchist underwent a significant transformation upon his arrival in Mexico. Traven is usually classified as an anarcho-syndicalist. In contrast, Marut was an individual anarchist following the ideas of German philosopher Max Stirner (1806–1856), who taught that the individual, in order to realize his inherent powers, must shed all vestiges and limitations of his life to emerge as what he termed *der Einzige* (the unique one). The first step in this direction, wrote Stirner, is to shed one's identity by adopting a new set of antecedents. Marut, following faithfully Stirner's guidelines, discarded the name he had inherited from his parents and henceforward used the unusual name of Ret Marut. His second metamorphosis would take place in Tampico when Marut became the writer B. Traven.

Marut, a recognized authority on Stirner in Munich, argued in his articles for the overthrow of the state and capitalism with the aim of securing personal freedom. He rejected party programs, political organizations, bureaucracies, and any form of state power, and he described his own political position as being so far to the left of the radical German parties that "his breath could not even touch them."[15] Marut rejected group action in any form; he believed, instead, in individual action. He argued that "the masses do not think because they cannot think. Therefore, we have [political] parties, programs, and leaders. But you, the individual, can think."[16]

Marut's political opportunity came with the Munich Soviet Republic of 1919.[17] Being a strident critic of the military, of World War I, and of the bourgeois German press and its role during the war, he became the press censor of the *München-Augsburger Abendzeitung*, a Munich evening newspaper. The journalists, playwrights, and writers—among them Ernst Toller, Erich Mühsam, and Gustav Landauer—who had formed the republic proved incapable of resolving the chaos in the state of Bavaria. The newly elected Socialist government in Berlin sent troops to Munich to put a quick and bloody end to the Soviet Republic.

Ret Marut was one of the few survivors. Without a passport or identity papers, with a death sentence pending, he spent another two years in Germany, living underground, changing addresses frequently, and publishing *Der Ziegelbrenner* at irregular intervals.

A firm believer in the ability of the individual to regulate his own affairs without interference from governments or any other authority, Marut tried to incite passive labor resistance against the Versailles treaty. "I let my hands rest in my lap and the government needs twenty officials to force me to do something I do not want to do." He admonished workers not to buy food or clothes because this would help the bourgeois class to regain power. German workers, eager to return to normality, refused to listen to Marut's impassioned pleas. His remonstrations that "no God will help you, no program, no party, no leader, no vote, no crowd, no unity" failed to strike a chord with the German working class accustomed for decades to strict party discipline.[18]

Although Marut's attempt to preach Stirner's idea of passive resistance was a resounding failure, as B. Traven he revived the idea many years later in the guise of his Mexican character Celso Flores, one of the heroes of the Jungle Cycle. In *Die Troza*, Celso is forcibly held in a mahogany logging camp. After his first whipping, he simply puts down his axe and lies on the ground. He understands his monetary value to the logging operation and knows that nobody will dare whip him after such defiance.[19]

When Marut left Germany to look for greener pastures, he had a clear idea of what he wanted to do after his journalistic career there had come to an end.

> I have tried as a ballad singer, but because of all the overwhelming pressure of lies, darkness, and printer's ink [this career] ends with a scream from a wounded heart. I relinquished it after a few months. But, my dear, to place a grain in the soil and to watch it sprout, grow, and ripen and then to feed it to a hen and her chicks is more than writing ten Ziegelbrenner. Give me humans who can understand that. But because I cannot live and sow among people who cannot understand this, I suffer from my contemporaries and can only escape from them in one leap. I do not want to sacrifice my life to my contemporaries because I value my life more highly than to simply deliver it up to my contemporaries. . . . Therefore, I only have printer's ink at the moment.[20]

Printer's ink, however, was to remain his livelihood for the next fifteen years. This was not because he was unable to find any other way of making a living. Upon his arrival at Tampico, he unexpectedly found himself in a situation that looked as if the revival of the ideals of Marut was possible. Traven's writing career became a quest to realize the old ideals in a new world.

1

Traven in Tampico: A Revolutionary in Paradise

Traven and the Industrial Workers of the World

Erich Mühsam was the last associate of the Munich days to hear from Marut. In December 1922 he received a postcard from Rotterdam indicating that "in a few hours' time I shall board a ship to take me across the Atlantic. With this I shall have ceased to exist."[1] Marut's intention, it seems, was to go to Canada. He was forced, however, to return to England where he was promptly jailed as an illegal immigrant.

Marut remained in Brixton prison from 30 November 1923 until 15 February 1924. Even before he was jailed he had attracted the attention of agents of the U.S. embassy, who reported that Marut had contacted Charles Thomas Hallinan, "a journalist of the Left who had formerly been Secretary of the American Union Against Militarism." This contact was made possible by a letter of introduction from the Bureau of Labor in New York.[2] Hallinan did help Marut, and this relationship brought Marut to the attention of the American embassy, which reported in November 1923 that the journalist had been a contact for "a mysterious German named Ret Marut."

The U.S. agents were interested in Marut because he "came under the notice of the Police as being intimately mixed up with Communist circles here." In fact, neither Marut nor Hallinan ever had Communist leanings or connections.[3] It appears that the agents grouped all individuals and organizations opposed to the economic and social status quo under the all-embracing epithet "Communist." Among this loose array of organizations was the Industrial Workers of the World (IWW)—or whatever was left of it, since the union had been outlawed in the United States in 1917. It is possible that Marut was put in contact with an IWW member in London, perhaps by Hallinan, although there is no evidence for this. It is known, however, that the IWW was active in Tampico in 1924 and that Marut, who had never taken any interest in Mexico or its revolution and who had firmly set his mind on migration to the United States, suddenly, without apparent reason, turned up in Tampico.

There is some circumstantial evidence to support the possibility of a Marut/IWW connection. In December 1924, Traven, then a resident of Columbus in the state of Tamaulipas, wrote a letter in very poor Spanish to a postal official in González requesting him to return three packages of clothing and personal effects to the sender in the United States because "Sr. D. B. Traven en Columbus/Tamps" could not afford the customs duty of 127.50 pesos.[4] González, a small township some two hours' drive north of Tampico, is situated on the railway line connecting Tampico with the U.S. border. Just outside González the IWW had set up a small farm, presumably a way station for Wobblies en route to Tampico. In November 1923 the U.S. consul, Mr. Stewart, reported that members of the IWW from Los Angeles had "formed a colony" at González, with a man called Young in charge and another by the name of Phillips living with him. The nickname of the colony, Stewart informed the State Department, was 5L, meaning five liquors, because of the high alcohol consumption there.[5] After watching the farm for a time, Stewart further reported that some sixty members of the IWW, some of them leading figures in the movement, had taken up occasional residence.

The three packages of clothing mailed to Traven at González most probably were dispatched by Irene Mermet, an associate from his Munich days then living permanently in the United States. Traven must have given her González as a first-contact address, although he apparently never lived there for any length of time. Mermet later sent her personal letters to Traven in care of the Southern Hotel in Tampico. His business correspondence went to a post office box at Columbus.

The Marut/IWW connection is plausible for another reason as well. When the Büchergilde Gutenberg, Traven's first German publisher, produced an expanded version of the story "Die Baumwollpflücker" in book form, Traven renamed it *Der Wobbly*. The novel portrays the life of an itinerant worker, Gerard Gale, who tramps through Mexico from one menial job to the next, making a precarious living by his wits and on the breadline. The tenor of *Der Wobbly* indicates that Traven was impressed by

Wobblies, not so much because of their political radicalism but because of their working-class ingenuity and sheer toughness.

The IWW was very different from the labor organizations that Marut/Traven had known in Germany, where he had experienced a trade union movement that had become "respectable" after voting for the war grants in 1914. After the defeat of 1918 the German Socialist party agreed to pick up the pieces, always proud to be of service. The German working class and its unions consistently supported the Socialist coalition government in its efforts to rebuild Germany's international reputation and to suppress the more radical elements of their own membership. Marut had only scorn for such a government and little regard for the blindness and deafness of its supporters. The IWW presented a radically different picture, one that was bound to please him.

The IWW represented all those elements that were excluded from its competitor, the American Federation of Labor: women, blacks, immigrants, children, unskilled laborers, and seasonal and itinerant workers. In 1912 the IWW introduced sabotage as a regular weapon in its fight to improve wages and labor conditions. The three pillars of its ideology were the class struggle leading to revolution, antimilitarism, and antipatriotism. Marut's point of contact with the IWW was most probably its antimilitarism, which had expressed itself in a firm stance against U.S. intervention in the European war.

Like Marut, the IWW preached that the Great War was fought "to give the capitalists a greater slice of heaven."[6] Why, it asked, should workers fight for a country that was not their own? Although the organization failed to adopt an unambiguous anticonscription policy, many thousands of Wobblies and Socialists avoided the draft by leaving the country and heading south to neutral Mexico. Many came in search of work, especially in the oil industry of Tampico, where the highest wages were being paid and where there were preferential wages for white workers. Political radicals in particular flocked to Mexico because President Venustiano Carranza (1917–1920) had promised to leave them alone as long as they did not break any laws. Among those coming to Mexico were Irwin Granich (later called Mike Gold, a leading U.S. Communist) and the Socialist journalist Carleton Beals. Many Wobblies became active in the incipient Mexican labor movement.

The legal arguments leading to the outlawing of the IWW in 1917 were weakly formulated at best. Although the Wobblies' activities were labeled treason by the press, Marut was only too familiar with the role of the bourgeois press in suppressing voices opposed to the German war effort. Furthermore, the IWW was the first union organization encountered by Marut that did not bow to government pressure to become "respectable" but risked annihilation rather than betray its principles and membership. Thus, many features of the IWW would strike a sympathetic chord in the revolutionary Marut.

Although the systematic repression of the organization in 1918 and 1919 caused the IWW great damage, it was not destroyed and remained active well after the end of the Great War, especially in Mexico, where it became affiliated in 1921 with the newly founded Confederación General de Trabajadores (General Confederacy of Workers), the CGT. When Traven arrived in the summer of 1924, the IWW was still active in Tampico.

Tampico in 1924

Traven probably knew next to nothing about Mexico upon his arrival. Unlike other German anarchists, Marut had never taken any interest in the revolutionary developments of this faraway country. The argument that probably swayed him to try Mexico was its reputation for slack immigration controls. Calling himself B. Traven Torsvan, Marut arrived in Tampico in June or July 1924, when Mexico had just begun to rebuild its economy and to reshape its social organization after a decade of bloody civil war and revolution. In 1917, Mexico had emerged from the turmoil with the most advanced labor legislation of its time and a young and strong labor movement. Land reform was being introduced to satisfy the peasants' call for redistribution. To a new arrival with Traven's sympathies, it must have looked as if social justice had come to rule in Mexico.

Traven arrived at a crucial juncture in the country's history. In July 1924, General Plutarco Elías Calles, minister of the interior in the government of Alvaro Obregón (1920–1924), won the presidential election. Calles had risen to the highest office in a unique and spectacular manner. His candidacy was supported by the largest group within the labor movement, the Confederación Regional Obrera Mexicana (Regional Confederation of Mexican Labor), the CROM. Indeed, the CROM regarded Calles as its candidate, and he devoted considerable energy toward supporting the organization.[7] Calles's candidacy and its labor backing appeared to give the CROM extraordinary political clout.

One of the greatest concentrations in Mexico of industrial labor existed in and around Tampico, and this city gave Traven his first impression of the country. Tampico was one of the main ports along the Gulf coast, situated in the extreme south of the state of Tamaulipas, just across the border from Veracruz, and was the center of Mexico's important oil industry. Enormous profits were made by the foreign companies that owned the refining facilities and held the drilling concessions. The British El Aguila Petroleum Company, the largest operator, extracted 165 million pesos from Mexico during the height of the revolution between 1911 and 1920.

Tampico was a boomtown with, at the time of the 1921 census, a population of some one hundred thousand, most of whom were recent arrivals attracted by the "black gold." Mingled with the masses of Mexican workers were several thousand unemployed Americans and Europeans, competing with the Mexicans for the well-paying jobs. Seven major oil refineries offered employment and good wages; the majority of Tampico's population made a living either directly from these refineries or from service industries related to the oil business. In addition, the port of Tampico employed about one thousand men on the docks and another six hundred in the local electric company.[8]

Tampico's predominantly working-class population set it off from most other Mexican cities. A visitor, such as the newly arrived B. Traven Torsvan, would have a misleading impression if he assumed that it was representative of the whole nation, for Mexico was still essentially a rural country and industry played a minor role in the national economy. Tampico's labor activity also distinguished it from other Mexican cities. At the time of Traven's arrival, Tampico was shaken by a number of decisive strikes, all of which ended in resounding victory for the workers. On 1 September 1923 the employees of the city's electric company had laid down their tools in response to a 15 percent reduction in wages introduced by the American manager of the company, Harvey S. Leach, who had made himself unpopular in 1921 by threatening to close down a vital water pump when he and the city council could not agree on payment.

The official reaction to the strike was surprising. Instead of suppressing the strike, Tampico's chief of police offered the strikers protection, and the state's governor, César López de Lara, supported them with a personal check of 5,000 pesos and acted as negotiator between management and the workers. When Leach began to undermine the agreement thus reached, the governor suggested a second strike. The military commander of Tampico, General Lorenzo Muñoz, not only protected the striking workers but also allowed them to operate the tramways and the electric plant. In this way wages could be paid and the electric company, one of the city's major employers, was virtually taken over by the workers. Leach, after thirty-three years' residence in the country, was expelled from Mexico under the provisions of the Noxious Foreigners Act of the 1917 Constitution. His plant and properties were transferred to government hands.

A report on these events sent to the State Department in Washington pointed out that

> the attitude of the Government from the beginning of this dispute has demonstrated that it is determined to support and implant syndicalism in Mexico and intends to implement the extreme provisions of the labor section of the Constitution. The strike is not of the usual character of industrial strikes, for no question of wages is involved. It is rather an attempt to strengthen syndicalism and to apply radical socialist doctrines.[9]

Furthermore, the report charged, while the minister for industry pressed for a settlement of the strike, President Obregón and President-elect Calles both tacitly supported the workers. To all appearances, the strikers had more influential supporters than the city authorities alone.

During the strike, which cut most of the electrical power to the Tampico oil industry, El Aguila Petroleum dismissed workers, since its operations had come to a virtual standstill. In protest, El Aguila workers went on strike in November 1923. In February 1924 this strike was settled in favor of the employees, and the company was compelled to recognize the union and its right to negotiate. Meanwhile, Consul Stewart, keeping a close eye on this threatening situation, reported to Washington that "in this strike the workmen are aware of the fact that they have the support of the authorities, both federal and state, and that these will do nothing to offend them on the eve of the coming election."[10] A unified front against the American oil companies was new both to Tampico and Mexico. As recently as 1921, when the Mexican government had imposed a new tax on oil exports, North American oil companies had simply halted all operations and oil exports. Twenty thousand workers were laid off overnight, and when they became restless the oil companies induced the U.S. government to send warships to Tampico as a "cautionary measure." In 1924 no marines appeared.

During these strikes the workers received substantial moral and material aid from other labor unions. Over one thousand men took turns to stand guard on El Aguila's premises, and over 11,000 pesos were collected by strikers and their helpers. The strikers apprehended disturbers of the peace, expelled corrupt members from their society, collected lost goods, caught thieves, and persecuted murderers.[11] The workers demonstrated that they were capable of administering and regulating their own affairs, and their success generated an atmosphere of optimism and elation throughout Tampico. President-elect Calles even visited the strikers at El Aguila Petroleum.[12] Traven, who soon heard about the strikes, was so fascinated by what he discovered that he decided to give them his own literary treatment. The incident at El Aguila Petroleum also engendered a flurry of strikes in other Tampico oil companies, including the Mexican Gulf Oil Company, where in August 1924 workers staged a walkout similar to that at El Aguila and with comparable results. Traven could very well have witnessed this strike.

H. K. V. Tompkins, general agent for the Mexican Gulf Oil Company, concluded that the American oil firms were caught in the middle of an interunion dispute. Tompkins, Consul Stewart reported, explained that "there are two labor parties in Mexico. The CGT or Reds; [and] the CROM or Yellows, the latter being affiliated with the present government." During the CROM's labor convention at Ciudad Júarez the previous year, "the yellow or conservative element dominated the same; . . . in the recent conflict throughout the Republic [the de la Huerta Rebellion of 1923], except in Tampico, the Reds have lost ground."

Thus, Tompkins was establishing a vital distinction between Tampico and the rest of Mexico, noting that "the Red element is making strenuous efforts to combine all of the unions in this district under one head so as to dominate labor conditions and principally to call strikes on individual concerns and finally, of course, obtain control of the entire situation in this district. The Yellow element has practically lost out in Tampico."[13] Stewart made an important distinction between Tampico and the rest of the country: labor activity in Tampico was dominated by the CGT, whereas the government-backed CROM had difficulties gaining a foothold in the city; the rest of Mexico was dominated by the CROM. The strikes in Tampico had been initiated by the CGT element, but President-elect Calles was backed by the CROM and not by the more radical CGT.

The recently arrived B. Traven Torsvan, however, assumed that the Mexican labor movement was a unified body with an anarcho-syndicalist orientation backing a president of similar outlook. Traven failed to understand the difference between the CGT and the CROM and the competition in which the two labor organizations were engaged. In Tampico he observed the CGT at work and assumed that the "red" union also dominated the rest of Mexico. This would prove to be a primary source of Traven's misinterpretation of Mexican politics as drawn in his travelogue *Land des Frühlings*. Waking up to his misconception would later cause Traven considerable distress.

Mexican working-class traditions were essentially anarchist and radical; the first step toward a national labor organization had been taken in 1912 with the founding of the anarcho-syndicalist *Casa del Obrero Mundial* (House of the worker of the world). Preaching the "separation of organized labor and government as the crucial start to ending 'bourgeois' control of society,"[14] the *Casa* did not survive for long and was destroyed in August 1916 after the Carranza government suppressed a general strike. The anarcho-syndicalist traditions planted by the *Casa* were kept alive, however, and "the majority of the working class kept operating within the ideological framework of anarchist, syndicalist, and libertarian ideas."[15] This was especially true in Tampico, where the *Casa* had been a strong organization with great formative and educational powers over the working class. The creation of the CROM as a government instrument to control the labor movement ran against the strongly anarchist working-class traditions.

The CROM was founded under government auspices in March 1918, and its leader was Luis Napoleón Morones, "a fat, bediamonded labor faker," as Irwin Granich astutely called him.[16] Even Consul Stewart had reservations about the CROM, stating that it was "composed of a group of regular grafters."[17] Indeed, after Morones rose to become minister of labor and industry in the Calles cabinet, his and his associates' capacity for graft and corruption became legendary. The CROM's policy was to operate within the capitalist system. Its close association with the government placed its members in the political arena but did not assign them a role as "leaders in a new social order but rather as guarantors of regimes that set out to reform Mexican society but not to fundamentally change its capitalist character."[18]

The CGT was founded in February 1921 as a challenge to the government's manipulations of the labor movement. Forty-three unions totaling nearly fifty thousand members, including the Communists and the IWW, joined the CGT,[19] and opposition to the government's labor policy flourished, particularly in the most advanced industrial sectors. The powerful oil workers' union; the electricians, who had initiated the strike at the electric company; and the transport workers of Tampico joined the CGT. An American observer in the city wrote that the new union "adopted the stance that the workers themselves can look after their own affairs. That is why this labor organization is the most radical and revolutionary. Loathing every form of political action . . . the CGT rejects intervention by the government or any other power except that of the workers. The CGT believes that the workers can solve their own conflicts through direct workers' representation."[20]

The CGT's first actions were to call a boycott of all political groups, to employ militant direct action, and to call a number of general strikes. The government reacted fiercely to these challenges: CGT leaders were exiled or deported from Mexico, and activities of the workers were suppressed violently and without mercy. Almost from its founding, the CGT and the CROM were at war, the CROM enjoying the advantage of full government backing. The CGT was soon under siege everywhere except in Tampico, where it still dominated the labor scene by controlling the city's most powerful unions. Its primacy there was due to two factors. First, the state of Tamaulipas was rather late in establishing an arbitration and conciliation apparatus through which company pressures and union activities could be regulated. This offered unions a large margin for maneuver that they would not have enjoyed had Tamaulipas possessed more restrictive labor legislation.[21] The second factor was the attitude of Governor Emilio Portes Gil (1925–1928), who not only intensely disliked Morones, the CROM's national leader, but was also intent on building his own power base in the state with the help of local labor and peasant organizations.[22] The governor used the CGT to provide a counterweight to the CROM. However, once Portes Gil left the governorship of Tamaulipas and boards of conciliation and arbitration were established, the CGT was quickly tamed.

For the moment, however, workers' power increased beyond industrial matters. On 2 February 1924, *El Universal* of Mexico City reported that the unions of Tampico had prevented Carlos Pelayo Quintana, the provisional governor of Tamaulipas, from taking office. They had threatened direct action, and workers had menaced Pelayo Quintana and his brother while the two were dining in a restaurant. The following day, *El Universal* reported that Tampico labor leaders had threatened to detain Pelayo Quintana so that he could not take office.[23] Although several union leaders were arrested as a result of this extraordinary incident, the unions on the whole were successful. On 4 February, *El Universal* reported that Pelayo Quintana would not be governor but that a candidate preferred by the unions had been appointed in his place. Traven must have heard about these events because he faithfully reflected in *Der Wobbly* the impression of workers' power that these events had created.

Traven was thus privileged to experience an exceptional period of virtually unfettered union strength in Tampico. Twice within a short time he had been exposed to a labor movement that shared his anarchist ideas as well as proving to be successful on the basis of group action. The evidence suggests that the individualist-anarchist Marut was converted into the anarchosyndicalist Traven through his contact with the IWW and the CGT. Traven could not know at the time how short-lived the labor union strength in Tampico would be. When its decline began to gather momentum in 1926, he left Tampico to travel through the southern state of Chiapas, his illusions intact. This constellation of events occurring in one city was the immediate reason why he received and preserved a wildly unrealistic impression of Mexican politics. In the meantime, however, Traven was happy. Assuming that Tampico was representative of the rest of the country, he concluded that Mexico was the nation for which *Der Ziegelbrenner* had been looking. "All is green," he exulted, "the land of eternal summer. Oh, you beautiful, wonderful, old country, full of legends and songs! Mexico, there is no other like you on earth. I had to sing. . . . I sang from a joyful heart."[24]

Der Wobbly

Immediately after his arrival in Mexico, Traven began to describe in writing his newly adopted homeland. As soon as he had a mailing address, he began to send manuscripts to Germany. By September 1924 a first 105-page version of "Die Baumwollpflücker" was submitted to eleven German newspapers.[25] *Vorwärts*, the influential and widely read popular organ of the German Socialist party, accepted it. The story, for which Traven received 500 marks,[26] was printed in installments between 21 June and 16 July 1925, a major success for an unknown author.

The story of "Die Baumwollpflücker," as it was serialized in *Vorwärts*, describes the adventures in Mexico of an American drifter, Gerard Gale. There was no treatment in this version of the radical labor scene in Tampico. Either it took Traven a while to gain an understanding of what was happening around him, or, more likely, he first wanted to test the German market's acceptance of his descriptions of the labor environment. Traven's narrator Gale simply recounts the adventures and mishaps he experiences in his quest for work in Mexico. He has been attracted to Tamaulipas in the hope of finding work in the oil fields near Tampico, but the only employment he can find is picking cotton. This is the worst-paid and most back-breaking job in the area and, as Gale is told by several American cotton farmers, totally unsuited to a white man.

Through the mediation of one of the cotton farmers, Gale finds temporary work on an oil rig run by Americans. There he is well paid and well fed, his clothes are replaced, and he even wears gloves. But the good life does not last long, and he is soon laid off. One of his fellow cottonpickers finds him a job in a bakery where, in return for fifteen to nineteen hours' work, the men are given food, board, and 1.5 pesos per day. The story breaks off as soon as Gale begins working in the bakery, and the reader is left with the impression that Gale's life will continue in the same pattern without material improvement.

Much of the attraction of the story lies in its setting. Traven described graphically the shabbiness of the world in which Gale moves: the deserted railway station in the middle of the tropical bush, the desolation of the small village consisting of two wooden shacks and twelve Indian mud huts, the "accommodation" of the cottonpickers, their water supply a drum of infested water left over from the last rainy season. In Traven's depiction the cottonpickers sleep on the ground, with visits from tropical insects, snakes, and scorpions. During the day, they work under the blazing sun for wages of 6 centavos per kilo of picked cotton when the cheapest meal in a Chinese restaurant costs 50 centavos. The down-and-out Gale and his ragged colleagues fit well into this world, and "Die Baumwollpflücker" poignantly describes the labor exploitation to which they are exposed daily.

The dry humor of Gale's tone, his remorseless eye for the frailties of his fellow proletarians, and the palpable way in which the author described the shabby world of itinerant workers in Mexico caught the attention of Ernst Preczang, editor of the Berlin-based Büchergilde Gutenberg, the book club of the German printers' guild. He wrote to the post office box at Columbus and, after establishing contact with Traven, suggested that he expand the story so that it could be published in book form.

In late 1926 the enlarged version of "Die Baumwollpflücker" was published in Berlin. Now that Traven had made contact with the German trade union movement and found an interested publisher, he ventured on a detailed, although somewhat veiled, description of what he had witnessed in Tampico. The narrative of Gale resumes where the author had left off in *Vorwärts*, beginning with a description of life in the bakery of Señor Doux, a Frenchman. Although Traven never said that it was his intention, the picture of political and social circumstances that he drew fitted the Tampico of the time precisely.

In the same building where Doux has his bakery and café, there is a hotel. The hotel manager and Doux are involved in an ongoing fight over the water supply from a pump vital to both establishments and inadequate because of overconsumption. This, indeed, was a particular feature of life in Tampico; huge demands on its water supply were one of the greatest problems facing a city with overcrowded quarters and a rapidly increasing population.[27] The Doux bakery in Traven's book makes large profits because it ruthlessly exploits illegal immigrants and foreigners who cannot complain or get redress for their grievances. There are no work contracts, only the take-it-or-leave-it attitude of employers in a city with an oversupply of cheap labor.

Doux's peace of mind, however, is broken when the Mexican waiters of his café begin a strike instigated by the new waiter Morales. Gale observes that he can see "the syndicate of restaurant employees forming."[28] Morales presents Doux with a list of demands that the owner, naturally, refuses, and Morales is dismissed on the spot. The following day, there are pickets at the café, but Doux manages to hire two down-and-out Europeans who are glad to find work and do not understand that they were hired as strikebreakers. One of the men is a German; the American Gale approaches him and in German informs him about the strike situation, noting that strikebreakers are not protected by police in Mexico: "The police here are not at the disposal of the capitalist but at the disposal of the capitalist and the worker, and I must stress the word *and*. The police assist neither the capitalist nor the worker when they are involved in a quarrel. A strikebreaker has no business at all in this."[29] In this instance, Traven clearly acknowledged his identification with Gale, and for the third edition of the book the entire scene was deleted.

Gale cannot convince the German not to work for Doux, and that same evening the man suffers an "accident" in the form of two well-aimed blows to the head. Two policemen called to the scene are in sympathy with the strikers, as are many of the bystanders. The second strikebreaker resigns voluntarily, understanding that strikebreakers in Mexico sign their own death warrants. The injured man is delivered into the hands of the German consul who informs him:

> Yes, dear friend, this is not Germany. Strikebreakers are not popular here. We have a workers' government here, a real workers' government that stands by the workers. If there is a strike at the electrical company or the water supplier's, there is no technical emergency service like in Germany or in America. There is no water and no power until the strikers decide: we will resume work. The government is neutral in these quarrels.[30]

Traven was clearly informed about the strike history of the Tampico electric company and its manager Harvey Leach.

As Gale's story continues, the reader is told that one of Doux's regular customers is a police inspector named Lamas, who has accumulated a considerable debt in the café and feels obligated to aid the owner by having the pickets arrested. When the union secretary reports Lamas's actions to the chief of police, however, Lamas is demoted on the spot. The café is closed for two months, and Doux is forced not only to reinstate his workers and meet all their demands but also to pay a hefty fine to the syndicate.

Traven had incorporated into his story several features of recent strikes in Tampico such as the positive response to the strikers at the electrical company by Governor César López de Lara, the chief of police of Tampico, and General Muñoz. But the response of his critics in Germany was incredulous. A reviewer in one of the Communist party magazines sneered: "A strike breaks out and the workers' government plus its police help [the workers]! There is no indication of the background behind which such an episode must disappear. . . . But Traven sticks to it: the police are not the tool of the ruling class. 'Uncle Policeman' becomes the guardian angel!"[31] Even Recknagel, a scholar sympathetic to Traven, questions the author's credibility and writes that "this is one of the autistic fantasies [*Wunschwahrheiten*] that appear frequently in Traven's work: This is how the author would like to see the economic war and therefore he exaggerated and generalized in order to instill in his working-class audience the optimism of victory to inspire their actions against their exploiters."[32] Indications are that Traven was serious and that what he described was an understatement of what had really happened at Tampico in 1924 and 1925. The fact is, however, that he would probably never have found a publisher in Germany had he truthfully described the strikes against Tampico's electric company and El Aguila Petroleum.

In his account of the strike at the Doux café, Traven characterized Mexican trade unions, stating that

> in this country [they] do not suffer from a clumsy, bureaucratic apparatus. The union secretaries do not regard themselves as civil servants; they are all young and roaring revolutionaries. The trade unions here have only been founded during the last ten years, and they have started in the most modern direction. They absorbed the experience of the Russian Revolution, and they embody the explosive power of a young radical force and the elasticity of an organization which is still searching for its form and changes its tactics daily.[33]

Here, as in the remarks by the German consul to the injured strikebreaker, Traven offered his observations as being valid for the whole of Mexico. His descriptions, however, were accurate only for some of the CGT-affiliated unions operating in Tampico.

In preparation for republication, "Die Baumwollpflücker" had undergone more than a mere expansion in size. The title had been changed to *Der Wobbly*, and the book was now divided into two sections, of which the first retained the original title, only in singular form (*Der Baumwollpflücker*). The second part was called *Der Wobbly* and was the section that Traven had added to the original story published by *Vorwärts*. In the second part of the book, Traven paid homage to the IWW by setting out to correct the fearful image of the Wobblies left by the press campaign unleashed against the union in 1917. This campaign had portrayed Wobblies as veritable monsters; "cut-throat, pro-German . . . or . . . bolshevik, desperadoes who burn harvest fields, drive iron spikes in fine timber and ruin sawmills, devise bomb plots, they obstruct the war and sabotage the manufacture of ammunition—veritable supermen, with superhuman power for evil, omnipresent and almost omnipotent."[34] Traven's character Gale is no such person. Fundamentally a gentle man with an eye for satire, a bystander, an observer, and a victim most of the time, he has no superhuman characteristics but resembles instead this Wobbly self-portrait:

> I am as mild mannered a man as can be
> And I've never done them harm that I can see
> Still, when now they placed a ban and they threw me in the can
> They went so wild, simply wild over me.
>
> Once the "Bull" went wild over me
> And he and his gun where everyone could see
> He was breathing hard when he saw my union card
> He went wild, simply wild over me.
>
> Then the judge he went wild over me
> And I plainly saw he never would agree
> So I let the man obey what his conscience had to say
> He went wild, simply wild over me.[35]

Gale never acts in such a way that he could be identified as a Wobbly. Each time one of his employers accuses him of being a IWW member Gale protests: "I? I would not even think of it. It is not my fault if I always happen to be where all hell breaks loose. I never interfere."[36]

Traven implied that what earns Gale the title Wobbly is his way of living rather than his political activities. A victim of different forms of labor exploitation that he recognizes but is powerless to combat, he is a drifter, an itinerant worker, without home, family, or worldly possessions, like those marginal members of the working class the IWW had set out to organize. He is not a man with a mission, a "stirrer" or a labor organizer. Gale's outlook makes him a Wobbly as well: he sees the world through the eyes of the exploited because he suffers all the injustices and humiliations of working men.

However, Gale is not the perpetual victim because of his bad luck. He weakens his own position by trying to be what he is not. The "assorted rabble" (*zusammengelesenes Gesindel*) in the Doux bakery accept working conditions and salaries that no worker with "class pride" (*Klassenstolz*) would ever accept, but then, Gale points out,

> we had bourgeois pride [*Bürgerstolz*]. But with bourgeois pride the living conditions of the workers cannot be changed. Because the entrepreneur had enough bourgeois pride and he knew how to use it to his advantage. . . . We merely aspired to saving a little and to buy a small business or amass the money for the trip to Colombia. We tried to pluck from this field as much as we could. Whether those who had to live on this field after our departure [had enough] or would die, was none of our concern. Each person is his own best friend. When grazing on this field, if there is not enough grass I pull the roots out as well. After us the deluge. What am I concerned with my fellow slaves?[37]

Traven knew only too well what happened to a working-class organization when it aspired to become respectable. Gale's failures and mishaps with employers demonstrate beyond a doubt that his ambition to rise within the capitalist system is doomed, and that he will never be able to leave his position at the bottom of the ladder. Therefore, he commits a second error. If he cannot realize his bourgeois ambitions, he reasons, he can at least appear as a bourgeois. Gale buys clothes far more expensive than he can afford. How could he have appeared before the señoritas in the sort of clothes the natives wore?[38]

This bourgeois delusion was enhanced in Mexico because of the special perks available to a white man such as Gale. Wherever he goes with his ragtag fellow cottonpickers, he receives preferential treatment. The perks, however, bring no real advantages or improvements; they are merely temporary diversions from an otherwise unbearable situation and give Gale a false sense of superiority over his fellow proletarians. The

Mexicans in Traven's account never fall for such divide-and-conquer tactics. Backed by a sympathetic government, they know what they want and how to obtain it. Unlike Gale and his fellow Americans, they do not try to succeed within a system of injustices; they change the system first.

This was the message of *Der Wobbly*: Of all the different cases of labor exploitation depicted, only one is successfully resolved—that of the Mexican waiters in the Doux café. No other situation Gale experiences is resolved before he moves on. The Mexican waiters, moreover, are not only successful because the city authorities back them; their success comes from having been organized by the waiter Morales and from their subsequent solidarity. Gale, the solitary individual with his bourgeois delusions, remains the victim of the social and economic situation he tacitly accepts, whereas the Mexican waiters succeed through group action. This change in attitude was the single most important step that Traven had taken away from the individualist-anarchist ideals of Marut. Only the examples of the IWW and the CGT could have induced such a radical change in outlook.

The City of Tampico

A by-product of Traven's portrayal of the lives of itinerant workers and proletarian life in general was a detailed description of Tampico, the only such description available in literature. Traven produced two books in which the shabbiness of this city plays an important role: *Der Wobbly* and *Der Schatz der Sierra Madre*. In the latter, the American Dobbs, unemployed, drifting, and destitute, spends his nights in the notorious rooming houses of Tampico. Following Gale and Dobbs around the city, the reader sees the seedy, working-class side of Tampico. Of all its many visitors, Traven was the only one who found the foulness and decreptitude of downtown Tampico worth describing, although a group of health inspectors also was interested in its unsalubrious conditions. A comparison of Traven's account with those of the health inspectors demonstrates the accuracy of his observations.

The Hotel Oso Negro, the rooming house where Dobbs every now and then could afford to sleep, was a typical Tampico tenement:

> In the courtyard stood the rotten and decayed wooden shacks that formed the hotel. All these shacks had small, narrow and dark chambers without windows. In each bedchamber stood four to eight bedsteads. On each bedstead lay a dirty pillow and an old, worn-out blanket. Air and light entered through permanently open doors. Nonetheless, the chambers were always stuffy because all rooms were at ground level and the sun could enter only partly into each room. There was no current because the air in the courtyard stagnated. The air was made worse by latrines without flushing water. Besides that, there was a wood fire burning in the yard day and night with large tins of laundry boiling on top. The hotel also harbored a Chinese laundry.[39]

The shabbiness and overcrowding of such tenements were not the result of greedy landlords alone. It was forbidden to put up wooden houses of less than two stories. Therefore, "the inhabitants of the town center were condemned to live in old wooden structures."[40] The Oso Negro, close to the plaza, was obviously such a building.

Dobbs pays 50 centavos for one bedstead per night. A private room—a tiny partitioned space with a double bed—is said to cost 1 peso. This, according to Traven, was the equivalent of two meals in a Chinese restaurant, ten packets of cigarettes, or five glasses of *café con leche* with French bread.[41] The Oso Negro, despite its dirt and decay, was expensive. To spend one night there would have been an unaffordable luxury for the cottonpickers. But the rates of the Oso Negro were in line with the rest of Tampico, where a small third-class room "in the low lying area of the warehouse and business district of food wholesalers cost twenty pesos a month."[42]

In "Die Baumwollpflücker," Traven described how these wooden structures performed under the extreme tropical weather conditions of Tampico:

> It was a large wooden box with an iron roof. Light entered only through the door and through hatchways that had neither glazing nor fly wire. . . . Beneath this sleeping cave had been thrown old egg cartons and lard boxes, old ropes and rotten rags. During the rainy season all this converted into a horrid morass and the ideal breeding ground for thousands of mosquitos. . . . Since the roof leaked, we always had plenty of water in our rooms as soon as the tropical thunderstorms broke. During the last month of the rainy season this happens every half hour. Naturally, we also got wet and our sleep consisted of pushing the bedsteads around under

such spots of the roof that we suspected would not leak. But the rain followed us with persistent malice wherever we tried to take refuge.[43]

Repairs were minimal because, due to the extreme housing shortage in Tampico, the shacks brought good money in whatever condition.

During the hot months the shacks, with their corrugated iron roofs, became veritable ovens. Having to work there, Traven pointed out, meant that "you can only collapse or grow into a skeleton." It was not possible to stay inside such a room during the day because one "would have turned into dried meat instantly."[44] The crowded and fetid housing conditions were made worse by a general scarcity of water and toilet facilities. A shower at the Oso Negro cost 25 centavos, "and the water was cold and scarce," Traven wrote. To avoid this expenditure, Dobbs goes to bathe in the river. The Carpintero Bay and the mouth of the Tamesi River were huge open, makeshift public toilets and bathrooms. Thousands went there for their bodily necessities and for a bath at the same time. This contributed to the general fetidness of the air, and the smells of decaying organic matter mixed with the strong smell from the petroleum refineries.[45] As Traven observed,

> the refineries exhaled clouds of smoke and gas. This gas settled in the lungs and the windpipe where it pricked like fine needles. It caused a slight cough. When the wind drove the gas clouds across the big city, the whole population felt as if they were in a poisonous oven. Those unaccustomed to it or newly arrived felt insecure and frightened. They kept gripping their throats and tried to sneeze or to blow their noses and could not understand what was happening. Many of the new arrivals felt they were dying. The piercing sensation in their throats and lungs was too poisonous.
>
> The old and accustomed ones took it easy. As long as this piercing, poisonous gas drifted through the city, gold ran through its streets and life looked bright from whatever side one looked at it.[46]

The ground was also polluted. On his way to the Pánuco River ferry, Dobbs observes, "the whole road was covered with oil. . . . To the right was the river. . . . But the water was covered thickly with oil, and all objects deposited by the incoming tide and the river were also covered with thick, gooey oil. The road where we walked was a morass of oil in many places. The oil had escaped from broken pipes or simply seeped up from the earth. Oil and nothing but oil wherever one looked."[47] Subsequently, the oil boom created a casino atmosphere of greedy exhilaration. Traven, well aware of the connection between excessive exploitation and ecological devastation, remarked that those

> who lived here only thought of oil, only thought in terms of oil and the possibilities for life connected with oil. Whether you worked or speculated, it was always oil. . . . This is new territory here. Everyone has only one thought: To grow rich and to do that as fast as possible. Never mind what becomes of your neighbor. This is how the oil people do it, the mining people, the merchants, the hotel owners, the coffee shop owners and everybody who has a few bucks with which to exploit something. If he has no oilfield, no silvermine, no clientele, no hotel guests to exploit, he will exploit the hunger of the ragged workers. Everything must bring money, and everything does bring money.[48]

Tampico was a city of great tolerance. The usual censors of manners were almost absent. The extended family, the most effective watchdog, hardly existed among the working men, most of whom had migrated to Tampico alone, and church pressure could hardly be felt. Traven was delighted with this tolerance and saw it as one more self-regulating feature of a proletarian society. The police, he pointed out, were unconcerned with the morals of the city's inhabitants, accepting that "they can look after themselves." Nor did the police need to supervise such things as closing hours. Bars and cafés simply shut down when the last customer left, Traven reported.[49] This general tolerance produced the impression that humanity prevailed amid all the squalor. The Oso Negro, in all its shabbiness, was a thoroughly decent place where anonymity was strictly observed and nobody, especially not the female inhabitants, was bothered. Nobody had imposed this order; it had emerged and was generally respected. Despite its decay and unhygienic living conditions, Tampico was the city for which Marut had been searching. Traven, however, a smart dresser and particular about his clothes and accustomed to certain comforts of middle-class life, drew the line at living actually in the squalor of Tampico. He contented himself with roaming the city and observing what he described so vividly in his books.

The Proletarian Writer and His German Publisher

In the first edition of *Land des Frühlings*, Traven mentioned that he once held a position as a "private teacher with an American farmer's family in Central America." His pupil, the farmer's young daughter, was then eleven years of age, and the "family lived some one hundred kilometers away from the city" on the railway line.[50] This rather sedate job as a private teacher is the only one in the array of adventurous jobs Traven claimed that he held for which there is some evidence. He occupied the position for the first two years of his stay in Mexico until he left for his trip to Chiapas in May 1926.

The "little girl of eleven" was born in April 1914, and she recalled that Traven entered their household when she was about nine years old. Her parents were both Americans, and her father, besides farming, traded in properties. The family lived in the small town of Cuauhtémoc, today a forty-five-minute car ride north of Tampico along the railway line. The railway station at Cuauhtémoc was then called Columbus, and it was here that Traven had his post office box. He lived in one of the properties owned by the American farmer together with another man, "also a foreigner, in an American colony."[51] Traven, who primarily taught the little girl English, had plenty of time on his hands, much of which he used "to read poetry behind closed doors." He "frequently went to Tampico" but "rarely received visitors." Traven obviously did not want anybody to know that he wrote stories for publication in Germany.

With the acceptance of "Die Baumwollpflücker" by *Vorwärts*, Traven, living in the security of the American colony, began to cultivate a proletarian image with stories of personal hardships, which were obviously meant to stress the authenticity of his writings. *Vorwärts* obligingly prefaced "Die Baumwollpflücker" with some introductory words about the unknown author: "The author B. Traven is talking from his own bitter experiences. . . . The author knows proletarian life in Mexico and North America. As an oil worker, clearing jungles, driving mules, hunting and trading among the wild Indians of the Sierra Madre where 'savages' still hunt with bows and arrows and clubs. . . . His residence is still thirty-five miles away from the nearest place where he can buy ink, as he told us in his letter."[52] Cuauhtémoc, a major railway station, was hardly so removed that ink could not be bought there.

In his early correspondence with the Büchergilde's Preczang, Traven included a photograph of the house where he claimed to have written most of his short stories under "the most apalling bodily torment. . . . Mosquito plagues during certain hours of the day, were so dreadful that I had to bandage my hands and head in order to withstand the attacks of hundreds of thousands of swarming mosquitoes."[53] This house, however, built on stilts, with a wide verandah and a second story, looked not only solid, well kept, and rather comfortable when compared to some of the tenements of downtown Tampico, but also as far as tropical architecture went it was rather elegant.[54]

It can be assumed that Traven paid little or no rent to his landlord and employer in exchange for the lessons that he gave the daughter. He received additional financial assistance from Irene Mermet. In his first letter to Preczang, dated 5 August 1925, Traven pointed out that "a friend from the United States" had loaned him some money so that he could buy a typewriter "and a few pesos more so that I did not have to hunt for a job but was able to write. At the present moment I am looking for a job because the money is finished."[55] He applied for work to El Aguila Petroleum but was unsuccessful since the large American oil companies were dismissing "dozens of white people," and he had little prospect.[56] In answer to his job application, Traven received a formal, typewritten, negative reply. He would hardly be honored in this way had he applied for a menial, temporary job such as Gale or Dobbs was likely to seek. Considering that one year later he introduced himself in Chiapas as "Ingeniero [engineer] Torsvan," connected with oil exploration in Tamaulipas, and that he was invited to participate in the prestigious Palacios Expedition to Chiapas, Traven certainly did not offer his services as a simple "oil worker" as he had told *Vorwärts.*[57]

Although Traven received his business letters through his post office box at Columbus, his private letters from Mermet were addressed to the Southern Hotel in Tampico. This building was sufficiently well known that no street address was needed. The most elegant and expensive hotel in Tampico, it was the preferred meeting place of the American and German communities.[58] Traven must have visited the Southern Hotel frequently and had contacts there in order to use it as a mailing address.

This situation, as well, would have been foreign to his working-class character Gale.

Elsewhere, Traven describes writing "in an Indian hut in the jungle, where I had neither table nor chair and had to make a bed from a hammock such as you have never seen, from bits of string tied together."[59] Comparing the realities of Traven's life in Tampico with his protestations about how lowly and miserable it was, it can only be concluded that, if Traven ever lived and worked under such conditions, he must have done so voluntarily. Why, then, did Traven think he had to exaggerate the adventure of his life? One possible answer is that he was not confident initially that his stories would ring true to a working-class audience. He fabricated his own proletarian biography in order to enhance the authenticity of the proletarian experiences of his narrator Gale. As soon as his first stories were accepted, however, he dismissed Gale and his pose as a proletarian.

Ever since the Munich Soviet republic, Marut/Traven had taken a deep interest in the affairs of the working class, and it was only natural that, once he decided to become a popular author, he would want to write about what interested him. His early observations in Tampico, we can surmise, only reinforced this resolve, especially as the city offered such an exceptional array of working-class activities and experiences. Indeed, Traven did not have to live in hotels such as the Oso Negro in order to see what life on the breadline was like. Such tenements existed all over downtown Tampico for everyone to see, and drifters were hanging around the city in droves.[60] All Traven needed was to approach them and he would be told of adventures as they were experienced by men such as Gale and Dobbs. What Traven wrote about was commonplace in Tampico, but his stories were a great novelty to his audience in Germany.

When Preczang first contacted Traven, he assured the unknown author that he would not do worse with the Büchergilde than with any "private, capitalist publisher."[61] Better still, Preczang was interested in anything else Traven might write, thus offering the prospect of a long-term contract. At the time, Traven pointed out, he had a whole drawer full of manuscripts, among them *Das Totenschiff*, which incorporated some of his experiences on his odyssey between London and Canada. He offered Preczang this latter manuscript to be published while he expanded "Die Baumwollpflücker." The first edition of thirty thousand copies of *Das Totenschiff* (1926) soon sold out; Traven was an instant success with the Büchergilde's readers. By late 1925 he was on his way toward being able to live by his typewriter and "printer's ink." Preczang's offer was the best Traven had at the time, financially and ideologically. It brought him in contact with a German working-class audience on a long-term basis. As it turned out, the Büchergilde not only made Traven's fortune, but Traven made the Büchergilde's fortune as well. *Das Totenschiff* was such a success that membership of the Büchergilde increased in 1926 from eleven thousand to twenty-eight thousand.

The Büchergilde was only one year old when Preczang contacted Traven in Mexico. Although it was the book club of the German printers' guild, it was also open to other readers "who could not be rightfully objected to."[62] It was a nonprofit organization, and communication with the membership was maintained through the interunion newsletter *Die Büchergilde*, which acted also as the catalog of the publisher. The newsletter reported on the life and activities of the Büchergilde, competitions, raffles, and the opinions of its members and, at the same time, was used to introduce new authors adopted by the book club. *Die Büchergilde* became the first platform from which Traven launched his fabricated biography, which was to confuse two generations of journalists and researchers.[63]

Compared to the commercial book clubs or that of the Socialist party, the Büchergilde Gutenberg was very small. In 1927 it had 40,000 members, of whom 27,000 were printers. After the surprising early success of *Das Totenschiff*, the Büchergilde decided, with the consent of its author, to distribute the book commercially.[64] This was done through the Buchmeister Verlag in Leipzig, a publishing house associated with the Büchergilde but functioning as a commercial enterprise. Although all Traven books were first made available to members, they were soon after distributed by the Buchmeister Verlag. *Das Totenschiff* initially sold 70,000 copies to members, but once it was available commercially the figure jumped to 170,000 sold in 1931.

Traven started with royalties of 7.5 percent on each copy of his books, which were sold from 1.50 to 4.50 marks. With growing fame, this percentage probably doubled. Traven, however, was certainly one of the least concerned with money of the authors of the Weimar Republic. Not only did he stipulate that his books must first be exclusively available to members of the club in order to increase membership, but he also set aside 10 percent of his royalties from serialization in newspapers for the Büchergilde

Gutenberg to use for advertising purposes. Traven was happy with his publisher; their relationship was based on mutual trust, respect, and understanding. In 1927, Traven wrote to Preczang that he thought he had "fallen instinctively on the right haystack" when he landed with the Büchergilde because "only heretics understand heretics, only heretics can spread heresies, and only heretics dare to help other heretics."[65] The Büchergilde, however, was not as "heretical" as Traven believed initially, a fact he was not to recognize until 1933.

Early in his career, Traven had set an agenda for what he wanted to achieve with his books, explaining to Preczang that "workers must not honor authorities, neither kings nor generals, neither artists nor aviators. Every man has the duty to serve mankind to the best of his abilities, to make their lives easier, to bring enjoyment, and to direct their thoughts to higher goals. I fulfill my duty toward mankind as I have always done, as a worker, a sailor, an explorer, as a private teacher in isolated farms, and now as a writer."[66] In this ambition, the Büchergilde seemed his best collaborator, but what Preczang could not foresee was that Traven included trade union leaders among the authorities not to be honored—a lesson from his Munich days. Friction over Traven's uncompromising attitude toward German trade union leaders ultimately would cause the break between author and publisher.

For the moment, however, no disagreement darkened their relationship. Traven was the most popular author of the Büchergilde. By 1936 nearly 500,000 copies of his books had been sold in Germany alone. One of Traven's admirers explained that "workers and unemployed alike adopted Traven as their writer because he did not lull them to sleep with dreams. He stirred them up and he kept urging them not to rely on their organizations but to have self-confidence."[67] His readers understood Traven in exactly the way he wished to be understood. One of them commented that

> *Der Karren* pictures the life of a young Indian, who forces us to compare his life to our own. We realize that the methods of the capitalists to keep the working man unassuming are the same all over the world. . . . The life of a *carretero* [oxcart driver] is one long accusation against the ruling system. . . . The book *Der Karren* has been written for the oppressed of this world and it sparks a feeling of solidarity in all working people of the world, which gives them strength to fight the cruel enemy in brotherly union.[68]

The love of Traven's readers for their favorite author was sometimes expressed in touchingly simple terms. One woman began a letter to Traven by speculating about his nationality, but concluded that it did not really matter at all: "The main thing is that you are alive and that you give us such wonderful books." He should not feel so lonely, the letter admonished. "So many people love you and feel with you. We all look forward to each one of your new books."[69] Traven was accepted unconditionally by his audience and, in return, was also a caring author. Each new book came accompanied by a personal letter to be published in *Die Büchergilde*. Traven was not particularly modest in the way he evaluated his own works, but his letters always conveyed two important points: first, that what was presented was documentary material and that the author had spared no pains to explore remote and dangerous corners of Mexico; and second, that he had undertaken this difficult work for the sake of his audience. The full extent to which Traven cared for his readers only came to light when he began to risk his life with the publication of *Marsch ins Reich der Caoba* in 1933. For the present, however, Traven had little thought to spare for anything outside the revolutionary events he witnessed in Tampico.

Die weisse Rose

How deeply Traven was affected by the contagious atmosphere of working-class triumph in Tampico only manifested itself when *Die weisse Rose* was published in 1929. With this book, Traven revealed himself as a thoroughbred Mexican nationalist, something that was not only unexpected but also revolutionary in a man with the opinions of Marut. Many of Traven's foreign contemporaries were infected by the new optimism generated by Mexico's national rebirth, but few delivered themselves so uncritically and unreservedly to nationalist enthusiasm. Although his attitude seemed inconsistent with the ideology expounded in *Der Ziegelbrenner*, Traven perceived Mexican nationalism as a vehicle that was singularly suited to the goals of Marut. In *Die weisse Rose*, Traven gave the first indication of his unconditional commitment to the policies of the Calles government.

Die weisse Rose, although published four years later, was clearly written under the influence of events that occurred in

1925, particularly those surrounding the oil controversy between the Mexican and the American governments that reached a climax in that year. It also, however, shows fresh traces of the influence of the author's first trip to Chiapas in 1926 and of his "discovery" of the Mexican Indians and the qualities unique to their society. Thus, while the content of *Die weisse Rose* relies on stories that Traven heard in and around Tampico, their interpretations are partly influenced by his discoveries in Chiapas and partly by his conversion to Mexican nationalism. It appears, from evidence in the text itself, as if *Die weisse Rose* was an unfinished manuscript when Traven left for Chiapas in May 1926.

The central events of *Die weisse Rose*, focusing on the fraudulent appropriation by an American oil company of the Indian-owned White Rose Farm, combined elements contained in stories of similar violations that still circulated in and around Tampico in Traven's time.[70] Many of the land deals of the last decade of Porfirio Díaz's dictatorship were fraudulent, illegal, and violent. Many involved Edward L. Doheny, the founder of the Huasteca Petroleum Company, a subsidiary of John D. Rockefeller's Standard Oil of New Jersey.[71] These stories formed part of the folklore that sustained the virulent anti-American feelings expressed in Mexican nationalism.

Mexican nationalism and anti-imperialism directed against U.S. capital were part of the ideology that emerged from the revolution. Díaz had welcomed foreign capital in the expectation that investors, led by the United States, would industrialize Mexico. Instead, capital from outside the country invested in land, mines, and petroleum extraction. Thus, Mexico became dependent on revenue from the export of primary products and the import of processed goods, both largely to and from the United States. Many early revolutionaries blamed Díaz for having betrayed the country to foreigners; for them the battle against the old regime was identical with the battle against outside economic domination. To root out foreign influence, one historian has noted, became the objective of nationalism.[72] In this context, it was no accident that every employer and exploiter in *Der Wobbly* was given a nationality other than Mexican.

In the economic sphere, nationalism found its most forceful expression in Article 27 of the Constitution of 1917, which effectively canceled earlier laws promulgated under the Díaz government that had given subsoil rights to landowners. The Porfirian legislation, in conjunction with generous tax concessions, had lured British and U.S. investment to the Huastecan area south of Tampico, where rich oil deposits had been discovered. Mexico itself was predominantly an agricultural country with limited demand for petroleum. Most of its oil was exported, and the only earnings for Mexico were salaries, taxes, and lease rents. The profits extracted from the oil, however, were enormous. According to data from the Mexican Ministry of Foreign Affairs, oil production during the first decade of operations was enough to pay back everything the companies had put into the enterprise, and the remaining income was profit.[73]

Revolutionary fighting did not affect oil production in the way it interrupted many other economic activities. The Mexican oil boom lasted through the most turbulent years of the revolution, and oil was easily shipped from the port of Tampico. Production fell off only after 1921, when most oil companies stopped making new capital investments because the principal oil fields south of Tampico, known as the Golden Lane, began to draw salt water and could not be saved. Only asphalt-rich oil, the black goo Dobbs noted on his way to the Pánuco River ferry, was still in demand in the United States. The rejection of Traven's job application to El Aguila Petroleum in 1925 was a consequence of this contraction. From the Mexican perspective, the American oil companies left the country, having taken all and leaving nothing.

The earlier governments of Presidents Carranza and Obregón had tried in vain to gain some control over the foreign oil companies operating on Mexican soil. But President Calles was the first to make headway in returning control over development to Mexican hands. Thus, the aspirations of Mexican nationalism had become an important and highly visible part of the government's political program. On the last day of 1924 a law was passed that required foreign oil companies to have their land titles reexamined, and it also imposed a fifty-year limit on oil holdings. Together with Article 33 of the constitution (the Noxious Foreigners Act), this legislation would place severe checks on foreigners and foreign companies. Not unexpectedly, the oil companies protested the new legislation they regarded as confiscatory. U.S.-Mexican relations reached an all-time low as a result, and there were growing fears of direct intervention by the United States.

Traven, living in Tampico at the time, was drawn into the vortex of excitement and anticipation generated by the controversy. It was only in 1925, under the influence of the oil dispute, that he began to understand the full implications of the Tampico strikes. They were not just a product of unions confronting capitalist employers, he reasoned, but part of the nation's effort to fight the American stranglehold over the national economy. The excitement produced by President Calles's daring and provocative petroleum legislation came from the realization that Mexico, an underdeveloped, debt-ridden, and dependent nation, was challenging the capitalist world order by asserting the right to reform and control its own economy. Traven recognized the universal importance of this situation. It had been Marut's avowed goal to abolish capitalism, and the novelist Traven had not reneged on this aim. The confrontational policies of Calles and the enthusiastic support he received from the Mexican nation appeared to have a possibility of succeeding in an area where Traven, the individual, could achieve little. He therefore decided to give Calles his undivided support and to put his talent as a writer in the service of the Mexican government. Traven became what *Frente a frente*, the organ of the League of Revolutionary Writers and Authors, called "Mexico's best propagandist abroad."[74]

Die weisse Rose was Traven's first unequivocal statement in support of the measures taken by the Calles government to reassert national control over the oil industry. The story of the fraudulent acquisition of the White Rose Farm by the American Condor Oil Company, and the subsequent destruction of the farm and everything it stood for, was Traven's contribution to Mexico's fight against the impositions of U.S. capitalism and justification for this fight. It is certainly no accident that *Die weisse Rose* appeared in Mexico in a pirated edition in 1940 as a timely comment on the March 1938 expropriation of the oil industry.[75] At that time, Traven's early novel was seen as a valid and powerful justification for the drastic measures that President Cárdenas was forced to take. The novel juxtaposed two worlds so different that communication between them was impossible. One world was the White Rose Farm, which had been owned by generations of an extended family of Huastecan Indians; the other was that of Mr. Collins, owner of the Condor Oil Company, who covets the land of the White Rose Farm. The head of the

Indian family is Hacinto Yanyez (Traven's spelling), a man unaccustomed to thinking of the farm as his property since it was only "on loan to him. It was merely his so that he could administer it for successive generations."[76]

Life on the farm is slow, unchanging, and harmonious, a picture Traven draws with infinite tenderness and delicacy. The White Rose Farm is the idealized Mexican version of the anarchist dream of a self-governing peasant community. It is, Traven wrote, "a small nation but a real nation with a real king. Where the king is not the ruler, where he does not live in luxury [through wealth] created by his people, where the king is not more than an administrator, a councillor, where his royal privileges are not more than the responsibility for the well-being of those his forefathers have placed into his trust."[77]

The arcadian life is suddenly disrupted by the arrival of the Condor Oil Company. Unknown to Hacinto, the White Rose Farm is located on some of the richest oil land in the region. When he is approached by agents of Collins, the unbridgeable gulf between the two worlds becomes apparent. Hacinto is impervious to Collins's offers of money, although his argument that "land is eternal, money is not, therefore, land can never be exchanged for money" is entirely incomprehensible in Collins's world where money is the only value. The noble Hacinto repeats stubbornly that he cannot sell the farm because the families living there "will then no longer have land to cultivate corn." Traven explained that "the word corn was for him, the Indian . . . the same concept as 'give us our daily bread' is for Europeans. . . . Hacinto knew no other phrase because this phrase contained all human wisdom rooted in the word 'Land is bread, and bread is life.' "[78] Collins, however, needs the land of the White Rose Farm in order to pay a substantial bill incurred by his mistress. Ultimately, the farm is destroyed by the trivialities of his sordid love life. But Collins also is piqued by Hacinto's stubborn refusal to sell; land he wants and cannot have, Collins declares, does "not exist in the whole universe."

Kurt Tucholsky, one of the Weimar Republic's leading literary critics and writers, hailed Traven's characterization of Collins as the only full-blooded description of a capitalist in German literature. "The author knows what he is talking about," he added significantly.[79] The juxtaposition of Hacinto's harmonious world with the greedy, sordid world in which Collins operates highlights that "what Mr. Collins lacked most of all was a soul," as Traven put it. Collins does not want to live in harmony with the world around him but, instead, to conquer it. His world is the end product of the destruction of such life as the White Rose Farm embodies.

Traven's heart was with Hacinto and his numerous clan, but he was no nostalgic sentimentalist. When Collins cannot lay hands on the farm by legal means, he resorts to a series of stratagems that lead Hacinto to accept an invitation to San Francisco, where he is murdered and his signature on the sales contract falsified. Immediately, the oil company moves to destroy the farm by starting drilling operations, and all the families, whose home it has been for generations, become employees, "rows of Indians dragging pipes like slaves in chains." Their harmonious life forever destroyed, the peasant farmers become wage slaves. Instead of pitying their cruel fate, however, as a good sentimentalist would have done, Traven hastened to point out that

> the author of this story has no intention of creating false sentimentality and picturesque effects so that the reader can talk about the beautiful and touching story of the tender rose being plucked. Materially speaking, all those affected were now better prepared for life. . . . A new world opened before their physical and spiritual eyes, a world the existence of which they had ignored until then. . . . These people had lost a lot but also gained a lot from their loss. And the day came . . . when they would rightly say: We are richer now than ever before, we are greater now than our fathers [ever] were because today we are citizens of the world.[80]

Traven recognized that the arcadian life was restrictive and unchanging, a point he was to make again and again in his future books.

This optimistic conclusion to a story in which right and wrong were delineated so clearly still seemed remarkable. Tucholsky suspected that the ending was the result of a "somewhat shaken conviction," although Traven had no doubt that Hacinto stood any chance in the power struggle between the traditional way of life on a peasant farm and the greedy dynamism of a capitalist like Collins. This was the point of departure for a new crusade by Traven. From this book forward he consistently advocated the necessity of integrating the Indian population, which had been living at the margin or outside of the national economy and culture, into mainstream Mexican society. Traven developed this topic fully in *Land des Frühlings*, and it remained one of the principal themes throughout his entire work.

As he had done in his previous novel, *Der Wobbly*, Traven drew on local events and modeled his characters on local personages. His IWW companions, his associates at the Southern Hotel, and his neighbors in the American colony at Cuauhtémoc would have spotted immediately the parallels between Traven's character Collins and the oil magnate Doheny. Volumes have been filled with the true or alleged brutality of the founder of Huasteca Petroleum and the oil companies' history of "cleverness, deceit, bribery and even crimes,"[81] and of tax fraud on a grand scale.[82] Doheny, however, became so notorious that even other oil companies complained about his methods. By modeling Collins after Doheny, Traven not only portrayed a capitalist in action but also addressed himself immediately to the prevailing feelings among Mexicans to which people such as Doheny had given rise. Finally, Traven gave voice to anti-Yankee sentiments, and he fed them too.

Never before in his writing had Traven pilloried the United States as the haven of capitalism. The new estimate of Mexico's northern neighbor he had learned in Tampico, and the available evidence once again points to the IWW/CGT connection as the source. Traven set his novel a few months before the outbreak of the de la Huerta Rebellion of December 1923, which appears as the Huerta rebellion in *Die weisse Rose*. When Traven arrived in Tampico in mid-1924, the Obregón government had just defeated the Huertista rebels at a staggering cost: seven thousand dead and an expenditure of 70 million pesos. Traven's interpretation of the de la Huerta Rebellion closely mirrors the contemporary nationalist and socialist views of the uprising. He thought that it was a thoroughly reactionary event, guided by people "who deplored the disappearance of old and rotten conditions and who loathed everything that did not have the artificial glitter of *Porfirismo*." Traven had obviously heard that the whole uprising was antilabor, and he commented that "the Huerta people also attacked Yucatán and there shot the workers' state governor. To be on the safe side, they included his son as well. Wherever Huerta went, trade unionists and syndicalists were shot."[83] A former interim president, Adolfo de la Huerta was not as clearly antilabor as Traven believed. In fact, during his short presidency in 1920 he had been sympathetic to workers and their strikes.[84]

At the outbreak of the rebellion the American oil companies were accused of having a hand in the affair. Traven mirrored this view faithfully:

> Huerta started his rebellion as the oil companies had expected. Whether they had also ordered the timing of the outbreak will not be easy to find out in the near future.... The tankers of the American oil companies imported weapons in their empty tanks in order to stir up the country more and more.
>
> But Tampico, which Huerta could have taken so easily, was never occupied because from here the wealth of the country—the object of the civil war—was being exported. This harbor had to remain open so that everybody could see who had given the orders and where they came from.[85]

Contrary to what Traven's analysis might indicate, de la Huerta used the Obregón government's conciliatory attitude toward the U.S. oil companies as a justification for his break with the Mexican government, and he presented his rebellion as a fight between nationalists and traitors. Indeed, the oil companies played a very different role in the rebellion from what Traven had heard, and the truth would have come as a great surprise to him and his friends. Doheny had advanced 10 million pesos credit on taxes to the Obregón government, while other American companies had raised another 8 million pesos.[86] The Coolidge administration, for its part, had reluctantly agreed to sell arms to Obregón, a move that proved decisive in the resolution of the rebellion.[87]

After abandoning Veracruz the Huertista troops did indeed enter Tampico, as Traven wrote. They tried to extort tax payments from the oil companies, an old and well-tried tactic in the region. The American response to the rebellion, however, was negative, and the United States threatened intervention if shipping in either Veracruz or Tampico were interrupted. Tampico was not occupied by the rebels, and both ports were left well alone. Traven's report of these events was therefore seriously deficient, reflecting a view prevalent in Mexican nationalist and socialist circles that saw all U.S. activity there as being directed against Mexico.

Traven made a sharp distinction, however, between private and corporate American behavior. None of Traven's American characters, such as his narrator Gale or the farmers Shine and Pratt in *Der Wobbly*, was an unpleasant individual. Even the gold diggers of *Der Schatz der Sierra Madre* had little in common with the millionaire bandit Collins. Indeed, one of the important elements in the optimistic ending of *Die weisse Rose* is Traven's faith in the simple goodwill of individuals, in this case the engineers employed by the Condor Oil Company. The engineers aid the dispossessed Indians of the White Rose Farm whenever they can, helping them shift their possessions and teaching Hacinto's son to drive a truck; they "were always prepared to alleviate the pain and to help wherever they could." The engineers are as powerless against their company as are the Indians. This and their sheer human decency create a bond between the two groups.

In the same manner, Mexican anti-Yankee feelings were not directed against individuals such as B. Traven Torsvan, who paraded as an American citizen, or the young Carleton Beals as he bummed around Mexico, or the likes of Gerard Gale. In the novel, Gale, like the patriarch Yanyez, is drawn as a victim of the oil companies. Mexican anti-Americanism was not racism; rather, it was directed against oil companies, meddling ambassadors, arrogant secretaries of state, and obnoxious individuals such as Leach and Doheny. Mexican anti-Americanism was expressed as derision of the economic policies of the northern neighbor and its immediate representatives.

Mexican nationalism, however, did not exhaust itself in anti-American feelings. This was only its defensive-aggressive side. Its more important dimension was the rediscovery of the worth and the peculiarity of indigenous Mexican values. After centuries of neglect and decades of deprecation of the Indian population by the *científicos*,[88] the new nationalists hailed the Indian as the true symbol of Mexico. Traven, who had little contact with Indian communities before his first trip to Chiapas in 1926, embraced this side of Mexican nationalism even more fervently than its anti-Americanism. He was not just fascinated by the exotic qualities of the Indians but discovered something in their way of life, their social organization, and their economic performance that persuaded him even further that Mexico was the country where the fight against world capitalism had taken a tangible form. More convinced than ever that his guiding star had led him to the land of his destiny, he threw himself with energy into the fight for the Indian and against capitalism. His understanding of this side of Mexican nationalism only came after his trip to Chiapas. His treatment of some of the Indian or part-Indian characters in *Die weisse Rose* reflected that recent exploration and foreshadowed what was to become the nucleus of his entire work: his belief in the inherent worth of the Mexican Indian.

The contest between Hacinto and Collins is, on the one hand, a fight between individual and corporate power; on the other hand, it is a battle between two races. In the struggle against corporate power, Hacinto stands no chance. But the real weakness that causes his downfall is his status as an Indian: his death is ultimately caused by his own customs and traditions. Hacinto accepts the invitation to San Francisco, a present that turns out to be a trap, simply because he does not know how to refuse. "In this manner," Traven wrote, "the Indian was caught up in his own customs and character. And no man on earth is caught worse than in these things."[89] This theme recurs throughout Traven's work; most of the Indians of the Jungle Cycle end up in the logging camps because of their honesty, innocence, or sense of honor and duty. By the same token, the officials of Chiapas could send Indians to perish in the logging camps because they, like Collins, knew how to manipulate government power for their own ends.

One of the more complex characters of *Die weisse Rose* is the governor of Veracruz. The Condor Oil Company lodges a complaint with him concerning Hacinto's continued refusal to sell his farm, whereupon the governor takes the unusual step of traveling to the farm and staying there for a few days in order to put the oil company's complaint into perspective. The character of the governor was loosely modeled on Adalberto Tejeda, governor of Veracruz from 1920 until 1924. Tejeda was a native of the Huasteca region and knew firsthand the problems created by the oil companies. As governor, he was known for his radical policies in favor of workers and peasants. In 1922 he took Huasteca Petroleum to court for tax fraud, an unprecedented act of boldness by a Mexican authority against a powerful American oil company. President Obregón, anxious for diplomatic recognition by the United States and no doubt under pressure from Washington, intervened in the trial, which then had to be abandoned.[90]

In the novel Traven's "governor from Jalapa, . . . a man with dark skin," undergoes an extraordinary experience during his visit to the White Rose Farm:

> It happened quite unexpectedly that the Indian in his blood sud-
> denly began to stir . . . and therefore, he began to feel and sense
> with the Indians. Things he had never understood before, he now
> began to understand with his feeling and his soul. This home
> [*Heimat*] was a matter of the soul. This home was something that
> created men. . . . Thus the governor, from his Indian blood, reached
> the conclusion that no automobile, no Diesel motor, could ever be
> valuable enough to exchange for this home.[91]

The educated man, who "lived like a civilized person in a large
city," can see suddenly that "the color of his skin and the
melancholy in his eyes, the color and straightness of his hair
were so similar to Hacinto's that both could have been born
from the same mother." Beneath the veneer of his education and
city breeding, the governor becomes closer to his Indian self
through the contact with Hacinto and the White Rose Farm. His
Indianness is not only expressed in his features, his hair, and his
skin, but it is also part of his very essence. The development of
this character foreshadowed Traven's theory, fully realized in
Land des Frühlings, that anticapitalism is part of the genetic heritage of the Mexican Indian. Although politicians had never
fared well with Marut, Traven now cast all prudence aside and
endowed the governor of Veracruz with traits that he was to
attribute in *Land des Frühlings* to living politicians, especially to
President Calles. Traven was convinced that a Hacinto Yanyez
lived in every Mexican. This man, to whom money meant nothing
and land everything, was an integral part of all those Mexicans
who had Indian blood in their veins. The only obstacle preventing
this anticapitalist mentality from prevailing was the economic
stranglehold the United States had over the Mexican economy.

As a foreigner without papers or resident status in Mexico,
Traven could not actively participate in its politics, but he could
create propaganda and disseminate information about the exciting changes taking place in the country of eternal springtime.
It took Traven well into 1928 to realize how shallow and premature his judgment was on the progressive character of President Calles's regime.

2 *Land des Frühlings*: Ode to the Mexican Revolution

The Significance of Land des Frühlings

Traven's only travelogue is a logical next step after *Die weisse Rose*. In the earlier book, Traven described in fictionalized form the mechanisms leading to Mexico's underdevelopment and dependency. In *Land des Frühlings*, he gives an account of the country's struggle for political and economic emancipation. It is the pivot of Traven's work on Mexico, his only work of nonfiction and a unique historical document. It is also the summary of his experiences up to October 1926, including two years of residence in Tampico, a sojourn in Mexico City, and a trip to Chiapas undertaken in that year. In addition, the book contains a hodgepodge of speculation parading as scientific theories, gossip, anecdotes, and accounts of the author's personal bravery and courage, as well as autobiographical information that Traven deleted from a later edition.

Although *Land des Frühlings* is of uneven quality, it is a pioneering work in two respects. First, long before the term "Third World" was coined, Traven gave an account of Mexico's struggle against the foreign stranglehold over its economy. Four decades before André Gunder Frank presented his Marxist analysis of the connection between capitalism and underdevelopment, Traven anticipated many of his observations.[1] Second, Traven did pioneering work on the Chamula Indians of Chiapas. He was the first to notice the anthropological significance of their primordial life-style, and he gave us detailed, although sometimes faulty, descriptions of it.

Throughout the book, Traven blended reports of the reform measures taken by postrevolutionary governments with his discoveries about the Indian population of Chiapas. The two issues will be separated here artificially for the sake of easier management. They are, however, causally connected: Traven's observations in Mexico until 1926 only began to make sense as a

result of his trip to Chiapas, where he discovered in the culture
of the Chamula what he called the "Indian sense of community." *Land des Frühlings* is, therefore, an interpretation of Mexican politics in light of his discovery of one aspect of Indian
culture. It is Traven's own version of *indigenista* theories applied
to contemporary events, theories that he grievously misunderstood. His peculiar view of Mexican Indians and how he came to
acquire it will be shown in Chapter 3. What follows is a discussion of Traven's rendering of the reforms and achievements of
the Mexican Revolution.

Traven left Tampico in May 1926 to take part in an expedition to Chiapas. Although there were few parallels between
industrialized Tampico and rural Chiapas, he found the same
sense of dynamic progress emanating from the policies of the
CROM-backed Chiapan governor, Carlos A. Vidal (1925–1927),
that he found in CGT-dominated Tampico. It is not known
where Traven drafted the text of his travelogue, but the book
shows signs of its author having been in a great hurry to complete
it in order to return to the south for further explorations. It
seems that Traven isolated himself while writing, in that he
presented a viewpoint already outdated and unrealistic at the
time. He left Chiapas in October 1926, shortly before the reform
policies of Governor Vidal were annulled. Thus, the unique
conditions that had fostered political radicalism in the state, as
well as in Tampico, had ceased to exist long before *Land des
Frühlings* was published. In his writing, however, Traven assumed that the Mexican labor movement was a unified body
under CGT guidance, striving for one goal and with President
Calles as its agent. This is the ideological underpinning of *Land
des Frühlings*.

Traven's viewpoint reflects faithfully the heady days of the
early Calles presidency and its strongly reformist drive. Traven
described the literacy and health campaigns, the land reform,
and the struggle against the Catholic church from the perspective
of a radical trade unionist who observes the progress of reforms
at the grass-roots level. While traveling through Chiapas, he
observed trade union activities in small villages and the union's
dedication to reform and improvement, and he disregarded the
well-known corrupt practices of the CROM's national leadership.
In the letter to his editor Preczang that accompanied the manuscript of *Land des Frühlings*, Traven confirmed this specific perspective. "I think I may assume that my book is the first book of

a traveling investigator that is conceived and written from the emotional viewpoint of the modern proletariat. This is where it differs from all other travelogues."[2] Although his letter was a typical piece of self-advertisement, the "viewpoint of the modern proletariat" is the one cohesive element in *Land des Frühlings*. The work is Traven's most revealing statement, not only because it communicates much of his personality, but also because it is a milestone in his understanding of the Mexican Revolution.

Traven's least-known and longest work, *Land des Frühlings*, contains 429 pages of text plus 63 pages of photographs "taken by the author between May and October 1926." It has never been translated; American publishers have been reluctant to produce an English-language edition of the book because, as one has written, "it contains obvious errors which should not be perpetuated."[3] Most of these errors, however, are attributable to the immediate circumstances under which *Land des Frühlings* was written; many only appeared to be mistakes as events have proved them so.

Land des Frühlings is a product of its time, so much so that it is barely comprehensible when viewed outside the context of the early years of the Calles presidency. The point in time that Traven captured in the book is the year 1925. Looking back, 1925 has been called "the year of optimism."[4] In his first statement as president, delivered the previous year, Calles had promised that "all the efforts of the new administration will be directed . . . to balancing the budget." The nation, Calles pointed out, had to "get used to living on its own resources without resorting to help from abroad."[5] This speech was swiftly followed by action. Private and corporate income taxes were regulated, the long-postponed Bank of Mexico was established, and large irrigation and road construction projects were begun. The Banco Nacional de Crédito Agrícola (Bank of National Agricultural Credit) was established for the beneficiaries of the land reform, and Finance Minister Alberto Pani arranged to ease the burden of payments on Mexico's massive foreign debt. These measures laid the groundwork for the reconstruction of Mexico's economy and were completed in the administration's first year. Calles had not only made himself master of his own house, but he also had put his house in order with a spectacular display of initiative.

The financial measures were accompanied by social reforms in the form of stepped-up literacy and health campaigns, a rural school program, land reform, and anticlerical legislation, all designed to benefit the poorest of Mexico's rural and working-class population. Traven welcomed the measures enthusiastically, seeing them as the expression of a true restructuring of society following a successful revolution, as opposed to an exchange of one elite for another. Under the influence of his ideological preconceptions and the impressions he had received in Tampico, Traven believed that he was witnessing a shift of political power to the working class, which was now responsible for determining the cultural, economic, social, and political development of the country. The Mexican Revolution, in Traven's view, was a class war:

> At the beginning, the Revolution was basically the revolution of a clique. There were some groups and cliques eager to feed where the old boy Porfirio, nearly eighty years old, had been sitting so long. However, once the working class awoke, once it reached a knowledge of its own existence, once it recognized itself as a class apart from the bourgeois class, no war can be fought and no revolution of a clique can be started without the working class immediately appearing on the scene to take power.[6]

This was the central message of *Land des Frühlings*: the Mexican Revolution had succeeded without a written program, without a political party, without even explicit guidelines; it was a true working-class insurrection. *Land des Frühlings* was Traven's attempt to explain to his German audience why the Mexican Revolution had resulted in a victory for the working class, in contrast to the German experience of 1918, when the revolution had been taken over by bourgeois politicians and aborted with the connivance of labor and Socialist party leaders. *Land des Frühlings* was Marut's ultimate triumph.

The peculiarity of Mexico's working class—according to Traven, 90 percent of the population—was its unusual social and ethnic characteristics. Four fifths were pure Indians, Traven informed his audience. He did not define what a "pure Indian" was, but from the context it seems that he meant persons whose parents were of pure Indian blood and whose ancestors had never intermarried with any other race. Indians were people who retained their thick, straight black hair, dark complexion, and melancholy eyes as did the governor of Veracruz in *Die weisse Rose*. The remaining one fifth were mestizos, people of mixed Indian and European blood. Thus, when the working class gained ascendancy during the revolution, the Indians "knew from the beginning that, if the workers win the Revolution, the Indian question will be solved, because the Indian question is intimately linked to the worker question. In Mexico, the worker question cannot be solved unless the Indian question is solved first."[7] The Indians, Traven argued, "knew instinctively that it was a revolution for them." Traven did not differentiate between peasants and workers. In anarchist fashion, he assumed that their goals, in Mexico as elsewhere, were identical.

The Indian question, Traven explained, required the emancipation of the indigenous peoples. The mestizo minority should recognize that Indians were not only the numerically strongest element of the nation but also that national policies needed to be based on the Indian heritage of cooperation and anticapitalism. Traven was convinced that the future greatness of the Mexican nation depended entirely on the acceptance of that heritage as a guide for national policies. The Mexican Revolution itself, he thought, was a rebellion of "the awakening Indian culture against European civilization." His explanation for the recent turmoil of the revolution and the ensuing reform program was thus shrouded in a deep indigenist mystique that the author had great difficulty in explaining to his audience.

When Traven wrote *Land des Frühlings*, he was only acquainted with a small part of Mexico and unaware of the great regional differences within it. Still, he was quite prepared to generalize, and he labored under the illusion that what he observed in Tampico, Mexico City, and the small part of Chiapas that he explored in 1926 also must be true for the rest of the country. This led him to make a number of statements that were not only very unusual for a mistrustful and cautious man such as Marut, but which Traven soon lived to regret. One of these concerned the progress of emancipation of the indigenous peoples that, Traven thought, was well under way. "Any foreigner in Mexico who would attempt to insult an Indian, to mock him, to fool him, even if he were in rags or drunk, would immediately confront all the Mexicans around. Nobody would dare to cheat an Indian who comes to town to sell his produce. The Mexican is an extraordinarily polite, hospitable, and helpful person but in this matter he will not allow tomfoolery."[8] Even the Mexican police force was now on the side of the Indian, Traven noted. Should an Indian think that he had been cheated, he would go to the police straight away where "he will get justice because in cases of doubt nowadays police always side with the Indian."[9]

Traven believed this reformed attitude of non-Indians toward Indians to be the fruit of a material change that Mexicans
of Spanish descent had undergone during the revolution.

> You have to be aware of the high-bred race pride of the Mexican in
> order to appreciate what it means to him to draw the Indian into
> his cultural realm. And the fact that the Mexican does this in spite
> of his race pride, in spite of opposing feelings in his soul, this is a
> great and noble trait of pure humanity, one we never witnessed
> before in all human history. . . . Conquest here is peaceful and is
> carried out as a sacrifice of pride. Europeans are not forced to
> cohabit with colored races. Therefore, the European will never
> understand what it means for a master race to give up its pride in
> order to embrace, kiss, and call brother another man who, according
> to his education and inner feelings, he has to regard as inferior.[10]

This was a gross simplification of the indigenist attempt to
reevaluate and absorb the Indians' past and present experiences
into the Mexican cultural mainstream. It presented the activities
of a small group of intellectuals, artists, and educators as a
nationwide reality. The case of the painter and muralist Diego
Rivera, the difficulties he faced in convincing audiences to
accept his subject matter as art, indicates the scale of Traven's
exaggeration.

Traven's overly optimistic statements about the miraculously
changed attitude of ordinary Mexicans toward the country's
indigenous peoples suggest a source of information that blithely
ignored popular objections to Calles's reform program. It seems
that this same source also fed Traven the idea that the Mexican
government was run by the trade union movement. One of the
pieces of evidence cited by Traven in support of this latter claim
is the case of the takeover of Tampico harbor by the city's
stevedores. Traven presented this occurrence erroneously as a
common event in Mexico. "The stevedores of Tampico have
eliminated the entrepreneurs by refusing to work. They sabotaged everything and made [their employers' lives] hell. They
refused consultation, conciliation, agreement, or pact."[11] In early
1927, he informed his readers, the capitalist press and the capitalist shipping agencies had to admit that the takeover was a
complete success. The action itself, however, had occurred as
early as 1922, when eight hundred dock workers had formed a
cooperative guild, a fact of which Traven was apparently unaware. Before 1922 strikes at the docks had been endemic, load-
ing and unloading was chaotic, and crates were broken and

their contents stolen. This situation improved rapidly once the stevedores operated their own cooperative, and costs were lowered and handsome dividends could be paid. The cooperative was hailed as a model of effective and enlightened organization. Traven proudly echoed these conclusions but failed to mention that, when the same strategy was attempted at Veracruz, the result was very different and confusion not only persisted but also increased.[12]

Soon after the completion of *Land des Frühlings*, Traven returned to Marut's self-reliance on information gathering and processing. His subsequent work, although consisting of novels, is characterized by meticulous research. Traven created archives of photographs, notes, letters, pages of diaries, and artifacts to substantiate the contents of his books. The archives provided irrefutable proof that the author had spent long periods in the jungles of Chiapas researching the logging industry. Filling a room with papers and files was a remarkable feat for Traven, an anarchist who believed in burning personal documents and who actively discouraged biographers.

After the publication of his travelogue, Traven became painfully aware of the lack of realism reflected in it. He had raised false hopes among his readers, he believed, by listening to and reproducing information and opinions that he was unable to evaluate critically. He had failed in his responsibility as a writer, a responsibility he took seriously. The book published, Traven could only keep *Land des Frühlings* out of circulation by blocking further editions and translations. A second edition did appear in 1936—at a time when the Büchergilde, in exile from Nazi Germany, badly needed Traven books to boost its reduced membership. This edition, however, must have had a small run and been inconsequential, for most biographers do not even mention it. The author's reasons for approving this second edition are not clear, but they might relate to his intention after 1933 to stimulate protest against the Nazi regime. A third edition, revised and abridged, appeared in 1950, the last edition printed during Traven's lifetime.

Land des Frühlings was Traven's first and last commissioned work. When he was invited in 1925 to travel to Chiapas, he informed Preczang and received financial assistance from the Büchergilde.[13] In return, he was to deliver a travel book about this little-known southern state. The travel books published by the Büchergilde were noticeable for the detailed background

information on economic and social structure they provided
rather than for their concern with landscapes and natural beauty.
Land des Frühlings on the surface met these criteria well, until the
author realized some time later that his "emotional viewpoint of
the modern proletariat" was one he shared only with a small
group of his friends.

The Reform Program of the Calles Government

Traven's account of the reform program of the Mexican Revolution in the 1920s, although deficient and distorted in some places
and exaggerated in others, is a faithful reflection of the issues
that excited politically engaged Mexicans at the time. Generally,
the reforms were a manifestation of the attempts by
postrevolutionary governments to "forge a fatherland." The
campaign against illiteracy was the first visible realization of the
revolution's promises. Moisés Sáenz, undersecretary of education
in the Obregón government and one of the authors of the new
Mexican rural education program, summarized the program's
goal as an attempt to create "an institution that . . . intends to
bring about an integral culture. . . . This program aims to bring
water to villages, induce people to change their dietary habits,
teach Spanish, preserve or revive the artistic genius, or get
people accustomed to coordinated action."
    At the heart of this program lay the need for villagers to
learn to read, write, and speak Spanish. Its ultimate objective
was the integration of the "two million people who do not speak
our language, or barely understand it four hundred years after
the [Spanish] conquest." The program was particularly aimed at
Indian groups that had tenaciously clung to their preconquest
culture, such as the Chamula whom Traven met in Chiapas. The
rural school "as a cultural agency will establish communication
between villages and the whole of Mexico until material unity is
achieved. [It is also] an instrument of spiritual unity, without
which there is no homeland."[14] Roads, post offices, telephones,
newspapers, and books would sustain this national cohesion.
    Traven was keenly aware of the importance of the rural
school program. Access to information, in his view, was the first
step toward worker self-help and emancipation. The full extent
of his belief in literacy and education became clear only in his
novels of the Jungle Cycle, in which the Indian characters are

cheated time and again by officials bearing papers they must sign but cannot read. Traven's infectious enthusiasm for his topic stems from the fact that after decades of neglect the Calles government was apparently embarking on reforms that would permanently improve the situation of Mexico's poorest stratum, the Indian rural population. In turn, Traven noted, the Indians responded with eagerness and gratitude.

Many of the rural schools, sustained nationally on a modest yearly budget of 25 million pesos, were basic, often lacking furniture altogether, with the children squatting on the floor "with a piece of brown paper on their knees." This type of school, Traven observed, spread rapidly. "Where there is none today, there will certainly be one by next year."[15] This rapid growth was possible, he explained, because the villagers undertook to furnish the school buildings, while the government provided the books and teachers. Wherever he went, Traven told his readers, he found soldiers bent over their first-grade primers, learning to spell, read, and write, helping and teaching each other. Traven had observed firsthand the hunger for education. Before traveling to Chiapas, he explained that he had sat with children in class and had made excursions with the teacher alone and with the whole school. The teacher he referred to was probably María de la Luz Martínez, a primary-school teacher in Mexico City, who lived with Traven at the time and who most probably drew his attention to the literacy campaign. De la Luz Martínez had trained in the United States and was involved with the Francisco Madero School in Mexico City, which had been made famous north of the border by Frank Tannenbaum in an article entitled "The Miracle School."[16] Orphans and homeless children were educated there, and the school recruited new students through its former pupils. It was self-supporting and run by the students with minimal adult supervision, and it appealed to Traven because of its resemblance to the anarchist ideal of a self-regulating community.

Where the young education system could not cope, Traven wrote, the workers' organization would step in. On his way from San Cristóbal de las Casas to Tuxtla Gutiérrez, the capital of Chiapas, Traven passed through the small township of Ixtapa, where "even in such a remote spot so far away from the railway, surrounded by jungle and high mountains, you can find a branch of the workers' organization, where lectures are given every night and reading and writing is being taught."[17] The "branch of

the workers' organization" to which Traven referred belonged
to the CROM. The government-sponsored CROM had begun to
make its presence felt in Chiapas ever since the ascendancy of
Governor Vidal. What Traven observed at Ixtapa, however, was
part of the CROM's educational policy more by accident than by
design. The CROM's national leader, Morones, considered it "a
mere diversion that would keep the workers emotionally satis-
fied," while members of the CROM's inner circle proceeded to
use their positions to amass personal fortunes. The young intel-
lectual Vicente Lombardo Toledano, who ten years later rose to
become Mexico's most important labor leader, was put in charge
of the education program. To Morones's amazement, Lombardo
took his job seriously, sponsoring instruction in "anything that
would increase the general knowledge and class consciousness
of the workers."[18]

The small CROM branch at Ixtapa, far removed from the
cynical power politics of the CROM's national leadership, shaped
Traven's understanding of how the Mexican workers' movement functioned, and it complemented his earlier impressions
of workers' power and self-reliance in Tampico. For him, there
was no contradiction between his experiences in Tampico and
in Chiapas; consequently, he innocently referred to the Ixtapa
CROM branch as belonging to the "*rojos*, the Reds."

In the context of President Calles's New Economic Policy the
rural schools, and the Central Agricultural Colleges in particular,
were intended to teach the peasantry better and more profitable
methods of production designed to support increased consumption.[19] Technicians—including de la Luz Martínez—were
sent abroad to study and to improve the quality of the teaching
personnel. Calles had concrete economic goals; Traven, however,
perceived more transcendent aspirations in the educational
policies. Educating the proletariat, he proclaimed, would raise
Mexico to "the highest level of civilization," and only the educated Indian would be able and fit to melt with the rest of the
country into one great nation and thus create the modern Mexican
superstate of the future.[20] The Mexican people, Traven wrote,
were aware of these exalted goals and wholeheartedly supported
the educational reforms that favored the Indian population.
"The present government," Traven noted, "wants to create
conditions in the country such that the Indian can love it as his
fatherland." Once the Indians' separate status as an underprivi-

leged nation ended through a merger with European-Mexican society, the Indian identity, far from being lost in the process, would contribute to the creation of a totally new culture. "Never," Traven enthused, "in all the thousands of years we can survey, has anything so great, so decisive and powerful happened as what is visible now in its beginnings." The humble Indian was now the bearer of Mexico's future and therefore, "even if he [the Indian] came along in rags, even if he cannot speak a word of Spanish, the Mexican respects him more highly in his heart than he does a foreigner."[21]

The new care for indigenous peoples found its most exalted expression among the rural schoolteachers. Young girls, Traven wrote, born and bred in high-class families of the cities, often sacrificed their lives when they ventured forth "into the jungle areas to teach Indians how to read and write." When one of them succumbed to tropical disease, another immediately stepped into the breach. Their motivation "is nothing but a deep love for a cause holy to her, a love which is quite un-European, which you can only understand if you know the history of the nation and its liberation from powers who would like to load themselves with the natural wealth of this country." Looking back on the first years of the literacy campaign, Tannenbaum reminisced that anyone who had the privilege of knowing the enthusiasm of the educational movement and the zeal with which the first teachers went to their tasks would "have realized that what these teachers lacked in equipment they made up in enthusiasm, in loyalty, in leadership."[22] Traven, in characteristic fashion, assumed that the whole Mexican nation was filled with this spirit.

According to Traven, the only sector of Mexican society opposed to the education of the Indian population was the Catholic clergy, and he now began to single out the Catholic church as the target of his scathing attacks in the same manner in which Marut had ranted against the "public whore number one," the bourgeois press. The reason for the clergy's opposition to the literacy campaign, in Traven's view, was that the reforms of the Calles government severely curtailed its influence and rendered the church's role in education redundant. The reforms, Traven explained, aimed at a return to preconquest modes of production and traditions that excluded the clergy outright. He was convinced that Mexican Indians, in spite of four centuries of

European domination and indoctrination by the Catholic church, were endowed with a sense of community that was unselfish, group-minded, and anticapitalist. The new educational policies built on and fostered these particular traits of Indian culture, Traven believed, by adopting the cooperative traditions "of the ancient Indian communes." Traven pointed out that "in the northern and central states of the Republic, where the Indian has made considerable progress toward civilization, the modern idea of cooperatives has gained considerable ground over the last three decades."[23] Here again is Traven's anarchist ideal of the self-regulating community, this time highly productive and essentially modern. The image of this community was to haunt him until the end of his writing career, when he thought that he had found evidence of its establishment by Indian rebels from one of the mahogany logging camps of Chiapas.

Traven's vision of a united Mexican nation extended to his views on state politics. He was aware that governors enjoyed virtual autonomy vis-à-vis the federal government, but from his limited experience he concluded that all Mexican governors acted from the same motives. Further hampered by his ignorance of the split in the labor movement, he could not see that the policies, for example, of the governor of Tamaulipas, Portes Gil, were not the same as those of Vidal of Chiapas. Portes Gil backed the CGT in order to keep the CROM out of his state; Vidal was backed by the CROM and fostered the establishment of CROM branches in Chiapas. Traven referred to all of them as "labor governors" and as "men, real men. They keep the promises made to the workers before the election. In many cases, I would say, they go further than their promises as soon as they are in office."[24] The revolutionary spirit that united all Mexican politicians, Traven believed, was the shared determination to enforce the anticlerical legislation of the 1917 constitution and the militant opposition to foreign capital. "All governors in Mexico," he wrote, "like all men who give orders today in Mexico, are Mexicans first and foremost. Their socialism is a Mexican-Indian socialism. They are men with strong spines, they are politicians of the modern era. They have realized that capitalism in its present form must die if mankind wants to survive."[25]

According to Traven, the most important change in the Mexican political climate was a new attitude of respect toward the Indian. In Tuxtla Gutiérrez, he had an opportunity to watch Governor Vidal in action, observing that "whether a millionaire mine owner or the deputy of a remote Indian tribe enters the governor's room, he gets up, comes toward the man and salutes one as well as the other with the same polite gesture. Perhaps he has even more time and patience for the Indian . . . than for the mine owner."[26] Traven possibly had made similar observations in Tamaulipas, where Portes Gil had begun to build his own power base by organizing peasants into agrarian syndicates, distributing land, promoting rural education, and initiating an antialcohol campaign. Traven concluded that in the governor's office one could observe all the problems of mankind, of "capital and labor, of races and nations," being treated.

At the same time as Traven was writing appreciatively of the educational policies of the Calles government, there was strong and well-publicized evidence that some of the more radical governors, such as Tejeda of Veracruz, Felipe Carrillo Puerto of Yucatán, and Tomás Garrido Canabal of Tabasco, were developing regional educational systems in opposition to the central government's efforts. These "rationalist" schools strove to link the educational process with the socialist notion of the class struggle. Traven, however, never acknowledged these attempts, describing only government-sponsored schools; again, the author gave the impression that the whole nation was struggling in solidarity toward one goal. Had Traven grasped the significance of the rationalist schools, he would have understood that the national education program was part of the Calles government's drive toward the centralization and strengthening of its power, as was the struggle to eliminate the recalcitrant CGT. Such an understanding would likely have had a profound influence on his evaluation of the Calles presidency.

Concomitant with the literacy campaign was a drive to improve health care and hygiene. How closely the two were linked became apparent to Traven when he learned that the pupils of the industrial school in Tuxtla Gutiérrez spent their Sundays in their native villages instructing villagers not only in improved agricultural techniques but also in hygiene, health care, and dietary habits. The driving force behind the health campaign was President Calles, and its aim was to stamp out venereal disease, tuberculosis, smallpox, bubonic plague, cholera, and hookworm, all of which were still rampant in Mexico before

1923.[27] The campaign included new standards in handling food, medical supervision of brothels, and cleaning up such fetid housing conditions as those of downtown Tampico.

Traven paid scant attention to the fact that the health campaign, like the literacy effort, was initiated, directed, and controlled by the central government. This fact was not important because, he reasoned, the reforms were driven forward and controlled by the Mexican workers and their unions. "It is the workers, and actually only the workers, who continuously belabor the government and the state governors not to neglect public health care." Worker participation in the day-to-day operations of the reform program only confirmed Traven's theory that the Calles government and the trade union movement worked together. Ultimately, however, Traven misrepresented not so much the ways in which the reforms were carried out as their ultimate goal. Calles, it is now clear, aimed to create a "progressive, modern, capitalist society, broadly along the lines of Western Europe and North America, [favoring] a dynamic exporting economy . . . and [looking] to create an efficient state, staffed by a competent bureaucracy and professional army."[28] State-sponsored, secular education was to produce a literate and numerate population, loyal to the revolutionary state, being both contributors and beneficiaries of the envisioned progressive capitalism. Traven's enthusiasm had been triggered by the expectation, fueled by his optimism, that the reforms were leading to an anticapitalist Mexican "superstate," based on self-regulating cooperatives in the Indian spirit and unfettered by a centralized bureaucratic apparatus.

Despite his misunderstanding, Traven clearly grasped the strategies underlying the reforms. A wide diffusion of education was to be the first step toward molding a strong national spirit. The second step would be the material betterment of the poorest of Mexico's population in order to engender the cooperation and devotion necessary to forge a national renewal. Traven recognized land reform as the most important measure designed to achieve economic improvement for Mexico's poor; it was in fact an integral part of the program that emerged from the revolution and was incorporated into the 1917 constitution as Articles 27 and 28. Agrarian reform was the most difficult of all reforms to implement because it involved massive transfers of property, a complicated process in a country in which foreign interests controlled one half of the national wealth.[29] U.S. oil companies and landowners vigorously protested against the provisions of Articles 27 and 28 and were therefore considered the chief obstacles to successful reform by many Mexicans. Traven had touched on this issue in *Die weisse Rose*, but in *Land des Frühlings* he addressed it in such a way as to reveal that he, essentially an urban person, did not understand the complexities of the rural problems.

Traven criticized the land reform law of 1925, in force at the time of his writing, because it did not encourage large-scale agro-industry but rather allotted small pieces of land to ejidos, tradition-based farming communities that held land in common. "I know no other country," he pointed out, "where the preconditions for large-scale industry are better than in Mexico." Only large, cooperative farms equipped with heavy machinery, he argued, could permanently improve the living conditions of agricultural laborers. "If Mexico wants to become a modern superpower, it has to create something new, it must stress its peculiarity, it must be more modern than all modern superpowers."[30] Harnessing the country's natural wealth under Mexican guidance and ownership and issuing individual titles for family plots would lead to fragmentation and inefficiency. The modernity Traven had in mind was an updated version of the age-old Indian communal form of living and working that excluded private property and individual ambition.

The land reform law of 1925 was quite unconcerned with Indian traditions. It responded to heavy pressure from peasant organizations to realize the revolution's promise for land. Although the Calles government turned over more land to ejidatarios than had all previous governments, the president acted unwillingly and from political considerations alone. If he had attempted to postpone or even suspend land distributions, he acknowledged to a French diplomat, the agrarian movement would have turned into a force beyond control.[31] Communal farming found no favor with President Calles and he rejected it as inefficient because it harked back to Indian traditions that were unconcerned with productivity.[32] The most telling sign of Traven's lack of awareness about rural problems was that he did not realize that some of Mexico's poorest workers, the *peones acasillados* (resident agricultural laborers), were expressly excluded from land grants. In effect, land reform, like all the other reforms undertaken by the Calles government, was designed to strengthen the central government and to control centrifugal and factional forces. By making small farmers indebted to the central government for their land grants, a huge network of patronage was created. Calles once put this case bluntly: "The restitution of ejidos," he stressed, "is the best way of controlling these people [the peasants] by telling them simply: if you want land, you have to side with the government; if you refuse to side with the government, then there won't be any land."[33]

Traven's ambition to convey to his German readers a comprehensive picture of a model revolution is flawed on two counts. First, it is clear that the author assimilated a good deal of faulty information, which he further distorted by incomplete understanding. Second, he failed to take into account that Mexico's complex political situation in 1925 grew out of traditions and historical circumstances incorporating not merely a preconquest Indian past but also four centuries of colonial domination by Spain. In short, he made two contradictory assumptions that the Indian heritage had survived into the twentieth century and that the colonial heritage had been erased by the revolution. Apart from these mistaken premises, Traven was overambitious; he must, it seems, have become aware of his failure to convey a valid picture of Mexico's national political situation, because hereafter he gave his novels a limited regional setting that would allow him to explore the human and political complexities of his chosen theme.

The tentativeness of much of Traven's information can be gauged from his comments on Mexico's foreign policy, particularly as it was directed toward Nicaragua. In the mid-1920s the Nicaraguan Augusto Sandino and his struggle against the U.S. presence in his country became a cause célèbre for the Mexican Left. Mexican praise of Sandino came in the wake of President Calles's support for the anti-U.S. faction in Nicaragua's civil war. His refusal to toe the U.S. foreign policy line toward Nicaragua caused lasting damage to diplomatic relations between Mexico City and Washington. Traven commented at length on the diplomatic situation between the three countries. In one of the rare instances in which he acknowledged the source of his information, he quoted "a gentleman known to me" who had recently written in *Current History* (New York) that "the U.S. try to conquer Nicaragua with warships, heavy artillery, Marines, and the almighty dollar, whereas Mexico attempts the same with flowers, songs, and warm greetings of friendship."[34] The article was written by Carleton Beals, a journalist Traven most probably met through the U.S. photographer Edward Weston. Traven, in fact, gleaned all his information on Mexican foreign policy toward Nicaragua from this article and freely copied whole sections for the benefit of his German readers.

The same article by Beals discussed the affinity between the Mayan Indians of Mexico and the Quiché Indians of Guatemala. Traven, however, added his own interpretation of these comments, stating that "the American immediately criticizes the Mexican for imperialist tendencies as soon as he approaches his brother in Central America. But imperialist feelings are the last motive to guide the Mexican. He does not need to be imperialist, even if he had the tendency. The great Indian empire, 'The Federation of Indian Nations of America' will come about on its own."[35] On this point, Traven developed the argument far beyond the scope of the original article, superimposing a conclusion that had never occurred to Beals.

The evidence Traven provided for the development of an incipient "Federation of Indian Nations of America" was the emergence of the Indian as a factor in Mexican politics since the beginning of the revolution in 1910. "The political leaders of Mexico," Traven noted, "are no longer Spaniards or white men, they all have Indian blood." Differences in mentalities would cause an inevitable clash between Mexican politicians and their counterparts in the United States. This, to Traven, was exemplified in Mexico's attitude toward Nicaragua. "The workers of the Central American republics are perhaps more Indian still than the Mexican workers; and they are in a pitiful state of servitude under American capitalism. And it appears quite natural that they look upon Mexico as their liberator, because Mexico is the first nation on this continent to have turned against American capitalism and its lack of culture."[36]

These were the hopes of many members of the Mexican Left for their own country and for Nicaragua. Traven, however, expected considerably more. The events he witnessed in Mexico, he believed, would ultimately reserve a global role for Mexico alongside Russia and China. In these three countries, he wrote, the destinies of the world would be decided. The Indian awakening, the anticapitalism manifest in Mexican policies, and Mexico's rejection of European ideas such as bolshevism "for the first time in history permit the emergence of the idea that the

political and economic union of all nations on earth is possible."
If 1925 was "the year of optimism" for Mexico, then 1926 was
the year of hope for Traven.

The Struggles against the Catholic Church and the Workers' Movement

When Traven came in contact with Mexican nationalism, he also
absorbed the anticlericalism prevailing in radical union circles.
The struggle against the Catholic church, its wealth and influence,
was born of the same spirit as the fight for control over foreign
capital. Reform-minded Mexicans viewed the church as a brake
on social progress and a rival to the revolutionary state. Since
1910 the church had sided with the opponents of the Mexican
Revolution, and the bishops fought the anticlerical legislation of
the 1917 constitution that was designed to bar the clergy from
national politics. Their fight culminated in an unprecedented
strike by the clerics in July 1926, when Mass was suspended and
church doors remained closed.

In retaliation for the Mexican archbishop's disapproval of
the revolution's "socialist" line, sporadic violence had broken
out in Mexico City as early as 1921. Bombs were planted, and the
red and black strike flag had been hoisted over the cathedral.
These provocations were attributed to activists of the CROM.[37]
In October 1925, Governor Garrido Canabal of Tabasco decreed
that no priest was allowed to officiate in the state unless he was
married. This proclamation was followed by a campaign of
iconoclasm and wholesale destruction of churches. Garrido
Canabal did not incur the president's displeasure with these
drastic measures, since the Calles government was already
supporting efforts to establish a schismatic Mexican Catholic
Apostolic Church that would advocate an end to priestly celi-
bacy and a break with the authority of Rome. The new schismatic
church, however, did not enjoy much popularity at home.
Nonetheless, President Calles was certain that "clericalism now
signifies no danger at all."[38] International protest at the closure
of churches in Mexico was much in evidence, and Traven was
incensed at this unsympathetic response. He stressed the church's
hypocrisy in demanding obedience from its followers, but "when
the church is being asked to be subject to authority, to obey the

constitution and the law, then its purse opens and millions of pesos are spent on starting revolutions and boycotts."[39]

Many of the urban labor unions supported Calles, and in early 1926 one hundred eighty trade union representatives visited the president to demonstrate their allegiance. Calles thanked them warmly for their support at a time when international questions "must define whether or not Mexico is a sovereign nation."[40] On 1 August 1926 a crowd of forty thousand union members assembled on the Plaza de la Constitución to cheer their president.[41] In light of this show of support, Traven saw the hierarchy's closure of the churches from the viewpoint of the urban worker and disregarded the rush of ordinary people who wanted to marry in church, have their children baptized, hear Mass, and confess before the churches were closed. He proudly remarked that church services had been suspended for fourteen months and church buildings had fallen into ruin everywhere, with villagers using them as quarries. "Everywhere in Mexico where I encounter a church in such condition, I know that the hour has struck." But Traven only cited one location where he witnessed such neglect. This was at Zinacantán in Chiapas, a village of fiercely independent Indians. Traven merely passed through the village and could not know at the time that the church of Zinacantán had been closed for reasons quite unrelated to recent government policy.[42]

The principal fault of the church in Mexico, as Traven and others saw it, was its complete failure to help or to civilize the Indians.[43] Instead, the church "has done nothing but deepen and strengthen the superstition of these primitive people."[44] Therefore, it was easy for the workers' organization, Traven thought, to take the place of the church. "What [the workers] learn with the *rojos*, the Reds, appears to them much more important and useful than what the priest told them for centuries." The ceremonial functions of the church had already been taken over by the workers' organization, Traven wrote optimistically. Baptisms and marriages were celebrated before the local union secretary. "The trade union is the state for the worker, and if his marriage is recognized within the trade union, he does not give a damn what other people think about him and his wife." The available historical evidence about such marriages and baptisms, however, indicates that the secular occasions were isolated instances.[45] The ease with which the influence of the church could be phased out, Traven believed, stemmed from the fact that the Catholic faith never left more than a superficial mark on the souls of the Indians, and he thought that he observed a remarkable neglect of religion everywhere. Calles was even more confident, believing that every week that passed without religious services would lose the Catholic religion about 2 percent of its faithful. The habit of churchgoing, he confided to a foreign diplomat, could be broken and the Indian would forget it.[46]

The uprising of the Cristero peasant rebels must therefore have been all the more of a shock to Calles, his cabinet, and even the church hierarchy. Traven, like other observers in Mexico at the time,[47] had fallen victim to the error of thinking that anticlericalism was a universal belief rather than the ideological property of a minority in power.[48] The articulate and vocal trade union movement, representing urban workers, had given rise to this impression. Judging by contemporary accounts of the uprising, it seems that few people knew quite what to make of the Cristeros. Large sectors of the Mexican press, especially the metropolitan newspapers, fostered the impression that the church had stooped to connive at rebellion, and this opinion became widespread in 1926 and 1927. But the newspapers were under virtual censorship by the CROM, which had instructed its members not to print anything that the union did not approve, and recent research suggests that the Cristeros had acted on their own initiative, without encouragement or financial support from the church hierarchy.[49]

Traven's handling of the Cristeros reflects the CROM attitude of the time. In *Land des Frühlings*, he did not mention the Cristeros at all, despite numerous horror stories in the newspapers about atrocities committed by them in Jalisco and Michoacán. In early 1927, Cristeros had begun to rob trains. In March, Catholic rebels, to the shout of "Viva Cristo Rey!" attacked the Laredo-Mexico City train, killed the conductor and train guard, and made off with 100,000 pesos worth of government funds. The passengers were unharmed.[50] A more savage incident occurred the following month when the Guadalajara-Mexico City train was attacked by about four hundred men who murdered many passengers, poured kerosene into the Pullman carriages, and set them alight.[51] The Cristeros were said to have been led by three priests.

This second incident, which was reported in the international press, was taken up by Traven and incorporated into *Der Schatz der Sierra Madre*. After the attacking bandits—all mestizos, Traven stressed—had mercilessly shot everybody in the second-class carriage, they began to pour petrol through the broken windows, "then they threw lighted matches into the carriages. Like an explosion, the flames shot into the black night sky."[52] The first German edition of 1927 did not identify the attackers as Cristeros, but in the 1935 American edition Traven wrote: "With their war cry 'Viva nuestro rey cristo! Long live our king Jesus!' the bandits started the slaughter. With the same cry the signal was given to begin plundering."[53] This attack, he now stressed, was led by two priests.

In July 1927, while Traven was still busy writing *Land des Frühlings*, it looked as if the Cristero Rebellion had been suppressed successfully, and Traven had no specific reason to think that the Cristeros were more than an isolated group of fanatical mercenaries who had taken to banditry. The impact of the rebellion, in fact, was such that President Calles eventually found himself compelled by internal as well as external pressures to come to terms with the clergy, and the churches reopened for services in June 1929. It was after this event that Traven identified the attackers specifically as Cristeros, and the new reference looks now like belated revenge, as well as an implicit acknowledgment that the Catholic rebels had to be taken seriously after all. In 1927, however, under the influence of his just-completed trip to Chiapas, Traven firmly believed in the permanence of the church's exclusion from Mexico. His argument hinged once again on the newly discovered Indian spirit. The increasing Indian influence on politics, he wrote, brought a different approach to property rights, "very unlike anything Americans or Europeans ever thought of." Traven could not quite explain what the approach was, but he assured his readers that "the laws against the church are in the Indian spirit."

The revolutionary development of the exclusion of the church was, according to Traven, primarily due to pressure from the Mexican workers' movement, which stood behind all the reforms instituted by the Calles government. Looking back from the vantage point of 1932, Tannenbaum recalled the impression of great power that the CROM conveyed. "It seemed for a while as if labor was the most important influence in the State, and certainly Morones was perhaps next to Calles the most important member of the government."[54] Karl Kautsky, the German Socialist ideologist, remarked that "the [Mexican] proletariat is growing stronger and more independent and at present [already] governs the state under the Calles presidency. . . . It is obvious that all progress in Mexico, however small it may be, is only possible under the direction of the proletariat."[55] Traven echoed Kautsky's thought when he wrote that

> as soon as the trade union starts to dissociate itself from the state, as is happening today in Mexico, and no longer recognizes the authority of the state, then the state slowly disintegrates without committing violence. If you do not count the pure Indian population which is only nominally attached to the state, the power of the trade unions in Mexico today is already larger than that of the state. This is evident in all political struggles today in Mexico. Whatever the state intends to do, it is powerless unless supported by the trade unions.[56]

It took Traven and others several more years to understand that their impression was mistaken and that, in fact, the opposite was true.

Since Mexico lacked an entrepreneurial middle class, as Traven himself pointed out, the federal government was forced to take the lead as banker, investor, and creator of an infrastructure. These were the beginnings of the "entrepreneurial state," as one historian has aptly commented.[57] A necessary part of such a developmental strategy was firm control over labor. The CGT did not easily agree to this requirement. When in 1921 President Obregón asked a deputy of the newly founded CGT to give an outline of his organization's political stance, he must have been deeply displeased by the reply: "To us it is an unchanging and fundamental truth that there is no good government and never will be. The mere word 'government' means abuse of power. . . . The CGT is not a political organization. It is rebellious against government and for freedom. You cannot preach peace and harmony among wolves and sheep, among hangmen and victims, among exploiters and exploited, among capitalists and workers."[58] This statement echoed the ideology of Marut, but it certainly did not fit the image of the state that Presidents Obregón and Calles had set out to create. Because of its unwillingness to cooperate, the CGT soon became the victim of government action.

The CROM fared better because of its willingness to cooperate with federal authority. At its 1924 convention, a declaration was issued that "the goal of the CROM is not the destruction of capital but rather a harmonious consolidation of labor and capital." In November 1924 a document was signed binding the CROM firmly to the government machinery. This pact integrated the CROM into the existing capitalist order and made it dependent on the state.[59] In return, the CROM could now count on the coercive and financial powers of the government in its fight to eliminate rival unions such as the CGT. The immediately visible consequence of the state-CROM pact was a great reduction in strike activity, as independent unions, including the tramway drivers and the oil workers, were coerced to join the CROM. The full extent of CROM dependence on the government only became apparent at the end of 1928, when the state withdrew its support from the federation. Immediately, membership figures dropped, and the CROM's influence over policy dwindled.

The CROM management consisted of a small group of confidential associates of Morones. Decisions affecting the organization were frequently neither discussed nor even revealed to the membership. The CROM's operating style ensured that "the cleverest and fastest could lay hands on the juiciest posts,"[60] with the most profitable post held by Morones himself. He managed to amass a fortune in real estate and diamond rings "in order to show those bastard bourgeois that we can wear diamonds too," while building a substantial patronage and bribery machine. His personal life-style resembled that of an oriental potentate, and the disparity between life at the top and at the base of the union movement was enormous. Traven, who observed the often democratic rank-and-file organization on the shop floor, seems to have been unaware of the corruption in the CROM leadership. Had anyone told him the then-common joke that CROM stood for *Como Roba Oro Morones* (How Morones steals gold), he would probably have dismissed it as the "labor pains" of a young and enthusiastic organization.[61]

Despite the existence of a strong labor movement, industrial workers were not necessarily materially better off in 1925 than they had been during the Porfiriato. The fight for better wages was hampered by the CROM's policy of restraining strikes, and thus the "spiritual gain," as Traven called it, of the freedom to organize in most cases amounted to very little.[62] The right to organize, the author argued, made all the difference in the world because the most hungry peon has a future as a free man ahead of him "with all the treasures of the world of learning and beauty within his reach."[63] Since the fundamental problem of poverty throughout the Mexican working class persisted, all these treasures remained as inaccessible to the working man as ever. Traven's failure to understand the nature of poverty and its social ramifications is the most certain sign that he was never part of proletarian life in Mexico, as he had claimed to be.

One reason for Traven's unreserved praise of the Calles government was his belief that Mexico's politicians of the day all had Indian blood in their veins. This observation was also made by James R. Sheffield, the new U.S. ambassador and an inveterate racist. But what Sheffield saw as the "Latin Indian who . . . recognize[s] no argument but force" was to Traven a justification for the greatest optimism.[64] The Indian heritage in Mexico's politicians, Traven believed, was the best guarantee against any relapse into the capitalist past. Mexico's politicians, Traven wrote, "push through what they think is beneficial to the people, whether it hurts the capitalist or not."[65] Under the present leadership, Traven asserted, the Mexican working class was on the brink of a revolutionary change. "You only have to have a closer look at the intelligent layers of a non-European race in order to feel unconsciously what is happening in the world today. The Indians show a strangely expectant attitude to be ready to take on their great task, the same [attitude] I imagine intelligent workers have when they feel that the edifice of the capitalist economic system starts to totter, so that a good kick will finish it off."[66] This revolutionary fervor, in Traven's view, was led by the Mexican workers' organization that in turn was headed by Morones. Traven could not have been more painfully mistaken, but his comments do show that he had abandoned the proletarian pose of his character Gale and become what Marut had once been: a theorist on behalf of the working class.

Traven had perceived an essential difference between European and Indian modes of thinking and viewing the world. Basically, Traven argued, the Indian is nonaggressive: It would never occur to an Indian to "want to rule somebody else, convince him, or enlarge his own property on account of others." The Indian, Traven wrote, "does not want to stand out, he wants to be happy." But "in place of ambition, greed, and craze for power which motivate [the European's] actions, the Indian does not have a vacuum in his soul. There are other characteristics that cannot be called by names because they are characteristics that we do not possess and probably never will possess because they are particular racial characteristics."[67] This characterization might have fitted Indian peasants and the likes of Hacinto

Yanyez, but it certainly did not fit Morones, Calles, or any member of the cabinet. Traven was not so much mistaken in the way he perceived Indian peasants; his mistake rather lay in the gross overestimation of the influence of the Indian spirit on mestizo mentality. This emerges most clearly in Traven's treatment of the Mexican middle class.

Traven cited figures stating that a mere 10 percent of the fifteen million Mexicans were nonproletarian. It is certainly true that the labor sector, although smaller proportionately than Traven's statistics indicate, gave an impression of dynamism that the author and other observers readily perceived. But Traven went one step further. He began to explain away the existence of a middle class on racial grounds. He achieved this by splitting up the meager nonlabor segment into two groups. One consisted of the reactionary individuals pining for the return of Porfirio Díaz. This group, Traven believed, was doomed because of its numerical weakness and lack of government backing. The second, larger group was made up of individuals who, like the rural teachers, had given up their middle-class identities. They believed in the goals of the revolution and were ready, in Traven's words, "to embrace, kiss, and call brother" the Indian in order to form the Indian superstate of the future. For Traven, there was no question as to whether the upper and middle classes would yield gracefully to their former inferiors. They had no choice because the Calles government was opposed to their interests.

The European traits contained in mestizo nature—their disruptive individualism, indolence, and personal ambition—traits that had proved detrimental to Mexico, would be eliminated in a fusion with the Indian race. What Traven in fact expected was that the non-Indian element would voluntarily crossbreed itself out of existence, and he anticipated no objections. When he abandoned speculative analysis based on crude racial stereotypes, Traven had to admit that ordinary Mexicans were afraid of the indigenous peoples. This was reflected in the multitude of stories circulating that concerned the unearthly power of Indians. Apart from this, Traven conceded, ordinary Mexicans "do not care what the Indian does or how he passes his days." Traven offered these observations as universal truths, without acknowledging their contradictions. Only his second and third trips to Chiapas would reveal that relations between rural Indians and Mexicans from the cities, especially in Chiapas, were quite different. In the novels of the Jungle Cycle, his view of

Mexican city folk crystalized into the opposite of his 1926 vision. From this point on, every encounter in the novels between Indians and city folk ends in disaster for the former. Traven began to portray the Indian as a person who was unprotected by both government and workers' organizations before, during, and after the revolution.

3 Discovery of the Mexican Indian

Preparations for the Trip to Chiapas

In either late 1925 or early 1926, Traven spent some time living and studying in Mexico City with the renowned U.S. photographer Edward Weston. Presumably on the strength of this apprenticeship, Traven was invited to participate as the photographer in the first exploration of the southern states of Tabasco and Chiapas to be launched after the close of the armed phase of the revolution. This expedition, sponsored by President Calles and Undersecretary Sáenz, was led by the archeologist Juan Enrique Palacios. One of its aims was to find the breeding grounds of locusts that had devastated the two states during the previous year. Another was to explore and chart the recently discovered ruins of Yaxchilán in the Lacandon Forest of Chiapas. There were some thirty participants, primarily biologists, topographers, archeologists, ethnographers, doctors, and engineers. The only foreigners were Tannenbaum and Traven Torsvan, who at this time introduced himself as a Norwegian. The men met for a briefing session in the Ministry of Agriculture in Mexico City, where a photograph was taken to mark the occasion.[1] The original plan was to divide into two teams, each entering Chiapas from Tabasco via the ruins near Palenque. One group was to go to Piedras Negras and Yaxchilán in order to reconstruct the trip of Hernán Cortés; the second was to travel through the Lacandon Forest to the tributaries of the Usumacinta River and the recently abandoned logging camp of San Roman Tzendales. Their work in Mexico completed, the two groups were to join up again and proceed to Guatemala.

This plan failed completely. A few days before the expedition was to set out by boat for Tabasco a smallpox epidemic closed the borders of that state. Both teams were rerouted to Chiapas by train via the Pan-American railway along the Pacific coast. Time was too short, however, and the reorganization turned into chaos. Those members who made the journey to San Cristóbal de las Casas in Chiapas found that nothing was prepared. The first group to arrive, including Palacios and the photographer Traven Torsvan, had to travel to Comitán, eighty kilometers to the south, to buy animals for the trip across the Lacandon Forest. During their absence, the remainder of the expedition dissolved in disarray. Some members returned to Mexico City from San Cristóbal; others left from Comitán. In the end, only Palacios, Miguel de Mendizabal, and Tannenbaum carried on and nearly completed the itinerary. In his expedition report, Palacios wrote that his group departed San Cristóbal for Comitán on 3 June 1926. They went by car, "but the road was in lamentable condition and it became impassable once the rains started. We had to stop overnight at the hacienda San Francisco."[2] Traven reported the same experience in *Land des Frühlings*. It seems that it was at the hacienda San Francisco that the expedition's photographer decided to split from his companions and where he picked up his *mozo* (assistant) Felipe.

Traven did not acknowledge in his travelogue that he had been associated initially with a prestigious expedition. Instead, he gave the impression that he had journeyed alone with Felipe throughout and that his sole purpose was to see the Lacandon Indians, a small group of forest dwellers who had largely escaped contact with European civilization. His only comment was that "during the summer of 1926, I tried twice to enter the unknown land [the Lacandon Forest]. It was the reason why I had traveled to Chiapas in the first place. The first time I had made the mistake of joining a group which changed plans while at the edge of the district."[3] His second attempt, he wrote, was foiled by the sudden arrival of the rainy season.

Traven went to Chiapas quite unprepared and knowing next to nothing about the Lacandon Indians. He stated, for example, that they had been visited only once before "as far as I know, and then only along the edges," although the Lacandons had been visited and reported on since the middle of the nineteenth century.[4] Traven also claimed incorrectly that the Lacandons went naked. His ignorance, in fact, extended to the entire Mayan race, and he simply assumed that the Maya and the Aztecs formed one cultural entity. Although he picked up a few local details about Mayan history, he used his knowledge of Aztec origins to explain the peculiar forms of government he encountered among the Mayan Tzotzil Indians in the township of Chamula.[5]

The breakup of the Palacios Expedition was to have a much greater impact on Traven's development and understanding of Mexico than he could have known in 1926. Had the expedition been able to proceed according to its original plan, Traven would have seen the site of the San Roman Tzendales *montería* (logging camp) and become acquainted with the history of the lumber industry in Chiapas. The route he took with Felipe, however, did not bring him into contact with survivors of the horrors of San Roman Tzendales. When Traven learned about the grossly inhumane labor practices of the Casa Romano and its general manager, Fernando Mijares Escandón, two years later, the impact was tremendous. The Jungle Cycle, discussed at length below, was a stinging indictment of the federal and state governments for allowing these outrages against workers to go undisturbed even until the bankruptcy of the Casa Romano in 1925. Had Traven had any knowledge of San Roman Tzendales in 1926, we might assume, his travelogue would have been very different. Instead, he wrote, "my intention to visit the Lacandon Indians led me to their nearest neighbors, the Tzotzil Indians. And soon I found the Tzotzil Indians so full of countless interesting details that I was richly rewarded for my disappointment at not having seen the Lacandons. Whether or not I would have experienced and seen so many beautiful things with the Lacandons as I did with the Tzotzils still needs proving."[6]

Traven's trip to Chiapas was marred by misfortune. Not only did the Palacios Expedition dissolve, but to make matters worse, the author was injured in a fall. After he separated from Palacios, Traven arranged to travel through the Lacandon Forest with Franz Blom, an archeologist from Tulane University and an expert on Mayan ruins. Blom's wife, the photographer and ethnographer Gertrude Duby, recalled her husband telling her that Traven "was riding across an Indian bridge on horseback— stupid of him—and it collapsed. Traven broke his leg."[7] Traven subsequently developed a healthy respect for Indian bridges and warned his readers: "If you see a bridge, you cannot optimistically presuppose that it will hold. It held once, that's certain. But whether it will hold right now when I try to cross it by car or on horseback, I have to find out for myself. The only way of doing that is by actually riding across."[8] It was this accident, rather than "the early arrival of the rainy season," that prevented Traven from meeting the Lacandon Indians for a second time. It precluded, as well, his learning about the *monterías*, for traveling with Franz Blom through the terrain of the old logging companies would inevitably have introduced Traven to the horrific events that recently had occurred there. Traven's temporary immobility was, however, the reason why he took frequent short trips to Chamula, some fifteen kilometers from San Cristóbal, and so became knowledgeable about the Tzotzil Indians he encountered there.

His accident detained Traven in San Cristóbal much longer than he intended. During his enforced stay, he made extensive acquaintances among the German community of the town. One of these was a resident German lawyer, Ewald Hess, whom Traven first met in May 1926. Hess was a great connoisseur of the region and of the Indians of Chiapas. He wrote fiction for relaxation and showed Traven some of his productions which, according to the lawyer's daughter who acted as his secretary, Traven plagiarized and incorporated into *Der Karren*.[9] Traven also brought his camera to the Hess house and took a shot of the interior courtyard, which he incorporated into his travelogue under the caption: "The peaceful patio of a well-to-do citizen's house in San Cristóbal de las Casas."[10] Traven stayed for a while on the farm of Otto Schlie, a German who had made his money from sausage manufacture, and had regular contact with a Swiss trade unionist by the name of Aggerle, who also had a small farm outside of San Cristóbal. Traven spoke German to all of them.[11] This group provided him with the bulk of his information on Chiapas, especially concerning the more recent revolutionary past with which he took astounding liberties in his books. It appears, however, that Traven remained ignorant of the most momentous event in recent Chiapan history: the end of the so-called Mapache War.

In 1914 a group of Chiapan landowners, nicknamed *mapaches* (raccoons) after an episode during which their leader Tiburcio Fernández Ruiz and his men had to eat raw corn in the fields, had begun a guerrilla war against the Constitutionalist troops whom Carranza had sent to Chiapas to introduce reforms in the state. Unlike Tabasco, where as early as 1910 private individuals had raised armies in the name of Francisco Madero, the overthrow of the Díaz regime hardly caused a ripple in Chiapas. The impact of the revolution only began to be felt in the state in 1914, when Colonel Jesús Agustín Castro was appointed military governor, bringing with him his regiment of "northerners" from Durango. One of Colonel Castro's first acts was to issue a Workers' Law in October 1914, abolishing debt slavery and physical punishment, regulating work hours, and introducing a minimum wage. The Chiapan landlords resented this attempt by outsiders to threaten their livelihoods, which depended primarily on cheap and indebted Indian labor, and they went to war. The *mapaches* emerged victorious in 1920, and for the next ten years they resisted the introduction of the reform program of the Mexican Revolution. When Obregón became president in 1920 he hastened to make peace with Fernández Ruiz. All of the *mapache* leader's demands were met by the president, and Fernández Ruiz became governor of the state in December 1920.

Carlos A. Vidal became governor in May 1925, achieving office after a campaign marked by violence against a candidate backed by Fernández Ruiz. Vidal could assert his authority because he enjoyed the backing of the army, the CROM, the Partido Laborista (the CROM's political arm), and President Calles. His right-hand man was Ricardo A. Paniagua, leader of the Socialist Party of Chiapas, who saw to it that all workers in the state were unionized and affiliated with the CROM. Vidal soon forced out all the remaining employees of the previous government and reaffirmed Colonel Castro's decrees, which had been disregarded by the preceding *mapache* governments.[12] In 1926, Vidal established offices to investigate labor contracts in San Cristóbal de las Casas, Comitán, and Motozintla and to supervise the annual contracting of Indians for the coffee harvest on the Pacific coast. No such office was established in Ocosingo, capital of the department of Chilón and center for the contracting of workers for the logging industry. Governor Vidal also revived the Junta de Conciliación y Arbitraje (Central Board of [Labor] Conciliation and Arbitration), which had disappeared with the *mapache* victory. None of these reforms materially affected the northwest of the state, the area of the *monterías* that Traven failed to see in 1926 because of his broken leg.

Although Traven was unaware of the details of these reforms, he understood Vidal to be essentially a radical labor governor who instituted policies that worked in favor of workers. Traven referred to "Senjor Vidal" as "a wise and most progressive man," since the measures taken by him, if not radical on a national scale, were radical in Chiapas, where revolutionary reforms had been assailed and blocked since 1914. Traven was justified in calling Vidal innovative and progressive, and 1925 and 1926 were certainly years of optimism in Chiapas for anyone not a member of the clergy, a landowner, or an industrialist. Traven happened to be in Chiapas at just this opportune moment, finding confirmation for the impressions he had brought from Tampico. When Traven entered the department of Chilón on his next trip, however, in 1928, he realized that what he had observed in the Pacific lowland region of the state was not true for the more remote department, Chiapas's largest district. Chilón was old *mapache* territory, hostile to reform and an area that the arm of Governor Vidal never quite seemed to reach.

Sources of Information in Chiapas

In Chiapas, Traven entered a world beyond any he had ever imagined. Twenty-seven percent of the Chiapan population were Indians living in their own villages. The most picturesque of these was Chamula, which had managed to retain part of its communal land even during the Porfiriato, helping to preserve its social organization, beliefs, costumes, and customs. It was here that Traven was first struck by the enormous gap between himself as a European, the Chamula Indians, and the ladinos.

The term "ladino," although it does not appear in *Land des Frühlings*, is used here because it is a commonly applied name for non-Indians in Chiapas and throughout Central America. In fact, the term has special connotations that Traven, by omitting it from his work, deliberately ignored. Ladino denotes whites as well as mestizos, and it can include Indians if they live the life of a city person. Ladinos consider themselves superior to the Indian population because of their wealth, power, and culture, through which they identify with those who govern the country. Traven eventually began to apply the term ladino in exactly this sense, but in 1926 he was under the impression that the old tensions between the two social strata had been done away with as a result of the revolution's pro-Indian legislation and the attitude of Governor Vidal. Therefore, throughout *Land des Frühlings*, Traven referred to only "Mexicans."

Although a large part of his travelogue is ostensibly about Indians, Traven never defined what he meant by the term and used the word to include anyone who possessed some of their racial characteristics. What is more, Traven did not differentiate between the Indians of Chiapas and other Indian groups. Although he was aware of how diverse the cultures were, he concentrated on what united rather than what separated them. Traven's generalizations about Indians betray the influence of the racial theorizing and speculation that was rife in early twentieth-century Germany. Ultimately, the generalizations made Traven disregard the obvious tensions, even hostility, between the Tzotzil Indians and the ladinos of San Cristóbal de las Casas.

Timing, however, may have contributed to Traven's ignorance. In 1926 there was still an office of the Coffee Growers' Association in San Cristóbal, with a large, open recruiting yard attached. Some two hundred Indians were herded together there at a time, exposed to all weathers and without sufficient food, brought by the *enganchadores* (labor contractors) to work in the coffee harvest in the Pacific lowlands of the state. The tax collector of San Cristóbal made vast sums of money out of the work contracts, and a network of brandy producers closely collaborated with the coffee growers to step up consumption and debts. In 1923 a group of Indians were killed after they had demanded an increase in the food rations. Their grievances went unheard, and their deaths unpunished, because the city authorities were allied to the coffee planters who, in turn, were interested in maintaining their contracted Indians in debt to guarantee a workforce for the coming year.[13]

The coffee harvest lasted from October to February, and Traven stayed in San Cristóbal from May to August. He was not present to witness, therefore, the spectacle of the *enganchadores*, with their elegant sombreros and waxed mustachios, entering San Cristóbal with a herd of Chamula and barefooted Tenejapa Indians behind them, headed for the corral of the Coffee Growers' Association.[14] Traven, it appears, was ignorant of these contracting and labor conditions; none of his friends seems to have thought them worth mentioning. Thus, Traven felt justified in writing that an Indian who had been cheated would go straight away to the police where "he knows he will get justice." Traven claimed to have made this observation in San Cristóbal de las Casas.

While Traven was staying at the hacienda San Francisco, he bought a riding saddle at a *tienda de raya*. He was quite aware how such a company or hacienda store functioned: "Every hacienda maintains a small shop where passers-by can purchase the bare necessities of a traveler on his way. At the same time, this shop serves the purpose of getting the peons of the hacienda to work even more cheaply than they do anyway. Mostly, these people are not paid in cash but in vouchers for the shop."[15] Traven was also aware of the debt peonage of which the *tienda de raya* was a prime instrument, but, he stressed, such conditions of bondage had been abolished by the revolution. He pointed out, however, that "this system of slavery still operates unmitigated in all those districts where the power of the present government does not quite reach, and where the Indians are so ignorant that they do not understand what happens to them."[16] One of these areas was Chiapas, and one of the Indian groups affected was the Chamula. Traven had heard from official statistics issued by the Mexican government and from reports of American researchers that in the southern states of Mexico, "especially Oaxaca, Chiapas, Guerrero, Campeche, and Quintana Roo, more than 250,000 Indians still live in a state of absolute slavery."[17] But in 1926 he acknowledged no evidence of such conditions.

Traven stressed that he only used information derived from "what I have seen myself and of what—according to my knowledge of the country and of Indians—is believable and probable."[18] "Believable and probable" were criteria influenced by his experiences in Tampico and his trust in the Calles government. If *tiendas de raya*, debt slavery, and physical punishment still persisted in isolated pockets, he argued, it was only a question of time until they would be eradicated. Two or three weeks more in San Cristóbal would have shown Traven that the *enganchadores* were alive and well, and so was their trade.[19]

In order to bolster the authenticity of his information, Traven told his readers that he had lived in Chamula for seven weeks. This claim is unlikely, because no non-Chamula is allowed to stay overnight let alone settle there temporarily. Traven, like every tourist, went for day trips. Moreover, when he encountered his first "primitive" he realized how difficult and uncertain communication with tribal Indians was. Trying to draw a few words of Tzotzil from a young Chamula, he became aware of the huge conceptual gap between himself and the other man. In the end, Traven was reduced to speaking with Indians who knew Spanish. In the course of his seven-week stay, Traven wrote, he had become "the best known white person in Chamula because . . . I distributed several thousand cigarettes and quantities of sweets to the children."[20] Despite this, the Chamula only allowed him to observe and to photograph them; they revealed nothing of their rituals, administration, and religion to the blond, blue-eyed stranger in jodhpurs and pith helmet, who spoke bad Spanish with a hard German accent.

Traven boasted that he alone had discovered that the so-called *preparación* for the Fiesta de San Juan, the most important fiesta of the Chamula Indians, was actually an occasion to worship the ancient rain god. He had asked the municipal secretary and the teacher for information on the fiesta without receiving a satisfactory answer. Then he "asked [his] Indians to whom [he] could talk."[21] After initial hesitation—although, he says, "there are ways to make such people talk"—he discovered the truth. But there was nothing special about this revelation except to a stranger like Traven, who did not understand that the Chamula preferred their own saints' images and interpretation of religious festivals, and that the Church had tolerated these practices for centuries.

Tannenbaum recalled that in 1926 there was no Indian in Chamula with any knowledge of Spanish. The schoolteacher, therefore, had to employ a young child who had lived in the city to act as an interpreter.[22] "My Indians to whom I could talk" and "my Spanish-speaking Indians," as Traven called them, seem to have been one person, namely Felipe, Traven's *mozo*, who was, we know, not a Chamula at all. Felipe was an itinerant pottery salesman from Amatenango where the predominant Indian languages are Tzeltal and Tojolabal. It was quite unlikely that Felipe spoke Tzotzil. But he did speak Spanish well, which means that he was a ladinized Indian. The style of his approach to Traven—offering his services as a *mozo*—indicates that he was fluent in the ways of non-Indians. Felipe's status as ladino and non-Chamula necessarily puts what he told Traven about Chamula religion and rituals in doubt. Later ethnographers have stressed that ladinos are unreliable informants about Indian life because their knowledge of Indians is uncertain, although they might have lived all their lives among them. Traven claimed to be aware of this unreliability, yet he depended on ladino information for lack of any other sources and therefore likely fell victim to being misled.

One such example is Traven's detailed description of a Chamula courtship and the shyness with which it is conducted. As is only natural, when it came to the conclusion of the courtship the author was not allowed to be present. Instead he relied on information from someone also not privileged to watch, but who drew his own conclusions from what he could see and then broadcast his knowledge to unwary travelers including Traven.[23] When a young Chamula has chosen his bride, she is allowed to live in her future in-laws' house for a month to see whether it is acceptable or not. Observers of this custom, including Traven himself, assumed that as soon as the young Chamula couple have agreed to marry, they begin sexual relations. Only then would the young man go and see the girl's father, Traven wrote. He concluded that "the probationary wedding night is an institution for which to envy the Indian sincerely," and he called the Europeans "goddamn hypocrites" for not allowing such a trial run before marriage.[24] In fact, anthropologists have learned, Chamula are very strict in matters of sex and decorum. Girls are not allowed to talk to boys, not even to their future husbands, let alone have premarital sex.[25]

Traven accepted what is obviously an uninformed and casual ladino interpretation of the courting ritual. Had he understood the economic system in which the Chamula lived and worked, he would have seen that courtship could not be so informal. A courtship required wedding presents. The economy, however, did not produce profit in cash; in order for the young Chamula men to earn the money for presents, they hired themselves out to work in the coffee harvest on the Pacific coast of the state. Although he knew of the annual migration to the coffee plantations, Traven clearly did not understand, at the time he was writing *Land des Frühlings* in 1926, the precise purpose of it. Two subsequent trips to Chiapas would enlighten him concerning the Indians' economic situation, and he would accurately fictionalize the dilemma of a young Chamula in *Marsch ins Reich der Caoba*.

Traven attended the Fiesta de San Juan in Chamula on 24 June 1926. The only person he talked to at any length on that day was the municipal secretary, the representative of the federal government and the link between it and independent Indian communities such as Chamula. The secretary allowed Traven to sit in his office while he conducted his business. He explained his duties to the stranger and the purpose of his job, which Traven faithfully reproduced: "One of the most important duties of the secretary under the present government is to protect the Indians of his district against non-Indian exploiters of labor . . . and of Indian ignorance."[26] The job description given to Traven and recreated in the book closely followed the guidelines issued by the government for the position.[27] Two trips to Chiapas later, Traven found out how these duties were actually carried out. His portrayal of the character Gabriel, the town secretary of Bachajón in *Regierung*, indicated how much Traven had learned about the realities of Chiapan government.

One of the most conspicuous aspects of Indian administration and ritual, the copious amounts of alcohol consumed during every transaction, never earned Traven's mention. Whenever anything was decided or sealed, either among Indian officials or among Indian and ladino officials, it was always confirmed with aguardiente. The Indian hierarchy was virtually sustained by alcohol, which also played an important role at weddings, funerals, and fiestas. "You can't govern the village and settle disputes or give people justice," one Chamula commented, "without drinking aguardiente. . . . Separations, quarrels, land divisions, boundary disputes . . . everything is settled by drinking, by getting drunk." A tourist such as Traven, of course, was not privileged to witness such an official session. Otherwise, he would undoubtedly have noticed the ritual role of alcohol and likely not have made light of Indian alcoholism. Traven was aware in a general way of pulque being "a peril for a large part of the lower classes" and of the antialcohol campaigns in several states. But the Tzotzil, he thought, were casual drinkers "who get drunk with a few glasses only. In fact, he is not really drunk. He thinks himself drunk and acts as if heavily drunk."[28] The liquor he observed being consumed during the Fiesta de San Juan, Traven claimed, was brought in by outsiders, "some fellows from the Mexican towns." It seems that Traven did not understand the purpose of the traditional cowhorns filled with *comiteco*, the local brandy, which every Chamula had dangling from his belt during the fiesta.

It appears that Traven was not aware that Chamula was no ordinary town but a ceremonial center with a shifting population of officials. He referred to it as the "political center for the nation of the Tzotzil Indians" and as their "capital city." The notion of Chamula as a political unit would have been typical of the views of the municipal secretary who dealt only with this aspect of Chamula life. Traven appears to have been informed only about the six liaison officers—the mayor, four aldermen, and a recordkeeper—with whom the secretary conducted his business. For the Chamula, however, fifty-one religious officials made up

their government; although these officials had no legal standing, they regulated the religious and economic activities around
which the entire structure of the community revolved. Had
Traven known of their existence and of their importance to
Chamula, he might have understood that his judgment on the
demise of religion in Mexico was premature. One of these religious officials, residing in Chamula for his one year in office,
had sponsored the Fiesta de San Juan. He had risen through the
ranks of the hierarchy in charge of the statue of San Juan in the
church at Chamula. He had not only spent all his available
savings on this honor but probably also had gone into considerable debt. To pay his debt, he likely would have to hire himself
out as a seasonal worker in the coffee plantations.

Traven was unaware that the fiesta was a religious festival,
believing instead that it was comparable to a German country
fair, that is, a commercial and social event with a religious
pretext. But this comparison was quite mistaken. No money was
generated within the Indian community; there was only money
spent. The liquor, the candles, the firecrackers—all were goods
purchased outside of Chamula from ladino traders. The Fiesta
de San Juan was the yearly occasion when excess wealth created
within the community was spent. At the time, there was nobody
to dispel Traven's misconceptions and explain the close link
between the religious life and the economic and cultural activities of Chamula. It was only two decades later that ethnographers
of Harvard University began a systematic exploration of the
Tzotzil communities. Traven could only fall back on his own
observations and the biased explanations derived from friends
and acquaintances in Chiapas. Like his CGT and IWW friends,
these informants did not serve him well.

Otherwise, Traven went around collecting stories and opinions as he had done since his arrival in Mexico. He chatted with
anonymous people who told him about their lives and their
environment, and he stored away the information given him.
One incident neatly encapsulates the way he worked: "One
afternoon, when crossing the plaza [of San Cristóbal] to get to
the post office, a gentleman called me . . . and said, 'You are
interested in everything, no matter what it is?' 'Yes,' I replied,
'that is correct; I want to know everything, whether it is interesting
or not.' "[29]

Chiapas was a close-knit society in which people knew each
other and their histories and enjoyed a good gossip. Much of the

talk dealt with the Chamula. However, the stories repeated by the citizens of San Cristóbal, Traven stressed, were the least reliable, springing from a mixture of boredom and fear:

> The evenings in Chiapas are long.... The Mexicans and the strangers residing in Chiapas, so far from the centers of civilization, are huddled together in the small towns, totally surrounded by Indians so superior in numbers. They love to sit together on the long evenings and tell stories. The stories are always about Indians ... and every time the story is passed on by someone who heard it, it sounds more horrible. Everybody swears that their story is absolutely true.... One has to protect oneself against these story-tellers in order not to succumb to their influence.[30]

Traven was exposed for months to these stories and to the often derogatory tone in which they were delivered. Yet, he was able to articulate his own opinion and appreciation of what he saw. He delivered a positive account of those customs and beliefs that ladinos derided. They saw Indians as uncivilized, dirty, and uneducable.[31] It was exactly these claims that Traven rebuked by showing that Indians not only had cleaner habits than Europeans but that they were also highly gifted and intelligent.

Traven was glad to leave San Cristóbal de las Casas, as the town had begun to wear on him. In this isolated backwater he kept meeting the same people who kept telling him the same stories. "This is destructive to the human well-being if one is not an immediate member of this circle," he wrote. Together with Felipe, Traven set out by mule to Tuxtla Gutiérrez and along the Pacific coast to Mapastepec. From here on, Traven depended on his own observation and on Felipe for company. The first thing he learned from Felipe was the handling and driving of mules. Every now and then he had to lend Felipe a hand in packing and unpacking. Traven noted these details in *Land des Frühlings* and reproduced them in the Jungle Cycle, especially in *Der Karren*, where they added an important element of authenticity. In fact, Traven proved to be the only traveler of the 1920s who thought the Chiapan transport system worth describing in detail. On a particularly dangerous piece of road, Felipe and Traven joined an oxcart caravan, and Traven, with his usual inquisitiveness, talked to the *carreteros* (oxcart drivers) and asked them about the difficulties of their profession. He was well rewarded and for the next ten years drew on the knowledge he had gathered in a few hours. Indeed, perhaps unknowingly, he recorded a piece of Chiapan history. The old *camino real*, the "King's highway," is a wide paved road today, and the caravans of mules and oxcarts have long since vanished.

When the two travelers reached the tropical lowlands, Traven rejoiced: "How happy I am to be back in the tropics . . . and to observe a tropical sunset. . . . I don't give a damn about the mosquito plague! This is the entrance fee to the country of eternal springtime. There is nothing free in this imperfect world." After two years in Mexico, Traven had learned to cope with the tropical climate. The trip ended "for this year" at Mapastepec, where both took the train back to the station of Jalisco. From here, it is believed, Traven returned to Tampico where he had kept his house in the American colony.[32]

Traven and Indigenismo

Indigenismo had emerged from the revolution largely as an urban phenomenon. Many intellectuals came in contact with indigenous people for the first time during the battles of the revolution, and they began to view the Indian as the builder of the new nation and the revolution itself as the affirmation of indigenous values. Although Indians did not make the revolution, they came to be regarded as its conscience.[33] Indigenismo thus became a part of Mexican nationalism, and Traven became an indigenista when he became a supporter of his adopted land. Land reform and the education campaign were expressions of this new ideology, and leading indigenistas such as Moisés Sáenz, José Vasconcelos, and Manuel Gamio played important roles in devising educational policies.

In 1926 indigenismo was no more than a philosophy fostered and nurtured in the literary salons of the large Mexican cities, where Traven most likely came in contact with it. Its following was not confined to Mexico alone but was present in every Latin American country possessing a sizeable Indian population. Its spread, however, only obscured the fact that it was a philosophical fashion as yet unsupported by a solid body of scholarship. Although indigenista writings praised the worth of the Indian, it was never clearly established what "the Indian" represented. In Mexico alone, Indians were as different as the Séris of Tiburón Island, who used their bare hands and teeth to devour raw meat, and Benito Júarez, the nineteenth-century president of the nation. The approach to diverse Indian groups and cultures was undifferentiated because it was the declared goal of *indigenismo* to do away with the differences between them. This may explain why Traven, along with other *indigenistas*, generalized about "the Indian." Abolishing the differences between indigenous groups was envisaged as the only successful path toward the social and economic betterment of the Indian peoples. Each Indian was to be educated to become a Mexican, and the literacy campaign, President Calles pointed out, aimed to incorporate rural workers into the ranks of civilization.[34] Indeed, this was the essence of *indigenismo*: to absorb the Indian into Mexican mainstream culture. Such anomalies as the dual government system of Chamula and the refusal to abandon Indian monolingualism were to be wiped out. To the politicians in Mexico City, the Indian was a minority to be pitied, helped, despised, or admired, but always to be changed to conform to the majority in dress, speech, and ideas.

The twin pillars of Mexican *indigenismo* were the restitution of community land and education, but the envisaged outcome of these policies had nothing to do with the wishes of the Indians. *Indigenistas* expected them to create and run highly productive communal agricultural enterprises. Although, on the one hand, the indigenous cultures were hailed as anticapitalist, on the other hand, they were understood to be capitalist on a communal scale. Traven echoed faithfully these contradictory expectations. Education, membership in a trade union, the closure of churches, the abolition of religion, and separation from the land through large-scale agriculture, he maintained, would force the Indian's removal from his communal organization and spiritual world. All the measures enacted by the Calles government to help the Indian were designed to break through Indian separateness and to promote assimilation. In *indigenista* philosophy, the integration process was to be reciprocal: The Indian was expected to adapt to Mexican civilization, and the Mexican community at large was to adopt Indian ideas of collective work and farming. Traven shared with the government this line of reasoning. It was not until later that he came to understand the ultimate goals of government policies.

Like the *indigenistas*, Traven advocated *mestizaje*, the blending of Indian and European peoples that had been under way since the Spanish conquest. From this process was to emerge Vasconcelos's "*raza cósmica*," a homogenous Mexican people, undivided by cultural and ethnic differences and drawing on the strength of both of its components. Traven saw *mestizaje* as actual physical blending, whereas the Mexicans meant the absorption of the Indian into the greater Mexican community. The majority of *indigenistas* agreed on this latter goal; they merely debated the merits of different ways of achieving it. In Chiapas the way ahead was through the peaceful means of education. In Sonora a war was fought against the mountain Yaqui, who fiercely resisted assimilation and claimed return of their tribal lands. The war was fought under the personal direction of President Calles and ended with the near extinction of the Yaqui in 1929.

Traven's misunderstanding seems to have hinged on a question of definition. In Mexico, an Indian was defined in social terms, and Indians constituted the lowest stratum of Mexican society. Should a mestizo adopt an indigenous way of life, its traditions, occupations, habitat, dress, and perhaps even an Indian language, then he would be considered an Indian. For a Mexican, anybody who adhered to preconquest social organizations and traditions, who knew little or no Spanish, who identified with an exclusive group instead of with the rest of the hispanicized nation, was an "Indian." By the same token, an Indian could cross the barrier and become a ladino, if he made efforts to become *civilizado*—to live, dress and speak like a ladino.[35]

The Indian, however, in Traven's work is defined in purely racial terms. To Traven, the education, health, and land reform campaigns were all designed to render the Indian fit to intermarry with the rest of the Mexican population. He wrote: "In order to accept the Indian whom he [the Mexican] needs for the formation of this new race, he has to raise him to a higher level of civilization. For the moment this can only be done by raising the Indian to his own level of education." Traven asserted that "the biological sciences showed that the melting of two opposite races always produces a [new] race superior by a third or half to its components in resilience and resistance." The Mexican, he informed his readers, "strives like every young nation to breed a purely Mexican nation. He works in that direction quite consciously, especially since the revolution. He has the instinctive feeling that from an intimate union with the native population of this country, a genuine Mexican race can be shaped."[36] Traven thus introduced a racial element into the *indigenista* debate that was not part of the Mexican discussions. The simplest and most likely explanation for this apparent liberty is that Traven had not understood that the Spanish word *raza*, a word amply used in *indigenista* literature, was not the equivalent of the German word *Rasse*. Although each corresponds to the English word "race," the German always has a genetic context, while the Spanish *raza* means "nation" and is used in *indigenista* literature in this sense.

Traven never confronted the problems surrounding the entrance of Indians into Mexican society. It was, he thought, not an issue, since he saw Indian blood and influence everywhere, up to the highest political office. The Mexican *indigenistas*, however, praised the Indian and his innate qualities, at the same time that their political scheme clearly indicated that the Indian would enter Mexican society at the lowest level. The inadequacies of rural education alone would make sure of this. Indians would lose their separate identities and, in the case of Chamula for instance, would become subject to the Mexican authorities, having to accept mestizo direction and domination. This was precisely what indigenous peoples in general and the Chamula in particular had fought since the Spanish conquest. The ladinos of Chiapas were very much in favor of Indian incorporation into their society. They were also convinced that this would constitute real progress for the Indian, believing, as the Chiapan historian Angel Corzo wrote, that this involvement would finally rid the Indians of their superstitious beliefs.[37] In 1926, Traven had no notion of what Indian absorption into Mexican society would come to mean in terms of increased power and control of the federal and state governments.

When Traven left the realm of speculation, however, he had great reservations about mestizos. He called the "offspring of a white man and a pure-blooded Indian woman rather inferior in the first generation," filled with "destructive instincts."[38] The author had some unpleasant experiences with mestizos during his trip to Chiapas, and he called them variously murderers, thieves, and corrupters of Indian morals and taste. He also acknowledged the thousands of uprooted Indians living in and around the large Mexican cities whose destitution drove them to crime. He described them as "Indians grown in the quagmire of civilization of a Mexican suburb [picking up] the habits and views of those groups that grow everywhere on the dungheaps of civilization." These Indians, one concludes, had lost touch with their inherent concern for the welfare of the group. In

Chamula, Traven had an opportunity to observe an Indian "gathering" firsthand. He noted that the children were brought along to the Fiesta de San Juan "to implant in their young hearts a feeling of togetherness of all members of the tribe. This happens unconsciously and without premeditation."[39] According to this account, the community sense was fostered by education and upbringing.

Traven was oblivious to the dangers of *mestizaje* because he thought the Indian "sense of community" would safeguard against any abuse. When he tried to explain this sense to his German readers, he ran into trouble:

> The idea, rooted in the nature of the Indian about how people gather and organize in order to facilitate and beautify their lives, has nothing in common with the European idea of the state. It has nothing to do with the ideas of the communists either.
>
> It is extremely difficult to understand the notion of a gathering of the Indian, more difficult still to explain it. We have no word, no comparison, to link it up with. This idea of gathering is neither an idea of a state nor a free commune idea in a European sense.[40]

The closest he came to formulating this idea was when he explained that "in Europe, individual ambition prevails. Here among the Indians, there is communal ambition," and he cited copious examples of how communal involvement manifested itself in all walks of life. Traven was convinced that this sense was inherent in Indian nature and that it was located in the Indian blood. Therefore, he argued, the "Indian blood becomes stronger, even in those classes of the Mexican population who mainly deal in politics." Anybody who had some Indian blood possessed necessarily a commitment to addressing the needs of other people. Indian blood in the veins of the ruling politicians was the best safeguard, according to Traven, against any relapse into capitalism.

Traven could advocate the abolition of Indian languages, customs, religion, and traditions because he thought the essence of Indianness was safeguarded in the genes. The Indian, he thought, would enrich Mexican culture permanently with his racial heritage. But the ladinos of Chiapas, for instance, had no intention of learning anything from the despised "superstitious and dirty" Indians. They did not value the communal sense, which was to them something imagined by a civil servant "who had never seen an Indian in his life and who pretended he could take charge of the Tzotzil and Tzeltal Indians."[41] Traven was unaware, at the time of this visit to Chiapas, of this attitude of the local ladinos. He saw Indians entering Mexican society at all levels, at the highest in the person of President Calles himself, and at the lowest in the trade unions. It was Traven's firm conviction that in the larger world the trade union was a substitute for the Indian's closely knit community. The trade union, he wrote, "is closer to his sense of community and his social views than the state whose organization he cannot and will never understand." A powerful central state was against Indian nature, Traven thought, and the best proof of this was that the trade union movement was taking over the Mexican state. Traven managed skilfully to blend his own anarcho-syndicalist ideas with the ideas of the *indigenistas* to argue that ultimately the working class would win political and economic power.

Shortly after the publication of *Land des Frühlings*, Traven became aware of his misunderstandings and saw that although *mestizaje* for him promised the beginning of a great future for an Indian Mexico, for the federal government it signified the completion of the Spanish conquest after four centuries of tenacious Indian resistance to Mexicanization. Traven seems to have become aware of the political dangers posed by his book now that he was gaining an international reputation as an author. This may well have been another factor explaining his subsequent decision to suppress the travelogue.

Traven and History

Traven's newly adopted *indigenismo* inspired in him a new way of interpreting the past. The author generally had no patience with history; he was only concerned with living people, he wrote. His vision was directed to the future and he used the past as an arsenal from which he drew for his speculations about what was to come. He went to great lengths to prove "from history" the then fashionable *indigenista* theory that the cradle of mankind was actually in Mexico rather than in Mesopotamia, a theory that was avidly discussed by the leftist circle around the muralist Rivera, in whose company Traven might have been introduced to it.[42]

Indian history in Mexico, Traven pointed out, consisted of accounts of Indian rebellions. "The rebellions they undertook," he wrote, "were like the movements of a sleeping man."[43] There had been two major rebellions of Chamula Indians in the preceding one hundred years, the most serious of which broke out in 1869. In 1911 political manipulation of the Chamula nearly led to the dreaded *guerra de castas* (race war), or so it was said. In explaining and interpreting these rebellions, Traven had to rely on ladino accounts. He pared away all but the core information and then superimposed his own interpretation of what he thought these events would look like from an Indian viewpoint. Indian rebellions, Traven explained, always had the same goal: the restoration of the Indian communities. In 1869 the Tzotzil occupied the city of San Cristóbal de las Casas. The event left such a trauma that the inhabitants of the city now lived "in a permanent and subdued fear of the Indians living around the city. The physical as well as the economic situation of the city makes it easy for the Indians to starve its population. All they need to do is block all access roads to San Cristóbal and no longer deliver food."[44]

As Traven explained it, the 1869 rebellion was caused by social and economic factors. The Indians were pressed into forced labor without pay; Indians delivering food to the city were simply kidnapped; the value of their goods was lowered while prices were inflated for the goods they needed. Outside of the city, Indian land was taken away and lumber rights annulled. All these developments are well documented, but Traven's interpretation of these events was more controversial. In order to change their unbearable situation, Traven wrote, the Tzotzils decided to defend themselves and "to show the local population how dependent they were on Indians." They blocked all access to the city and, Traven continued, "went on strike, reinforced by a boycott and the elimination of strike breakers."[45] The ladinos of San Cristóbal, however, managed to break the blockade by trickery, luring the Indian leaders into the city and killing them. Peace was restored, even though the Chamula realized what had befallen their murdered representatives. From then on, Traven reported, Indians were treated with great respect in the city, "like extraordinarily large but good humored dogs with a reputation for ripping everything to pieces when irritated."[46] According to Traven, not only had the Chamula behaved like regular trade unionists trained in the tactics of the class war and of direct action, but they had also achieved a great moral victory. Traven had completely disregarded the most significant dimension of the whole uprising: that the Chamula had attacked San Cristóbal because the bishop had blocked their attempt to have their own Indian saints.

The most complete record of the 1869 uprising was written by Vicente Pineda, a local historian, and published in 1888. Pineda saw the struggle in apocalyptic fashion as a war of "savagery against civilization." The Chamula had been seduced by a city slicker called Galindo into believing that they possessed a talking statue of an Indian Virgin and, Pineda concluded, "the assembly of idiots believed it." Pineda's account of the siege of San Cristóbal contained an element about which Traven marveled until the end of his writing career. The Chamula won the battle against the few available soldiers who, Pineda wrote, "were horrified at the shrieks and whistles of the barbarians, at the pitiful cries of the dying ... at the brutal furor of the savages who know no feeling of humanity and pity and have no consideration for the vanquished."[47] Pineda then continued: "Fortunately for Ciudad Real [the old name of San Cristóbal] the Indians did not recognize their advantage." They failed to follow up their victory and, instead, retreated to their positions outside the city.

Pineda was baffled by this last point, as was Traven. But whereas Pineda had no explanation, Traven hypothesized that this failure to follow up a victory was another side of the Indians' "sense of community." Later investigators have noted the Indian leaders' inability to control men, their suspicion of conflict, and tireless advocacy of adjustment.[48] Traven never found an explanation for this peculiar event, but it puzzled and intrigued him, and he revived the theme in *Marsch ins Reich der Caoba* and *Ein General kommt aus dem Dschungel*. His knowledge, however, of this particular incident during the 1869 siege of San Cristóbal indicates that Traven was familiar with Pineda's account.

When the Chamula Juan Pérez Jolote recalled the events of 1869, in which his grandfather had participated, he disregarded the issues of ladino interference and the siege of San Cristóbal. He was interested exclusively in the religious question and the crucifixion of an Indian boy to create a "brown Jesus" that constituted an act of rebellion against the white man's religion. The whereabouts of the body of the brown Jesus was a closely guarded secret among the religious hierarchy of Chamula, whereas the cross can still be seen today in the church.[49] Thus, despite Traven's interest in the unique character of the Chamula's actions, his interpretation of the 1869 rebellion had little in common with Indian viewpoints.

In discussing the 1911 rebellion, Traven referred to an event in Chiapan history known as *el desorejamiento* (the ear cropping). When Traven arrived in Tuxtla Gutiérrez, he was shown photographs of a number of Chamula whose ears had been cut off with machete blows by a Mexican army officer in July 1911. Either Traven was never told the full story of this brutality or he did not understand its complexity; he simply proceeded with his own interpretation of the event, and in the process distorted the facts beyond recognition. Except for the actual ear cropping, all the other details Traven provided in *Land des Frühlings* had no bearing on the incident. Traven's presentation of the event reads:

> Even in the remote state of Chiapas, the Indians rose in the second year of the revolution. They had no weapons. With the primitive tools used in agriculture, they marched in a column to the governor in the state capital Tuxtla Gutiérrez, and there they were received in a civilized way. The troops of the conservative government waited for them on the road. . . . The soldiers captured some forty of them and brought them to the governor's palace where their ears were cut off. This horrible deed was executed in the most cruel manner. . . . Then these unfortunate creatures were officially photographed and sent home to their villages to tell their fellow villagers what to expect should they ever again dare to go to the governor and inquire about their ancient rights.[50]

Traven was unaware that this incident formed part of a war that was unrelated to the struggles of the Mexican Revolution. No Indians had risen in "the remote state of Chiapas" in 1911 or later. On the contrary, the Indians of Chiapas fought alongside their masters, and the incident of July 1911 formed part of a war in which the Chamula went to battle for the ladinos of San Cristóbal.[51] The 1911 war, between the old Chiapan state capital San Cristóbal de las Casas and the new capital city Tuxtla Gutiérrez, was started to redress political and economic grievances of the highland landowners. The leading citizens of San Cristóbal, with the help of promises of land, managed to enlist the services of Jacinto "Pajarito" Pérez, the Chamula leader, along with fifteen hundred of his men, who were fierce and cruel soldiers. Although the mutilation of a few captured Chamula was universally condemned, the warring ladino parties soon realized that the Chamula were difficult to control, and fears of a new *guerra de castas* were voiced throughout the state.

When the ladinos made their peace in September 1911, work began to eliminate El Pajarito, who was eventually executed.[52]

It is doubtful whether Traven would have been willing in 1926 to acknowledge the degree to which ladinos had manipulated the Chamula in 1911. The true background to *el desorejamiento* would have destroyed his *indigenista* vision of the race-proud Mexican willing to "embrace, kiss, and call brother" the humble Indian. But while Traven never understood the complicated background of the event itself, he never forgot the picture of the mutilated Chamula and revived it in a powerful scene in *Die Rebellion der Gehenkten.*

The rudest blow to Traven's optimistic vision of 1926 came from Felipe. At the railway station where the two parted, Felipe had gone immediately to buy himself ladino clothes. Traven sadly commented: "When I saw Felipe standing before me, feeling so happy in his stiff blue calico jacket, obviously not expecting anything higher from life than that this condition would last forever, it suddenly dawned on me that this self-sufficiency, this being happy with the given limitations, is one of the main reasons why the Mexican people in their great and preponderant mass are economically so backward."[53]

The Influence of Traven's First Trip through Chiapas on His Early Fiction

As soon as Traven returned north from Chiapas, he began to work feverishly. Among the manuscripts he produced while living at Cuauhtémoc must have been *Die weisse Rose, Der Schatz der Sierra Madre,* and *Die Brücke im Dschungel,* since all show signs of having either been completed or altered under the influence of the impressions the author brought back from Chiapas. The difference between Traven's pre- and post-1926 fiction is the author's greater awareness of Indian culture. Gale and his cottonpickers never meet any Indians, observing them only from afar. *Der Schatz der Sierra Madre,* which begins in the insalubrious rooming houses of Tampico, introduces half way through the novel tribal Indians living in small villages. In this book, Traven described an incident in which a traveling medical team, part of the government's health campaign, visited a village to vaccinate Indian children. The health workers ask the passing Americans to stop and make a display of being vaccinated in order to help them overcome Indian mistrust. Traven had first become aware of Indian mistrust of medical teams in Chiapas where the Indian boys from the industrial school in Tuxtla Gutiérrez "prepare the way for the government commissions presently traveling through the country in order to vaccinate the population. . . . In hundreds of cases, it would be quite impossible to vaccinate Indians. Small armies of soldiers would have to accompany the commissions."

Traven also made use of Chiapan geography. Dobbs's approach to the city of Durango in *Der Schatz der Sierra Madre*, the last lap of his solo trip carrying the gold, is not the approach to Durango at all but to Tuxtla Gutiérrez. Compare Dobbs's experience to Traven's own: "The road improved and by midday Dobbs could reckon that three more hours would take him to Durango. . . . The track was deep with sand and dust. . . . Whenever the wind rose or a sudden squall came over, a column of suffocating dust whirled up, and you could scarcely breathe. A fine sand was driven into the eyes, making them smart and blinding them minutes together." Traven could describe this piece of road so vividly because he had experienced it himself:

> From Chiapa de Corzo to Tuxtla Gutiérrez . . . it is only three hours on horseback. The last part of the road before Tuxtla Gutiérrez is quite painful to ride, especially in the heat of noon. . . . The road is open on both sides. No trees for shade . . . no rock, no hill. The mule sinks deep into the soft, powderlike dust. The smallest breeze stirs up the dust, it settles in the lungs and burns in the eyes.[54]

Dobbs halts his caravan under a tree to rest. "He turned his head," Traven continued, "and saw three men lying under the next tree. They were mestizos, down-and-out and in rags, fellows who perhaps had worked for a mining company long ago. . . . Whatever a town cannot do with, even on its rubbish heaps, it drives out on the roads." The three mestizos kill Dobbs in cold blood and scatter the gold dust in the wind, not realizing what they are doing.[55] During his approach to Tuxtla Gutiérrez, Traven observed just such unsavory individuals near the city: "The traveler frequently meets men from the trash heap of the big cities, hanging around here, close to the big cities, waiting for opportunities. It does not need to be murder. But a traveler can lose something. . . . Such opportunities develop under certain circumstances into actions which are no longer harmless, especially when two or three men are gathered to wait for an opportunity."[56] What is more, both Dobbs and Traven suffered a delay of two hours—Dobbs for losing two mules, Traven for taking the wrong way—so that both only reached the dusty stretch of road under the burning midday sun.

The daughter of Traven's friend in San Cristóbal, Ewald Hess, maintains that the idea of transporting gold in animal hides was plagiarized by Traven from her father.[57] This accusation would certainly fit the timing of the writing of *Der Schatz der Sierra Madre*. In Chiapas, Traven also had heard the story of how several people had spent a miserable night tied by their belts to a mahogany tree. This pitiful position was preferable to "being caressed by the paws of a tiger which they thought stalked nearby." Traven also incorporated this episode into *Der Schatz der Sierra Madre*.

Traven's first story dealing exclusively with Indians was *Die Brücke im Dschungel*, first published as a serial in *Vorwärts* between 14 May and 17 June 1927. Although the setting appears similar to the tropical region of Tamaulipas, Traven's Indians have characteristics that he had observed in Chamula. At the Fiesta de San Juan, Traven had noticed that "we need much music, noise and fuss in order to amuse ourselves. But here at this feast, the music consists of three Indians with roughly constructed guitars who file in and out between the people, play badly and sometimes sing along. Nobody pays them. The musician finds his reward in the fact that he is allowed to play and that somebody listens to him or calls him and accompanies his music with clapping."[58] Compare this with the comment made by old Garcia, father of little Carlos who drowns in *Die Brücke im Dschungel*: "Never mind. Garcia did not feel insulted when everybody ceased dancing to his fiddling. He did not mind at all. If there is somebody able to play better, why doesn't he step forward?"[59]

Traven's description of his parting moments with Felipe at the railway station in Chiapas appears in more than one book as well. In *Land des Frühlings*, he described Felipe as "proud in his new blue calico jacket that stiffly enveloped his well-shaped body like a barrel. Despite his patched shirt and his splattered white pants he had always looked like the native bronze-colored son of this beautiful country. The jacket, however, threw him with one stroke into the great mass of industrial workers; he, the beautiful Indian."[60] In *Die Brücke im Dschungel*, Gale receives the same shock when he suddenly sees the corpse of little Carlos all dressed up: "The mother dressed the child in the sailor's suit.

When she had finished, I looked at the corpse. A cold chill ran down my spine. With his torn, patched trousers . . . the boy had been quite graceful, a real child of the jungle. In this cheap sailor's suit, he no longer looked like the son of his native land."[61] The only part of *Die Brücke im Dschungel* that indicates that Traven may have begun writing the story before leaving for Chiapas is the fact that it deals with the oil industry. It was the American oil company that failed to provide a railing for the bridge. Ewald Hess's daughter claimed that the idea to let little Carlos slip on the bridge in American shoes, which his feet were not used to, also belonged to her father. Again, the timing suggests that this could be so.

The novel most strongly influenced by Traven's *indigenista* views and his experiences in Chamula is *Die weisse Rose*. The characterization in that work of both Hacinto Yanyez and "the Governor from Jalapa" suggests that Traven devised both personages after his return from Chiapas. In Hacinto Yanyez, Traven crystalized his ideal of the self-regulating community, something he never managed with his halting and uncertain theoretical expositions in *Land des Frühlings*. Hacinto Yanyez is one of Traven's most attractively drawn characters, but he is distanced from everyday reality. Not the slogging beast of burden, he is peace itself, the embodiment of Traven's own arcadian dream, which he had come to associate with the Indian "sense of community." Hacinto owned no property; instead, "what he owned was only on loan to him." Traven had learned in Chamula about this pattern of landholding in which each family received as much community land as it needed and no more than it could work. Because land was a communal patrimony, it was inalienable. Traven made Hacinto Yanyez sum up in a few immortal words what he thought were Indian attitudes to property and profit: "Land is eternal, money is not eternal, therefore land cannot be exchanged for money."[62] "The Governor from Jalapa" was Traven's fictionalization of labor governors such as he had seen in Chiapas, the "men with strong spines" who adhered to "a Mexican-Indian socialism," "politicians of a new era" who did everything in their power to help the Indian.

Traven spent a year completing his four manuscripts. It seems he finished each of those "in his drawer" and immediately bundled it off to Germany, where the publication of the four was spaced to give Traven the time he required for a return to Chiapas and further study of Indian life and culture. *Der Schatz der Sierra Madre* was published late in 1927; *Land des Frühlings* followed in 1928, together with a volume of short stories entitled *Der Busch*. Late the following year, *Die Brücke im Dschungel* and *Die weisse Rose* appeared. The first volume of the Jungle Cycle, *Der Karren*, was published at the end of 1930.

During Traven's adventurous five months in Chiapas, an economic crisis of major proportions had arisen across the country. The reform program of the Calles government was expected to be financed by oil revenues, but in 1926 income from taxes on oil exports suddenly began to drop alarmingly. Competition from Venezuela, Colombia, and the United States produced an oil glut, and diminishing output from Mexican oil wells compounded the crisis. If this were not enough, in the same year India and China, Mexico's principal clients for silver, switched to the gold standard. Thus Mexico's two principal sources of export income dried up in one year. Trade in general went into a crisis, provoking growing unemployment and violent strikes. On the land, the impoverishment of the rural population increased. The crisis reached such a point that government employees could not be paid for weeks. In 1927 the crisis was sufficiently serious for the United States, Mexico's principal foreign investor, to send financial experts to investigate the economic situation. Led by the new ambassador, Dwight Morrow, the U.S. banking experts became "the new masters of the Mexican house."[63]

In Tampico, right outside Traven's front door, the CGT-dominated petroleum workers went out on strike. But this time there was no worker-state solidarity. Instead, President Calles sent troops to El Aguila Petroleum's plant.[64] Yet, Traven remained oblivious to all these events while he worked through the experiences he had had in 1925 and during his 1926 trip to Chiapas. What Traven wrote in September 1927, "fourteen months after the closure of the churches in Mexico," and what he passed off as the current Mexican political reality, was already history. The publication of *Land des Frühlings*, *Die Brücke im Dschungel*, and finally *Die weisse Rose* between 1927 and 1929 seemed to indicate that Traven continued to believe his idealized version of the Calles government's policies right until the last months of the decade, but he realized the nature of his mistakes well before the end of 1929.

4 The Turning of the Tide

Traven's Second and Third Trips to Chiapas

The only luxury Traven allowed himself between October 1926 and October 1927 was to participate in the summer school of the national university in Mexico City. The subjects he chose clearly reflected his needs; he enrolled for courses in Spanish, South American literature, Mexican folklore, Mexican archeology, and the Mexican Revolution.[1] Traven returned to Chiapas in December 1927 and explored areas of the state he did not see during his first trip. He took day-to-day notes, which allow us to reconstruct the route he took that year. Typed, in often curious English, mostly cryptic, always brief, they record usually no more than dates, times, place names, distances, and temperatures. Although there are only a few scattered pages, they correspond precisely to the routes described in *Der Karren, Regierung,* and *Marsch ins Reich der Caoba.*

For his second trip, Traven came prepared with letters from the Museo Nacional in Mexico City. The letters asked the reader to help the bearer, Señor T. Torsvan, with whatever he needed.[2] Traven must have realized during his first trip that the assistance of local authorities in finding mules, guides, and accommodations could be valuable. This trip, like the previous, did not start well. Traven had hired a mule driver who did not seem very happy with his *patrón* and wanted to leave. The boy accompanying them was "absoly ineffic [*sic*]." Their animals strayed at night and developed sores, "esp. the big horse." Despite, as Traven wrote optimistically, being "well prep. for all kinds of trouble in the road," they were plagued by fleas that accompanied them the entire length of the trip. Moreover, one of the horses seems to have suffered a bad fall ("horse falls from the road down"), and the group also experienced a heavy earthquake.[3]

The last stop before the travelers reached Comitán was at Zapaluta, a small township situated on the road connecting

Tapachula and San Cristóbal de las Casas. Their arrival coincided with the Fiesta de Caralampio (the local patron saint) and the marimba played all night.[4] According to his notes, Traven stayed only for one night, yet he produced an account of the fiesta for *Der Karren* as if he had witnessed the whole two weeks of celebrations. Behind all the color and bustle of the occasion Traven could only see the commercial interests and greed of the Catholic Church, which "did its biggest business for the year" in those weeks.[5] Traven gave his readers a lively picture of the hypocrisy, token devotion, prostitution, deceit, gambling, and the general licentiousness and corruption of the local authorities, conveying the impression that all the non-Indians taking part wanted merely to make a financial killing. Against the background of this fiesta the touching and chaste love story of Andreu Ugalde, one of the two heroes of the Jungle Cycle, and Estrellita is set. The treatment of this event determined the tone of the entire cycle, in which the Indians are all pure souls and the innocent victims of ladino corruption and greed. But it also shows that, although Traven's views matured over the years, he never learned to accept the religious rituals and beliefs of the Mexicans as an inherent part of their culture.

Traven's notes end on 11 February 1928 in Comitán. We know, however, from the memories of a family with whom he stayed that Traven traveled on from Comitán to San Cristóbal de las Casas and then northeast into the hot lowlands around Ocosingo and Palenque, the home of the Tzeltal Indians. On his way from Ocosingo to El Paraíso—a trip reconstructed in great detail in *Marsch ins Reich der Caoba*—he had an important encounter that was to influence deeply his future adventures in Chiapas. Traveling only with his mule driver, and with the neck of his beast hung with cameras and photographic equipment, he met Manuel Bulnes, son of Enrique Bulnes, the owner of the farm El Real, near Ocosingo. Traven was invited to stay at El Real, where he was received with the customary generous hospitality of the Bulnes family. He introduced himself as Torsvan and handed over a card with "Ingeniero T. Torsvan," explaining that he was connected with the oil industry in Tampico and that he was American. He also announced that he was a writer. To his great relief, he could speak English to Enrique Bulnes, who quickly realized that "Ingeniero Torsvan" was neither American nor English.[6]

El Real was the last stop on the journey in and out of the Lacandon Forest, and it was therefore of strategic importance to all travelers to the jungle. Large Mayan ruins had been recently discovered there, and most foreigners who came to this remote area were in search of more archeological remains. This was also Traven's purpose, and he spent his time riding about the countryside with another of Enrique Bulnes's sons, José, collecting Mayan images, pottery remains, and artifacts. For longer excursions into the forest, the Bulnes family provided Traven with a competent guide, Amador Paniagua. A resident of Ocosingo, Paniagua was a Tzeltal half-caste who spoke Spanish and Tzeltal and had worked in the mahogany logging camps of Chiapas.[7] The two penetrated the Lacandon Forest as far as the Usumacinta River, where Traven took a collection of "forty-six photographs of the jungle dwellers on the western banks of the Usumacinta. All photographs have been taken personally by T. Torsvan from February 1928 until June 1928."[8] They traveled from Ocosingo via El Paraíso, Santa Clara Lake, Busijá, Anaité, to Nuevo Filadelfia, the only operational logging camp Traven ever saw.

For the first time, Traven, accompanied by a former *montería* worker, crossed mahogany logging terrain. If Traven had not heard about *monterías* earlier during this trip, the company of a lumberjack would inevitably have given Traven his first knowledge of the industry. What is more, Paniagua and Traven got on well together. Given Traven's curiosity and the circumstances of a lonely and often dangerous trip through the forest, long conversations between the two men were likely. We know that Traven left Chiapas at the latest in early July 1928, because he once more joined the summer school of the Mexican national university. It appears that he spent part of 1929 in California, where he received a letter from Paniagua expressing his delight at the prospect of traveling together once again.[9] In December 1929, Traven returned to Chiapas for the third time, reaching San Cristóbal on 23 December and staying there for Christmas. During his sojourn in the town, Traven took a step that clearly revealed his interest in investigating the stories he had heard about the *monterías* during his previous trip. He contacted Emilio Varela, who had been the accountant of the largest mahogany logging company of Chiapas, the Casa Romano. The company had gone out of business in 1925, and Varela now acted as the

Casa Romano's liquidator.[10] Traven asked Varela for a letter of introduction to Sergio Mijares, who worked at that time at a *montería* called Pico de Oro.

Sergio Mijares was the nephew of Fernando Mijares Escandón, general manager of the Casa Romano and the most ill-reputed *negrero* (slave dealer), as the most cruel in his profession were commonly called, between the Guatemalan border and the port of Frontera in Tabasco. Mijares Escandón met a grisly end by the order of Tomás Garrido Canabal, governor of Tabasco, in 1924. His nephews Sergio and Fernando had worked with him and had helped spread terror throughout the vast logging zones of the Casa Romano. When the company went out of business in 1925, the movable goods of San Roman Tzendales were transferred to Pico de Oro, a logging tract situated in the old "Marqués de Comillas" concession on which the Casa Romano had rented vast stretches of forest land. A visit to Pico de Oro would have brought Traven into direct contact with a person who had helped Mijares Escandón inflict many of the cruelties that were later described in the Jungle Novels.

The purpose of his trip, as Traven proposed it to Varela, was to inspect the ruins of Las Tinieblas in the old territory of Los Tzendales. Traven became aware during his second trip that making open inquiries into the recent horrors of labor practices at San Roman Tzendales could be dangerous, and that pretending to be an archeologist would be the most acceptable pretext for finding the information for which he was searching. It seems, however, that Traven did not undertake the trip to meet Sergio Mijares, judging by the fact that the letter of introduction by Varela is still in the Traven Archives. San Roman Tzendales, however, became Traven's model for the Montellano *monterías* featured in *Die Troza* and *Die Rebellion der Gehenkten*.

During his first trip to Chiapas in 1926, Traven had assumed that the agricultural workers of Chiapas were as much involved in revolutionary change as were the industrial workers of Tampico. With the discovery of the *monterías* and the system of debt slavery that provided their labor force, Traven not only realized that he had been mistaken in 1926 but also that the most pernicious system of exploitation of agricultural labor in Mexico had never ceased operation. The discovery of this unchanged and backward rural sector of Chiapas was such a shock to him that he dedicated the remainder of his literary work to the

Indian agricultural worker of Chiapas and the systematic exploitation of him. The labor-backed administration of Governor Vidal, he found, had not left the slightest mark on this part of the state.

When Traven returned to Chiapas in December 1927, Vidal was dead, murdered on the road between Mexico City and Cuernavaca by agents of the federal government. Vidal had made a fatal mistake by backing his old friend, General Francisco R. Serrano, in his election campaign for president against the "official" candidate Obregón. While Traven attended classes during the summer of 1927, former President Obregón decided to run once more for the presidency. This amounted to a serious violation of the 1917 constitution, one of whose articles, emerging from the revolution of 1910, was the principle of nonreelection. The constitution fixed the term of Mexican presidents for four years without any possibility of return to office; ten years later, Obregón decided to succeed his successor, Plutarco Elías Calles. Governor Vidal objected strongly to Obregón's reelection and the constitutional changes it required, and he took a leave of absence from the governorship to become Serrano's campaign manager. Obregón's renewed candidacy, however, enjoyed the full backing of President Calles and a host of powerful political parties and groupings. In 1926 an analyst attached to the U.S. War Department commented that Mexican governors who wished to retain their posts needed to be in accord with the federal administration.[11] This was proven dramatically true; for opposing Obregón's campaign, Vidal paid with his life. His murder and the subsequent events in Chiapas were clear indicators of the increasing strength of the central government.

Vidal's murder on 2 October 1927 brought a complete change of political power to Chiapas. On the following day, the commander of the Tuxtla Gutiérrez garrison received orders from President Calles to take control of the state government. Police captured Luis Vidal, the murdered governor's brother, who had been left in charge. As soon as Vidal handed over the state treasury to his captors, he was shot together with leading Vidalista officials, including Ricardo A. Paniagua and the municipal president of San Cristóbal, who was killed for the simple reason that he held this important office under Vidal.[12] A statewide witchhunt for Vidalistas and socialists began. On

27 November 1927, Federico Martínez Rojas, a long-time *mapache*, entered Tuxtla Gutiérrez as the new state governor. He was accompanied by Tiburcio Fernández Ruiz, the *mapache* leader, and his men, the Ruizada, as they were known. Fernández Ruiz had hoped that Obregón's presidential ambitions would mean a return to power of the *mapaches* in Chiapas.[13] He was proven right more quickly than he had anticipated, and the return of the landowner party to power brought a swift dismantling of Vidal's reforms. Indeed, one of the first laws signed by the new *mapache* governor rekindled the old tradition of Indian forced labor. The law ordered village authorities to recruit every male in Chiapas to help repair bad roads in order to encourage commerce. Those who did not want to contribute labor could pay the Junta de Caminos an amount equivalent to the value of their labor.[14] This meant that every Indian in the state would be forced to build roads without pay and that ladino officials would line their pockets with money paid by those who could afford to evade their obligations. Traven was aware of these traditions and of their revival.[15]

Traven left San Cristóbal on 27 December and arrived on 29 December at Ocosingo, where he stayed for a few days. On 8 January 1930 he moved on toward El Real. When he crossed the Naranjo River it was already dark, and by the time he was near El Real, crossing the Santa Cruz River "in canoe," it was night. Traven arrived at the farm that same night at 7:10 p.m.[16] He recreated the details of this trip in *Marsch ins Reich der Caoba* as days one and two of don Gabriel's convoy, although he renamed El Real "La Condesa."

Traven spent a few days at the farm roaming the country-side and taking photos.[17] On 14 January he set out for Santa Isabel and Capulín, where he stayed for several days taking photos of Lacandon Indians. This excursion was marred by bad weather, and the mules had to be "loaded and disloaded" again and again because the small rivers and creeks had swollen with the rain. The horse slipped constantly, and they traveled most of the way in the "greenish darkness" of the jungle.[18] Traven resurrected the difficulties of this trip in *Marsch ins Reich der Caoba*. The journey took him as far as the Laguna Lagarto and the Lakes of Ocotal between the Perlas and the San Pedro rivers. Later on in February, Traven returned to the jungle. This time he reached the Usumacinta River and, on 3 March 1930, the Agua Azul *montería.* Traven's track is exactly the one traveled by don Gabriel and his convoy in *Marsch ins Reich der Caoba*, and Agua Azul is the model for the camp where Andreu Ugalde and Celso Flores, characters in *Die Troza*, first work.

Traven gathered much of the information on the logging industry and *montería* life at El Real itself. There he found himself surrounded by the best possible sources. Enrique Bulnes, with his brother Manuel, had the most detailed knowledge of the timber industry of Chiapas. Although neither of them had worked in a logging camp, their family had owned the oldest timber interests in Chiapas. The Casa Bulnes had gone out of business in 1914, but its central logging camp of San Quintín continued in operation under a new owner, the Casa Vega, until 1927. The data gathered for the few studies of the Chiapan logging industry that have been undertaken have come mostly from the Bulnes brothers.[19] Always generous and urbane, the two answered freely all questions about the logging industry of Chiapas before and after the efforts of B. Traven had called international attention to its working conditions.

As an additional source for Traven's research, there were still plenty of *montería* workers alive in 1930, many of whom had seen the horrors of San Roman Tzendales, or Los Tzendales, as the main camp of the Casa Romano was generally called. Many *monteros* (timber fellers) had stories to tell about their personal sufferings, the sadism of Mijares Escandón and his overseers, disciplinary measures in the camps, and the ways in which they had originally been trapped into *montería* work. At El Real there was no shortage of men who could tell such stories. Chicle gatherers, crocodile hunters, *monteros*, archeologists, treasure hunters, adventurers, and the odd tourist such as Traven all spent one or several nights at El Real before entering or leaving the jungle. There were nights when up to two hundred men were camped on the grounds. Before going to sleep, they would sit on the breezy verandahs of El Real exchanging news, telling old and new stories, and recounting anecdotes. Anyone listening to the men talk could not help being initiated into jungle gossip. These were the stories for which Traven was looking, although he recorded none of them on his surviving journal sheets. By 1930, Traven could speak "passable Spanish," according to Enrique Bulnes, which enabled him to actively interrogate his informants, thus releasing a torrent of stories.

In Chiapas, Traven remarked, a traveler was known to everybody in the village or township; they knew what he looked like, how he was dressed, what sort of animal he was riding.[20] Men connected with the jungle all knew each other or at least knew of each other. The *monteros*, once they survived the harsh world of timber felling, were not a gray or anonymous mass of people. They were colorful individuals known to everyone between Tenosique and Ocosingo and identified by the stories attached to them. One *montero*, Villanueva, became known for having seriously damaged the ruins of Yaxchilán when he ripped out several mahogany trees growing on top of them.[21] Juan Celorio, son of Pancho Celorio, a labor contractor whose story Traven retold in *Marsch ins Reich der Caoba*, had a lame foot and was known as El Cojo.[22] Others were known for murders they had committed; many were known for drinking bouts in Tenosique or Ocosingo, a valiant deed, or an injury. When such men met after prolonged periods of silence and loneliness in the jungle, they sat and talked for hours. Palacios, the anthropologist Oliver La Farge, and the Swiss ethnographer Duby have all left accounts of these exchanges of information. As Traven pointed out, night falls early in Chiapas and exchanging stories was the only available form of entertainment during the long evenings.

When news of what Traven had published under the title *Die Rebellion der Gehenkten* finally reached Chiapas, the Bulnes family was astonished. Nothing of what was narrated there had been told Traven by any member of the Bulnes family. The German coffee planters and estate owners with whom Traven was in regular and friendly contact were not pleased by what they heard or read.[23] They discouraged Traven from ever returning to Chiapas and, according to his widow, he even received death threats. The Bulnes family remained an exception. Its members maintained some intermittent, friendly correspondence with Traven, who continued to mail them Spanish newspapers from San Antonio, Texas, and birthday cards for which he always received their thanks.[24] Traven heeded his former friends and only returned to Chiapas twenty years after the book's publication, during the filming of *La Rebelión de los Colgados*, and even then he traveled incognito. In the 1930s, however, he spent much time in San Antonio, training for his pilot's license. He had acquired a half share in a small aircraft for the express purpose of making access to the Lacandon Forest easier.[25] But he never returned.

Traven's informants did not know how he would use the information they supplied him, as the author never revealed to his erstwhile friends that he planned to use the data against them and to take up the cause of their Indian laborers. To defend themselves against Traven's accusations of ruthless exploitation, many former friends pointed to the misunderstandings and misrepresentations in Traven's work. They argued that much of Traven's information was simply wrong. The most vocal of the landowners was Pedro Vega Martínez, son of the last owner of the San Quintín logging operation. Vega was the only person to have attempted to repudiate Traven in writing by presenting accounts of *montería* life as he had seen it in his youth at San Quintín. The differences between Vega's and Traven's accounts are stunning, and yet they are both truthful, as will be shown later.

In one of his books, Vega has described how he thought Traven collected his biased and often untruthful information. On his travels between Ocosingo, El Real, and the edge of the jungle, Traven met one of Vega's many uncles, a man called Fulge, Vega wrote, whom "the devil may boil on slow fire. He was the shame of his family and a punishment on Ocosingo." After being sacked from several *monterías* because of his big mouth and general uselessness, Uncle Fulge was finally sent home from Los Tzendales. On his trip back, the dispirited Fulge met the German Torsvan:

> Unfortunately, from El Cedro Uncle Fulge went to El Triunfo on the way to Ocosingo, and there he met Herr Thursband [Vega's spelling of Torsvan], the author of a book that Abel read and which is called "The Rebellion of the Hanged." In several days of [shared] living at El Triunfo, with the venom and the lack of manliness of my relative, coupled with the sadism of the German plus the minimum respect for our dignity, this ignominious miscarriage came to light.[26]

Pedro Vega has also pointed out in no uncertain terms that, if Traven ever had the idea of returning to Tenosique or Ocosingo, "where the sons of those men live who cut off ears and hanged others," he would not have been well received.[27] Traven's *montería* novels, according to Vega, were an insult to every decent *montero*, full of improbable inventions and lies.[28] In Vega's opinion,

Traven's inquiries were shallow and the inquirer gullible. This reaction conveys some of the outrage and indignation that many of Traven's Chiapan friends felt when they recognized their own images in his novels.

The wealth of information Traven collected during his last two trips to Chiapas fueled his writing for ten years. From that point forward what he depicted was a circumscribed but easily recognizable world. His new novels were characterized by a careful choice of material on the one hand, and the author's accumulation in his private archives of supporting evidence for his claims of abuses of Indians on the other. It was obviously Traven's goal to make the abuses known worldwide, and thus to implicate the state government of Chiapas and the Mexican government for allowing them for so long. This was dangerous business for an author without secure residence status in Mexico, and from now on Traven rightly began to fear for his safety.

Traven must be credited with being the first writer to take note of the labor conditions in the mahogany logging industry of Chiapas and thus to preserve the memory of an important chapter of Mexican labor history which, without him, would probably have been forgotten. Still, there were many details about logging that he misunderstood or of which he remained ignorant. His detractors, such as Vega, who are true experts on the logging business of Chiapas, seized on Traven's mistakes in order to dismiss his accounts of *montería* life. Although the five Jungle Novels consolidated Traven's fame as a writer of uncompromisingly anticapitalist convictions, he has never been accepted as the chronicler of Indian exploitation in Chiapas in that historians, as well as former *monteros*, have denied him such recognition. This denial would have caused Traven much consternation, but, above and beyond purely technical mistakes, he had begun deliberately to skew his evidence for a range of political purposes, the first of which was to express his increasing disenchantment with the Mexican Revolution.

The Reelection of Alvaro Obregón and the Institutionalization of the Revolution

The federal agents who shot Governor Vidal eliminated everybody connected to General Serrano's election campaign, including the candidate himself. Thirteen crosses on the old road from Mexico City to Cuernavaca still mark the spot of the assassination. The killings removed all obstacles in the way of Obregón's renewed presidential aspirations, and his reelection became a foregone conclusion. Obregón's candidacy enjoyed wide support because it formed a focus for political opposition to President Calles, his labor policies, and the enormous power wielded by CROM leader Morones. Eventually, virtually every political party and grouping, including the Communist party, found reasons to support Obregón,[29] and Morones and the CROM drifted into political isolation. In effect, the Obregonista campaign was evidence that revolutionary enthusiasm had congealed into revolutionary rhetoric, and that short-term political goals had become dressed up with revolutionary phraseology. The revolution, it seemed, was about to abandon its political program and become a personal vehicle for ambitious politicians. Traven became acutely aware of the hollowness of the new political rhetoric, and in the Jungle Cycle he began consistently to pillory the hypocrisy of Mexican politicians.

Obregón was elected president on 1 July 1928; on the 17th of the month he was shot dead by a religious fanatic, and the powerful Obregonista bloc was suddenly left without a focus or leader. The Obregonistas accused Morones of complicity in the murder despite ample proof to the contrary; under their pressure, President Calles did not hesitate to sacrifice his old friend and supporter. The labor leader was forced to leave his post as minister of labor and industry, thus breaking the CROM's power over national politics. When Emilio Portes Gil became interim president in the autumn of 1928, his long-standing feud with Morones broke out into the open. The labor leader called on all CROM officials holding public posts to abandon them forthwith,[30] effectively weakening his position even further. With government protection withdrawn, Morones and the CROM were pushed to the sidelines, and the mainstay of Traven's argument that the Mexican labor movement was about to take over state power collapsed. Morones's fall from grace openly demonstrated the CROM's dependency on the state.

At the same time, the radical labor fringe, represented by the anarcho-syndicalist CGT, also began to decline. Amid constant attacks by the CROM and the federal government, the CGT struggled to maintain its independence from political commitment in an environment of changing political requirements. From 1926 onward, a trend toward *liderismo*, an abrogation of democratic procedures in favor of rule by one leader, and "the quiet path of conciliation and opportunism" became discernible.[31] As more and more states established—CROM-dominated—boards of arbitration and conciliation, the ideological position of the CGT became steadily more obsolete. The "yellow devils and false apostles of the working class," as one CGT speaker called the CROM, had completed their job before their own demise.[32] The CGT became so demoralized and financially weak that it finally struck a deal with the central government in 1930, which left it on the "verge of collaborationism."[33] When the federal *Ley del Trabajo* was promulgated in 1931, a labor organization based on direct action became redundant. In 1936 the two former enemies, the CGT and the CROM, now both powerless and languishing, united to better compete with the newly founded Confederación de Trabajadores Mexicanos (Federation of Mexican Workers), the CTM.

Under the impact of the deepening economic crisis, many of the irrigation and road construction projects of the Calles government had to be abandoned, although the worsening conditions were not solely responsible for the projects' foundering. "Ignorance, lack of foresight, haste and even naïveté," together with widespread corruption among government officials, finished off many projects.[34] A contemporary pointed out in 1923 that he had been reliably assured that of all the Mexican governors only two could be called honest, and that it was a matter of luck to find a governor who, besides enriching himself, would also do something for his state. "The majority keep it all and leave nothing."[35] These were the same governors Traven had praised so warmly for their prolabor and anticapitalist stance. By 1928 most of Traven's signs of hope for the great Mexican anticapitalist superstate of the future had begun to crumble.

While he was in Chiapas exploring the recent horrors of the mahogany logging camps, an event occurred in Mexico City that must have robbed Traven of any lingering illusions about the direction the revolutionary movement was taking. In March 1929 the Partido Nacional Revolucionario (National Revolutionary Party), the PNR, was founded, a signal that the Mexican Revolution was about to leave its "revolutionary" phase and enter the stage of institutionalization. When Traven heard about the foundation of the PNR he must have been reminded of Max Stirner's observation that only insurrection will liberate the individual, while permanent revolution will ultimately create its own structures.[36]

When President Calles stepped down from the presidency in September 1928, he announced that the age of caudillos was over and the new era of "institutions and law" was beginning.[37] Portes Gil, the new interim president, made the same point when he stressed that "men who know how to be loyal to men should be replaced by men who know how to be loyal to institutions."[38] The foundation of the PNR was Calles's solution to the political upheaval created by the murder of Obregón. Meant to prevent the civil disturbances and repeated military coups that had previously complicated presidential successions, the PNR brought together under one banner all the warring factions that could provoke a repetition of the de la Huerta Rebellion. All political groupings considering themselves "revolutionary" were to be unified in the PNR, which would become "a pact of union and solidarity . . . that would unify a vast national organism and all fighters of the Revolution above and beyond private tendencies and interests."[39] The party became the sole focus of all revolutionary power, and membership in it became the criterion by which the status of a political current or individual was determined.[40]

The PNR did not boast any particular ideology. Its program was full of internal contradictions, proposing support for workers, farmers, and capitalists, and reconciliation between all social classes. In reality, the program appealed to the urban middle class,[41] a drastic change from the labor-oriented policies of 1925. With this new definition the term "revolutionary," as Traven understood it, was rendered meaningless. It soon became clear that the purpose of the PNR was in its role as kingmaker; the strongest political organization, it would nominate the presidential candidate and therefore determine who would win the election. Its virtual identification with the government guaranteed that the whole force of the state apparatus was at its disposal. Thus, the PNR was the instrument for the institutionalization of the presidential succession. Indeed, the first to feel the full impact of this new power constellation was José Vasconcelos, the 1929 candidate of the Partido Nacional Antireeleccionista (National Antireelection Party), who ran against the PNR's official candidate Pascual Ortiz Rubio. Vasconcelos and his aides were harassed and his campaign was sabotaged systematically,[42] culminating in the killings at Topilejo on the road to Cuernavaca, where one hundred corpses were discovered in March 1930. Investigations revealed that they were the bodies of Vasconcelista elements who had disappeared mysteriously after an attempt on the life of Ortiz Rubio.[43]

The effectiveness of the PNR became apparent during its founding congress in March 1929, when the Escobar Rebellion, the last military uprising aimed at unseating the central government and imposing its own candidate, was easily defeated. Political stability aside, it did not take long for another, more hidden purpose of the PNR to emerge. The choice of the politically ineffectual Ortiz Rubio indicated that the PNR would serve as an instrument through which ex-President Calles could rule the country as éminence grise. With the help of the PNR, Calles managed to transcend the last element of the revolutionary legacy, the principle excluding presidential reelection. During what became known as the *maximato*, Calles ruled through a number of puppet presidents. When Ortiz Rubio began to show signs of independence, he was quickly undermined and then forced to resign in 1932. His successor, Abelardo L. Rodríguez, was Calles's willing instrument.

With the help of the PNR, Calles did not need to violate overtly the principle of nonreelection as Obregón had done; instead, he effectively circumvented it. How little Calles himself was concerned with law and order became apparent when he placed his son Alfredo, who was not yet old enough to hold office legally, in the state legislature of Tamaulipas, and then tried to force through an amendment to the state constitution to reduce the age for gubernatorial candidates. His sons Rodolfo and Plutarco were already governors of Sonora and Nuevo León.[44] His behind-the-scenes politicking demonstrated that Calles still believed in government by personal relationships, despite his professed faith in the virtues of institutions as regulators of the life of the nation.

The PNR was a government party and its links with state power operated at all levels. Party discipline was maintained by expelling undesirables and nonconforming elements in an environment in which no effective political career was possible outside the party.[45] The early days of organized labor in Tampico, when CGT unionists sent the appointed governor packing, were now a distant memory. During his 1929 election campaign,

Vasconcelos summed up the new state of affairs: "The truth is that most of our revolutionary illusions have been extinguished."[46] Calles, whom Traven had admired for his revolutionary vigor and his independent and innovative policies, had permanently changed the political landscape of Mexico in a way unacceptable to the anarcho-syndicalist from Munich.

With the establishment of the PNR, political opposition was made possible only on the fringe. The 1929 election campaign no longer addressed itself to real issues; instead, it produced a veritable "torrent of oratory" and grand displays of political opportunism.[47] Traven, who had become highly sensitive to political rhetoric in his Munich days, began to portray Mexican politicians as using oratory to hide short-term goals and personal greed. In truth, many of the politicians of the time who produced high-sounding oratory about their revolutionary fervor were more or less openly connected with different forms of corruption. Calles himself was implicated in diverting funds from the Banco de México to help build his sugar enterprise,[48] and in those states where President Obregón or Calles or their generals had personal interests, land reform was severely hindered.[49] The most notorious example of an entrepreneurial politician was Obregón, who turned himself from a middling Sonoran farmer into a millionaire, but the effects on the country of politicians' greed were disastrous. In the northwestern states agriculture shifted from food production to export-oriented crops under the guidance of the Sonoran presidents Calles and Obregón, a policy that ultimately distorted the national economy to the point where Mexico had to import corn, beans, and sugar.[50] This development was in sharp contrast with the agricultural cooperatives Traven had predicted in the "more advanced north," helping to convert Mexico into a "superstate." By 1930 the most optimistic observer was forced to acknowledge that the revolution had bred a new elite, led by the Sonoran presidents, who, in time-honored fashion, used state office to enrich themselves. It became impossible to disregard the continuities between the Porfiriato and the Calles *maximato*.

To complete Traven's disappointments, in 1929 the churches of Mexico were reopened and religious services resumed. Mexicans flocked to hear Mass, have their children baptized, and their marriages blessed. In 1928, President Calles, who had approached the anticlerical campaign with almost prophetic zeal, had been under such severe internal and external pressures that he reached an accord with the clergy. With these developments, all of the factors Traven had cited in *Land des Frühlings* as being guarantees of permanent revolutionary change in Mexico had vanished, and 1930 marked the definitive end of Traven's epoch of hope and optimism. More important, however, was the disappearance of a political environment in which labor unions such as the CGT, and anarcho-syndicalist ideas in general, could flourish. Its passing meant that Traven risked drifting into political obsolescence unless he directly opposed the Mexican government. True to himself, Traven chose exactly this path.

A Change of Direction

Traven never explained to his readers or to his publisher why he changed his position so radically between the publication of *Land des Frühlings* and *Der Karren*, and no one seems to have questioned him about the shift. Not even Traven's critics noticed the oddity of *monterías* and debt slavery existing in the country of eternal springtime. The living and working conditions of indebted laborers that Traven began to describe in the Jungle Cycle were virtually unknown outside of Chiapas, and they were not even known to many people within the state. The new novels began to disseminate information that would publicize for the first time these illegally and often clandestinely perpetuated labor conditions. Traven's exposé implicated both the Chiapan and the federal governments, and he risked the application of Article 33. Traven was aware of this danger and from this point forward began to protect his identity more carefully.

At the same time as he was beginning to conceal his identity, Traven began to stress that his novels were based on information he himself had seen or heard and that he had gone to great lengths to procure for his readers. In the letter introducing *Regierung* to the Büchergilde, he noted that "the author . . . does not write fairytales for grown-ups, so they can go to sleep easier; he writes documentaries, nothing more than documentaries, which he presents as novels in order to make them more readable."[51] Traven began a curious and often desperate balancing act, disguising factual information in fiction and then giving his fiction a twist to serve as a political parable for his readership, who were worlds removed from the logging camps of Chiapas. This convoluted strategy produced such a tangle of intention and reality that most of his readers missed Traven's finer points. Ultimately, the author created a web from which he found it impossible to extricate himself.

To add to the confusion, Traven set his novels during the time before the revolution of 1910, "to show Europeans the true causes and reasons for the revolutions and rebellions which have rocked the Mexican nation for the last twenty years," as he wrote in the letter accompanying his new novel. In that same letter, Traven contradicted himself, stressing that "as proof of the closeness of the events and circumstances [described in *Regierung*] to the date of its publication, let me say that the Indian revolt against the decree of the governor . . . occurred on New Years Day 1929." An entry in Traven's travel notes confirms this circumstance: "Ch[amula] elects pres. each year, and each year from another of the four barrios of which the nation is composed. 1929.I.1. pres. xxxx was told by gov. not to resign, stayed in office, town was besieged and surrounded. I.1. by nation, at 10.00 pres. and his whole family killed. When after phone call soldiers arrived, not one Indian was to be seen. Killers never found."[52]

Pretending that his novels were set in the past must have appeared to offer protection to the author from possible prosecution in Mexico. His strategy seems to have worked, since there is no evidence that the government made efforts to persecute the author. He was at risk: Despite attempts on his part, he could not keep knowledge of his books from reaching Mexico, and for a Mexican reader there was no need to point out that Traven described current conditions. In 1936 the Mexican popular-front journal *Frente a frente*, in an article about *Der Karren*, *Regierung*, and *Marsch ins Reich der Caoba*, noted that "although all the stories 'officially' take place during the times of Porfirio Díaz, in reality they deal with contemporary events surrounding the exploitation of workers in the south of Mexico."[53] Moreover, Traven increased the risk he ran by perpetuating his mistake of treating as national conditions that did not bear such generalization. Although he focused the setting of his novels on Chiapas, he continued to imply that the labor conditions he described were common throughout Mexico. Traven not only ran the risk of offending the Chiapan landowners, who had

regained political power in the state, but also the national revolutionary elite, who had established themselves as the new
hacendados.

In fact, in the northern border states of Sonora, Chihuahua,
and Coahuila, for instance, peonage never reached the levels
seen in labor-scarce and isolated Chiapas. Proximity to the United
States and the existence of industry and mining along the border
offered alternative and high-paying work opportunities. Landowners in these states had to treat their peons well if they
wanted to retain their labor force. The north, as a result, offered
its peons a markedly higher standard of living than did the
south.[54] Even the ubiquitous *tienda de raya* took on a different
function in such areas as the cotton-growing Laguna district of
Coahuila, charging lower prices as an added incentive to attract
the labor force.[55] It was the relatively well-off peons in the north,
and not the most oppressed and exploited workers of the Valle
Nacional in Oaxaca or the slaves of the Casa Romano, who were
the first to join the revolutionary armies forming in 1910.[56] Thus,
Traven's simple assumption in the Jungle Cycle that oppression
bred rebellion is not supported by the available historical evidence. Traven's greatest error, however, in the eyes of the
Chiapan landowners was not his erroneous judgment but his
unwitting embrace of the unpopular Colonel Castro and his
Workers' Law of October 1914, which had abolished debt slavery, physical punishment, and *tiendas de raya* in Chiapas, and
led to the *mapache* war.

Castro had expected an enthusiastic response to the promulgation of his *Ley del Trabajo*. Instead, "although [the peons] were
the beneficiaries of the law, they remained indifferent and supported the *finqueros*."[57] One of the reasons adduced to explain
the peons' loyalty to their masters is the complicated network of
mutual obligations known as the compadrazgo system. Traven
equated the term compadre with "godfather," and he remained
unaware of the political dimension of compadrazgo, although
he must have been familiar with incidents such as occurred at El
Real in 1917, when the local Tzeltal Indians killed an agent sent
by the Constitutionalist Army to incite them to burn the farm.
The Indians had gone to seek advice from the Bulnes family
first, and they were informed that "Carranza and his men are
children of the devil."[58] The trust shown toward their *patrón* by
the Tzeltal may well have been used by the Bulnes family to
create a private army to defend its property, an army of the kind

that Fernández Ruiz, the *mapache* leader, formed among his *mozada*, the *peones acasillados* living on his properties.

The close personal relationship between *patrón* and peons in Chiapas was primarily a product of the modest size of land-holdings. Unlike many other areas of Mexico, where individual landholdings like those, for example, of the Terrazas family of Chihuahua could be enormous, grazing properties in Chiapas averaged thirty-five hundred hectares, while most other agri-cultural properties did not greatly exceed four hundred hectares. Nearly 90 percent of the land in Chiapas belonged to fincas whose owners, as a rule, lived on farms inherited from their ancestors,[59] and 57.7 percent of the rural population lived on fincas and were dependent on them for their livelihood. This personal and economic dependence on the *finquero* ultimately determined that the peons went to war for their masters, often against their own interests.

The *finqueros* of Chiapas felt threatened by the Workers' Law that canceled their peons' debts, recognizing that the law went right to the heart of their seigneurial privileges and threatened the economic basis of the state.[60] Colonel Castro had stated that the new legislation was for the benefit of the "victims of relent-less exploiters whose vile practices will not be stopped by any-thing."[61] Given how deceitfully the peons' accounts were kept on many farms of Chiapas, as well as in *monterías* and other businesses employing illiterate Indians, the need for this legis-lation was plain. However, peonage conditions within the state of Chiapas varied greatly. The German coffee planters of Soconusco, for instance, had never managed—nor had they ever really tried—to maintain a system of coerced labor as did the Casa Romano.[62]

The pious *finqueros* of Chiapas were particularly outraged over Castro's anticlerical legislation, which drove most priests out of the state, closed convents, and prohibited publicly dis-played signs of the cross. Constitutionalist soldiers broke into churches and vandalized them, stealing everything of value and prompting Tiburcio Fernández Ruiz to declare war on the "acts of vandalism of Carrancismo." Initially, these acts had consisted of little more than the usual cattle stealing and confiscation of crops in order to feed troops and generate extra money for officers. But the vandalizing of churches by an unpopular mili-tary governor was viewed in Chiapas as the abuses of an army of occupation. Thus Castro enforced his new legislation with the help of soldiers, whose forays into the countryside often "took the form of punitive raids against the haciendas, churches, and occasionally towns." In many cases, the Constitutionalist soldiers had to force freedom on the reluctant peons.[63] At El Real, the Carrancista officer paid with his life for his efforts.

After the murders in August 1915 of a number of Chiapas's notaries, the Constitutionalist governor decreed a policy of "concentration." Civilians were herded into guarded population centers to facilitate the maintenance of tighter control. Crops remained unattended, and what was left was pillaged by the Constitutionalist soldiers, resulting in famine throughout the state. These desperate and unpopular measures drove more and more Chiapans into the *mapache* resistance until a veritable army was created. Although the military governor of Tuxtla Gutiérrez self-righteously attributed the expanding *mapache* war to the landowners' opposition to the Workers' Law, Salvador Alvarado, chief of the Constitutionalist Army of the Southeast in Yucatán, blamed the uprising on the abuse of power by Colonel Castro and his subordinates.[64] Many *finqueros* in Chiapas responded to the Constitutionalists' efforts by introducing a double book-keeping system. They continued their traditional labor practices and kept one register with all the accumulated debts of their peons in the old manner. Another set of books showing the cancellation of all debts was ready to be presented to the federal labor inspector, should one ever venture into *mapache* territory.[65] The *finqueros*, it is clear, did not expect the Constitutionalists to remain long in power.

After the *mapaches* won their guerrilla war, an armistice was signed on 24 February 1920 between the *caudillo mapache* and an emissary of President Obregón. The *mapaches* were transformed into a "new revolutionary force" under the command of Fernández Ruiz, the "born chief of Obregonismo in the state," and they were allowed to retain their arms in order to guarantee peace.[66] The *finqueros*, who had not paid taxes for the previous six years, were given another three tax-free years, and the federal government promised to build a railway across central Chiapas to give the coffee planters of the Pacific coast access to the Gulf ports of Tabasco. As a token concession to the land reform articles in the constitution, peasants in Chiapas were to be given state land. The *mapaches* had won all the way.

In 1921, one year after he became governor of Chiapas, Fernández Ruiz was forced to introduce an agrarian law. Obregón and Fernández Ruiz, however, reached an agreement to minimize its effect and, consequently, the agrarian law stipulated that only estates exceeding eight thousand hectares would be included. There were only seventy such estates in the whole of Chiapas, many of which were inaccessible logging zones in the Lacandon Forest.[67] Thus the estates of the Chiapan landowners were safe, and life went on as it had for generations, the old social system of the peon's dependence on his master unaffected. When President Calles in 1925 declared agrarian collectivism to be at an end, the efforts at land reform under Governor Vidal were curtailed before they could gather momentum. For villagers and peons this meant that life did not change substantially in spite of the turmoil of a revolution allegedly fought on their behalf.

Because the revolutionary cause, represented by the Constitutionalist army, had been so destructive for the state of Chiapas, it became possible for Fernández Ruiz to parade as a new "revolutionary" force, despite the fact that his only interest was in maintaining the status quo. Reaction had thus become the revolution in Chiapas, and what Traven discovered in 1928, therefore, was a state whose social and economic structure had been preserved nearly intact since the days of the dictator Díaz. All Traven needed to do to create a vision of Porfirian times was to describe what he saw around him. What Traven did not understand, though, was how this state of affairs had come into being. Moreover, he now began to denigrate a social order that many of his Chiapan friends had fought long and hard to preserve.

Der Karren

It appears that Traven left Chiapas some time in mid-1930. Since *Der Karren* was published in Berlin late that year, it seems likely that the novel was finished by the time Traven left. Manuel Bulnes maintains that Traven spent a total of four months at El Real between 1929 and 1930.[68] He never saw Traven write, however; for this activity the author had rented a small farmhouse outside of Ocosingo. Access to this house, it seems, was via a code word using the letters of the name Traven: Tiene Razón A Vivir Entre Nativos (He has a right to live among natives).[69] A regular and welcome visitor to the farm was Victorino Trinidad, the schoolteacher in Ocosingo. He was a knowledgeable and well-spoken man, and together the two went exploring along the Lacantún River and in the neighborhood of Ocosingo. Trinidad had been a teacher in the Indian township of Bachajón for several years and was, no doubt, an important source of information for Traven on the abuses that the Bachajón Indians had suffered at the hands of the ladino authorities. Much of Traven's next volume, *Regierung*, was informed by this knowledge.

The central character of *Der Karren* is Andreu Ugalde, a Tzeltal Indian and the son of a peon on a farm in northeastern Chiapas. The reader follows Andreu's development from a bright and gifted boy until manhood as a *carretero*. Andreu's life is nearly destroyed when he goes to the *montería* to work off his father's debts. The intelligent Andreu is wasted in a senseless and grinding system of organized exploitation, and ultimately only the rebellion of the hanged prevents his death. It is clear from the novel that Traven intends to use the character Andreu to show that debt peonage in Chiapas was in fact debt slavery, and that debt slavery was no different from slavery pure and simple. In Tabasco and northeastern Chiapas, the novel demonstrates, it was not uncommon for a master to "sell" the debt of his peon to a logging company, especially to such a voracious consumer of labor as the Casa Romano, a practice little removed from selling the peon himself.

In *Der Karren*, Traven sketched the legal and social conditions that made debt slavery possible and discussed how the system operated in Chiapas. The estate on which Andreu is born, and where his father serves as a peon, is paternalistically ruled. Andreu is taken into the house at the age of nine to perform domestic services. "Given" to his *patrón*'s daughter and her husband upon their marriage, he is sent to school, a privilege, however, not so much designed to benefit Andreu as to provide an educated worker for his new master's shop. Andreu is never paid for his work, since he "belongs" to the household, and living conditions are harsh. Ultimately, the debt that sends him to the *montería* is created when his father buys bedding for the boy at the estate's *tienda de raya* because the new *patrón* does not see the necessity to provide a blanket and mat. Andreu is only released from the shop, and comes to work as a *carretero*, after the shop owner loses him in a game of cards. Andreu's third *patrón*, don Laureano, is the largest freight carrier in the state. Thus, by the time Andreu has grown up and before the boy has seen employment in the *monterías*, Traven had firmly established that what he described was outright slavery along the lines of the pre-war American South.

In the part of the novel in which Andreu begins working for don Laureano, Traven inserted a scene that exposed the nature of the difference between Chiapan slavery and that of the American South. Slavery was illegal in Mexico, Traven pointed out, but the peon's debt fulfilled the function of a law effectively sanctioning slavery, binding the peon as inexorably to the estate as any slave law could have done. Andreu has to have a debt before he starts work as a *carretero*. Consequently, he is charged with the loss that don Laureano sustained by accepting Andreu's services in lieu of cash in the card game. Through this trick don Laureano obtains him for free, and there is no way in which Andreu can dispute the manipulation.

Physical punishment of peons was common and expected in Chiapas and Tabasco. Peons could be placed in the stocks, whipped, and jailed at the master's will, with the peon's voice mute before the law, a point Traven stressed again and again. Throughout the novel, Andreu knows that his master would, "without hesitation, seize the next best piece of wood, a stick, or a length of pipe, and hit it over his head, should he fly into a rage."[70] He could also be whipped to death, the penalty for killing an Indian carrying a maximum fine of five hundred pesos in Chiapas. How ingrained and persistent these conditions were in northeastern Chiapas can be gauged from the fact that the Instituto Indigenista reported at least a dozen cases of outright slavery as late as 1952 in the districts of Tenejapa, Huistán, Abasolo, Oxchúc, and Ocosingo.[71]

Traven also pointed out the important role sexual exploitation played in the enslavement of the peons' wives and daughters. The two Indian girls featured in *Der Karren*, Estrellita and Rosario, both suffer from sexual persecution by their masters and as a consequence lose their jobs. Only by entering the world of the *carreteros*, who enjoy special status among the indebted workers of Chiapas, do they find a degree of security that not even their fathers' homes can afford them. The strength of the *carreteros* does not come from "syndicates and trade unions," Traven remarked pointedly, but from a voluntary organization built on mutual help. "Nobody helped them, they only helped themselves. But they defended themselves with a brutality and surety that nobody could escape."[72] This was the first in a series of remarks Traven began to insert into his novels, warning his readers against the fallibility of trade unions and their leaders. Yet, even the privileged *carreteros* were subject to one danger that hung over every peon's head. Their *patrón* could decide to sell them to the *montería*, as happens to Estrellita's two brothers when they are unable to discharge their father's debts after his death. Later in this study it will be shown that Traven exaggerated here, in that not every Indian could be sold in such a manner. But in Traven's representation, being sold to a *montería* in Chiapas was the equivalent of being "sold down the river" in North America.

After Traven had firmly established that Chiapas was a slaveholding state, he began a delineation on race and class lines. Every non-Indian, be he mestizo, Spaniard, or German, was either a slaveholder or profited from the slaveholding system, whereas every Indian was a slave or a potential slave. The common ladino, Traven explained, did not work. Once he reached maturity, he endeavored to scrape together four or five hundred pesos, marry, and then buy a small shop. His wife would run the shop, making it profitable through skill and industry, paying her husband pocket money, whereas his most distinguished task in life was to produce as many children as possible for his wife to bear and bring up. "He is always merry, friendly, contented with the world and other citizens. Otherwise he engages in politics. . . . He always carries a revolver in his belt. During elections, he attempts to snatch a post as mayor, chief of police, vendor of duty stamps, tax collector, or postmaster. Should he become mayor, then all his friends get good posts too."[73] Election results, in Traven's eyes, were determined by who was the best shot.

The ladinos in Traven's account operated within a system that not only permitted the ill-treatment of an Indian boy like Andreu but also demanded it. According to Traven, it was the Catholic Church that instructed the faithful "to leave the Indian in his innocence and ignorance." By giving its blessing to actions that were not commensurate with Christian charity and virtues but rather designed to enhance ladino power, a population of "worthless hypocrites" had developed. Traven claimed that it was under the influence of the church that state laws institutionalized the helplessness and dependence of the Indians. The historical record shows instead that state laws were adjusted to the economic advantage of the *finqueros*, and that the laws ensuring "that the *carreteros* would not be raised above the bullock which pulled their *patrón's* cart" were not the making of an all-powerful Chiapan clergy.[74] But with the church and the law on his side, as Traven viewed it, there was no reason for any ladino to act differently from his neighbor. Differences in behavior were determined by the degree of abuse, not by its absence or presence.

Traven, however, was realistic enough to see that the helplessness of the Indian peons was not merely a result of the worldly and spiritual powers that were arrayed against them. His earlier observation in *Land des Frühlings* that the Indians lacked ambition and were conservative now became crucial in his explanation of debt slavery. Their inferior status, Traven explained, was accepted by the Indians as "destiny, unchangeable in the same way as water flows downstream and not upstream. Most of the reasons [for their backwardness] are due to characteristics, customs, and habits of those Indians. But the main reason was the desperate ignorance of the Indians and the skill of the large landowners, in conjunction with the church, in keeping the Indians in ignorance."[75] Only Indians who had been mentally as well as physically removed from their communities, he now argued, could ever conceive of the notion of rebellion.

When in *Der Karren* Andreu becomes a *carretero*, he has been in daily contact with ladinos for years. He is a citified, albeit full-blooded, Indian like all the other *carreteros*, most of whom can read and write, and all of whom speak Spanish fluently. Yet, their society is quite different from the world surrounding them, and Traven contrasted it with the ladino society, stressing that the *carreteros* adhered to neither rules nor codes. Viciousness was alien to them, and the ever-present profit motive of the ladinos was absent from their interactions. They were of such selfless purity that "none of the *carreteros* would have ever denounced a comrade, either to take revenge or to get into the good books of his master. This was against their nature," Traven stated.[76] The Indian *carreteros* and their women possessed an instinctual, untutored sense of right and wrong. Although Andreu and Estrellita meet in an environment of the crudest sexual excesses, their meeting remains pure and untouched by its surroundings. Traven deliberately disregarded evidence of millionaire Indians as ruthless at exploiting their brethren as any ladino, or of those Indian caciques who sold their people for money to haciendas and *monterías*.[77]

Traven's depiction of indigenous peoples as the representatives of a gentle form of undoctrinaire socialism and cooperativism was the only element he could salvage from the ruins of his 1926 vision. From now on, he would maintain this simple and artificial opposition between good (Indian) and evil (ladino) to the point where he began to stereotype both.

Regierung

Despite his usual claims of intimate contacts with Indians, given voice in his letter to the Büchergilde—"[the author] lived, resided, danced, sung, and walked with Indians, mule drivers [and] *carreteros*"—Traven's information about the township of Bachajón and the Bachajón Indians was obviously derived from non-Indian sources. His experiences were similar to those of all other investigators at the time. The anthropologist La Farge and the archeologist Blom stressed in 1925 that they were indebted to local farmers such as Manuel Bulnes for their information.[78] The two investigators pointed out that the Bachajón Indians had a bad reputation for murderous violence and brutality. Murders committed by them "are sometimes so appallingly brutal that one could think them committed by an abnormal or degenerate people." At the same time, the two visitors pointed out that "these were the most independent Indians we met, controlling their own lives and way of living, and they are left very much alone by the neighboring Ladinos." Traven described the Bachajón in very similar terms, stressing, like La Farge and Blom, that they were usually peaceful people, and that disturbances were always the result of outside interference.

La Farge and Blom had some personal contact with a group of Bachajón Indians who were anxious for the two strangers to make their complaints known to the government in Mexico City. Government agents, the Bachajón reported, levied unjust taxes, the Indians "were forced to work for the municipal president of Ocosingo and did not have time to look after their own cornfields, and . . . they were bothered [for work] by the managers of the neighboring properties." This was nothing new in Bachajón. In 1911, for example, the male population had been dangerously depleted because of forced recruitment for the *monterías*.[79] In May 1926, in a situation similar to that of the Bachajón, the Indians of nearby Cancúc engaged a scribe and directed their complaints directly to the Ministry of Labor in Mexico City. They claimed they were now worse off than before the revolution. Agents came and forced them to sell their pigs and grain at low prices and the same agents bribed their leaders with alcohol. Traven also incorporated these frequently encountered features into *Regierung*. He now realized that Indian caciques could easily turn into *"charros,"* landlords who cared nothing for the welfare of their tenants.[80]

Evidence of official corruption was as easy to come by as stories about the brutality of the *monterías*. The town of Ocosingo itself had a well-known history of corruption and graft. One of the men who covered up for Fernando Mijares's cruelty, and who traded him men for a handsome profit, was the *jefe político*, the prefect or district administrator, of the town.[81] Moreover, elections in Chilón were customarily rigged and private armies of pistoleros made their presence felt at the ballot box.[82] The municipal presidents of Ocosingo made sure that they earned their share from every fair by levying taxes, especially on the Indians, in exactly the way Traven described in *Regierung* and *Marsch ins Reich der Caoba*. There is, therefore, abundant evidence to support Traven's accusations concerning corruption among government officials.

It is all the more astonishing then to read Traven's explanation for corruption in Mexico as he expressed it in his introductory letter to the Büchergilde. There he falls back on the racial theories that he had expounded so unsuccessfully in *Land des Frühlings*:

> Such a melting of races . . . produces necessarily explosions. During the racial melting process, the notions of justice, honesty, personality and honor must become shaky, as well as [the understanding] of such crimes as theft, murder, deception, corruption, graft, cheating, and forgery. For this reason, during such periods of racial equalization, men of corruption, imperiousness, despotism, vanity, lack of scruples, and [men] of crime, find opportunities to satisfy their instincts at the expense of the rest of the nation and humanity in general.[83]

This was a complete reversal of the position Traven had taken in *Land des Frühlings*, where he had argued that the same "racial melting" process produced a new and better mentality. Although Traven still believed in the good intentions of the Calles government, which now recognized "the Indian, every Indian, as a Mexican citizen whose rights are equal to any other citizen, for whose welfare the government is responsible," Traven now admitted that there was a huge gulf between the administration's theory and its practice.

To this setting, Traven now added his own thoughts on government and on the power emanating from it. In his introductory letter he pointed out: "Government is the same everywhere: it is always suppression of one part of the population in favor of another part of the same nation. What people need is organization and administration. What people don't need is government and, therefore, they have to abolish it." He identified government as the expression of political power; abuse of power among those close to its source was the inevitable consequence. As Traven succinctly put it: "He who has power and does not use it, is an ass." *Regierung*'s don Gabriel, who has been appointed *secretario de municipalidad* (town secretary) of Bachajón by a friend in political office, was Traven's prototypical government representative. Gabriel, the author indicates, never acts in such a way as to benefit the town; he merely disrupts its peaceful life. When Gabriel begins to learn how to make money from his office, Traven remarked, "These were forty-five pesos in his pocket. He knew how to govern."[84] The historical truth of this attitude on the part of ladinos was neatly illustrated in a letter written by the municipal president of San Cristóbal de las Casas to the undersecretary of the Ministry of Labor. The municipal president complained that the indigenous workers did not volunteer to work for ladinos and preferred to work their own—insufficient—lands. Measures should be taken, he suggested, to destroy this laziness that was so typical of the indigenous race.[85]

Politics in Chiapas, according to Traven, had nothing to do with administration or organization and was, instead, an end in itself. Positions were created for no other purpose than to generate income for a ladino, whose incentive to hold office was never the quest for prestige or responsibility, as was the case with the Indians, but always greed. Since the government only paid nominal salaries, the opportunities for personal enrichment were limited only by the inventiveness of the individual. In all cases, the bill had to be paid by the Indian population, who had no defense against this system. A large part of *Regierung* is taken up with a description of the activities of the *secretario*, and Traven concentrated on showing the opportunities for exploitation open to holders of this office. The secretary's duties had not changed since Traven first reported on them in *Land des Frühlings*, but the author's vision of them had. In the later book he acknowledged the possibilities for graft associated with the position, in part, it can be safely assumed, because he had been exposed to reports of how Indian townships were administered in the department of Chilón.

Traven had also revised his ideas on alcoholism among Indians, acknowledging, as he had not in *Land des Frühlings*, the moral devastation caused by brandy, especially when it was sold on credit. He now clearly perceived that alcohol was the strongest weapon ladinos wielded in their ongoing exploitation of indigenous peoples, and this special Indian weakness becomes in *Regierung* Gabriel's main source of income. The Indian Gregorio, who cuts his brother-in-law to pieces with a machete, acts under the influence of brandy sold by Gabriel. During his second and third trip to Chiapas, Traven must have experienced drunken Indians; he wrote in *Regierung*: "It seems to be part of the Indian's nature that he is easily influenced by brandy, especially the kind sold to Indians. Many Indians lose total control over their actions under the influence of brandy. Anybody who knows Indians, is aware of this; and if he does not know, he will learn faster than he fancies."[86] Traven made an about-turn as well on the issue of the Indians' loyalty to their community. He now saw that estrangement from his community made the Indian sense of duty and involvement disappear. Traven drew a sharp line between the "civilized Indian and the citified Indian, [who] are as alien to the primitive Indian in their ability to understand hidden and inexplicable motives as is any European."[87]

The ultimate powerlessness of the Indians vis-à-vis Gabriel was depicted by Traven in a scene of great power and compassion. The parting of the murderer Gregorio from his wife is as touching as the love story between Andreu and Estrellita. The wife loses her husband simply because Gabriel sees the opportunity of arranging a free trip to San Cristóbal on the pretext of escorting Gregorio there. The parting of husband and wife is a compelling description of pain, loss, and mourning, and this pain is genuine and articulate despite the fact that Gregorio appears to be nothing but a beast of burden, "dirty and full of lice, baptized a Catholic and yet a heathen, less educated than a dog, greedy for brandy, with hands used to work and hard as ebony, the hair on the forehead rubbed thin and bald like the pressure points on the back of a mule. A figure in the slaughterhouse of the caprice of those who rule over the land and the race."[88]

Ladinos regarded Indians "as cattle," according to Traven. "What is that Indian to me?" Gabriel asks himself, when he suffers a moment's regret after witnessing Gregorio's parting from his wife. His hesitation, we are told, is rooted in the sort of "compassion shown toward a horse that looks at you with sad eyes and the faint hope that man can help him since God had no mercy on him." Don Ramón, a labor contractor for the *monterías*, who will later teach Gabriel his trade, exhibits the same attitude: "A lousy Indian does not matter"; what does matter are the *"jefes políticos*, the municipal presidents, and the chiefs of police [who] all want to live." This indifference toward Indians, and the Indians' degradation at the hands of the powerful, had now become Traven's most prominent theme. His ladinos regard an Indian as a commodity created for their special benefit. Ramón sums up the situation thus: "What is the Indian otherwise in the world for? He only causes us trouble. He was born to work." This attitude is shared by every ladino in Traven's novels. Yet, none of these characters is an outright villain. Each, Traven tells us, is merely the victim of greed and a "perpetual need of money." The degree to which each possesses or lacks scruples about exploiting Indians determines his profits.

Traven was aware that unscrupulousness alone could not explain the degree of exploitation practiced by ladinos; the Indians, he argued, contributed to their oppression. The Indians' ignorance and meek acceptance of the impositions put upon them led the ladinos to believe that ruthless exploitation as a beast of burden was all the Indian was worth. By 1930, Traven had concluded that the ladinos of Chiapas would never attempt to meet Indians on their own ground or (as he had tried to do) understand what motivated them. The bigoted, conceited, and narrow-minded ladino characters of Traven's novels were not capable of such mental effort. It was the Indian who would have to learn to adapt himself to the other's ways in order to beat him at his own game. This learning process begins to be enacted in Traven's next novel, *Marsch ins Reich der Caoba*.

This process, in Traven's view, could only begin once the Indian was removed from his community. The world of the independent indigenous settlements, his argument ran, was held together by a network of traditions and regulations whose transgression was unthinkable. To act like a ladino, to take up the other's ways, would be to break those strictures. What is more, the Indians who honored their traditions had no reason to break with the past, because they were not motivated by greed but by a sense of communal justice. Deceit, for example, is inconceivable to the Bachajón chieftain who falls victim to Gabriel's lies. In addition, many of the greatest calamities that befall the Indians in Traven's novels are due to illiteracy. In effect, the ladinos' greatest business, the author shows us, was Indian ignorance itself. As Andreu tells Estrellita: "Those who know how to read and to write cannot be easily deceived with contracts, debt registers, and government orders. If the peons on the fincas knew how to read and write, then the *finqueros* could not keep them in debt and slavery and sell them when they pleased."[89] The case of the Indians of Cancúc, who took the extraordinary step of complaining to the Ministry of Labor, indicates that more than literacy alone would be required to solve the Indians' problems. The ministry replied to their petition that they would have to direct their complaints to the local authorities—the same authorities, presumably, that condoned or assisted in their exploitation.

The novel *Regierung* comes full circle when Andreu Ugalde is reintroduced into the plot. He is, in fact, expected to become one of Gabriel's victims once the ladino has thoroughly learned his new trade of trafficking in human beings as a labor agent for the *monterías*. The prospect of striking it rich has finally erased his rudimentary conscience. As Gabriel's convoy of indentured laborers forms at Ocosingo, Andreu meets his future friend Celso Flores, and between the two of them they begin challenging the system with increasing skill. In the course of their march to the *montería*, the subject of Traven's next novel, the two friends find out that the source of their suffering is not the power of the ladinos but their own weakness.

Marsch ins Reich der Caoba

With his next book, Traven left the somnolent world of the fincas and began to focus on agricultural industry in Chiapas, where the two worlds of ancient rural traditions and industrial labor exploitation most strikingly coexisted. Traven's new theme concerned coerced labor in which corporal punishment, usually applied as the penalty for a misdemeanor, was geared toward production. These practices were well known in Mexico from the experiences of the Valle Nacional and the hemp plantations of Yucatán, but the fact that much of Chiapas's mahogany export industry also relied on forced labor was virtually unpublicized. Although John Kenneth Turner, the author of *Barbarous Mexico*, and Henry Baerlein, a correspondent for the London *Times* who confirmed many of Turner's findings, had good sources of information in the country, neither of the two journalists had heard about the nearby *monterías* of Chiapas.[90] In January 1926, almost two years after the closure of the Casa Romano camps, an article appeared in the metropolitan *El Universal* titled " 'Infernos' Also Exist in Mexico."[91] The article seems to have inspired the fifth annual congress of the CGT in 1926 to order the printing of a pamphlet describing the horrors of the *monterías* and to send a team of three investigators to Chiapas.[92] It appears, however, that although the order was given, the plan was never carried out.

The world that Traven now began to describe formed part of the neoslavery that emerged predominantly in southern Mexico at a time when slavery was being abolished nearly everywhere else in Latin America. A sudden increase in the demand for tropical products and the opening of railway lines between the remote southern states and major seaports made large-scale agricultural exports from the region feasible for the first time. Neoslavery was the answer to labor scarcity in tropical states, where debts were systematically used to provide a legal basis for labor coercion.[93] Huge profits could indeed be made from the new agricultural industries. Except for the hemp plantations in Yucatán, the new agricultural estates were nearly all owned or managed by foreigners, who had come to Mexico not just to make a living but to make a fortune. Traven traced this development through his depiction in the novel of the history of the Spanish-born Montellano brothers, whose cruelty and greed ultimately cause the rebellion of the hanged.

Neoslavery generated substantial revenue for the Díaz government, and in order to assure industrial peace a body of rural police, the rurales, was created, whose purpose was to quell peasant uprisings and return escaped peons. Nature aided the task of the rurales in the southern states; Chiapas, Tabasco and Yucatán were isolated, and those who fled from the region had nowhere to go. The Díaz government also created a legal situation that barred every avenue of escape or redress for the peon. A large apparatus of civil servants was built up to supervise the coercive mechanisms with which the production of tropical commercial crops was increased. Rural police, *jefes políticos*, judges, and frequently also the clergy formed a formidable alliance of worldly and spiritual powers against the illiterate peon. The purpose of the alliance was to keep the peon working and to squeeze as much out of him as possible. The exposure of this system became Traven's primary concern.

When in the novel Andreu joins Gabriel's convoy at Ocosingo, he has only a hazy notion of what awaits him in the *montería*, and is aware merely that he might not come back. The first solid fact he learns about the timber industry is that a peon, once trapped in a *montería*, cannot escape. The story of Celso Flores, who is tricked at Ocosingo into another year's contract against his will, teaches Andreu this valuable lesson. Moreover, the march to the *montería* confirms to Andreu that from now on, more than ever before, he is considered a beast of burden. He is exposed, consequently, to the abuses of such brutes as the *coyotes* (overseers) El Zorro and El Camarón, instead of the casual and thoughtless brutality of his former masters. Along the way, Andreu witnesses the "accidental" deaths of both these *coyotes*, and he soon realizes that his new friend Celso is getting revenge on his tormentors. Although Celso has displayed considerable cunning in dispatching the two, the author implies, his wrath is essentially misdirected, because the dead men were merely a part of the system that oppresses him. But by killing the two, Celso has his first sweet taste of vengeance and power.

The new circumstances of his life accelerate Andreu's learning process, and Traven was prompted to begin to analyze for his readers, much in the style of Ret Marut, the nature of state power: "All four [Celso, Andreu, and the two *coyotes*], like the whole troop, were subject to powers stronger than themselves. But all power relies on recognition. There is no power that exists in its own right like a universe regenerating itself. No dictator is powerful enough that his power could not be circumvented. No dictator can command where there is no will to obey him."[94] The reliance of authority on recognition, then, becomes a second theme of the book. Unlike Marut, who argued for individual action, Traven developed a scenario in which a voluntary union of like-minded men, without leadership or organization, can achieve more than an established and politicized trade union movement. The basis of effective action, he began to argue, was first an understanding of the enemy's tactics, and then the development of a concerted and unified strategy for dealing with his actions. Therefore, Celso would only become really effective once he stopped operating alone, and he would only gain true strength once he shared his goals with the other muchachos working alongside him. Traven described the process of voluntary organization in more detail in *Die Rebellion der Gehenkten*.

While on the march to the *montería*, organized opposition is impossible, because the new friends have only a rudimentary understanding of the forces that determine their fate. They cannot see past Gabriel and the *coyotes*, whereas in reality, Traven pointed out, "their fate was determined by the dictator Díaz whose actions in turn were influenced by the idea that the welfare of Mexico was only assured if capitalism reigned free."[95] Not even the mahogany companies or their employees, Traven remarked, could be blamed for the fate of the Indian peons. They "only worked for a salary." It was the forces of capitalism that dictated the actions of everybody, from the dictator down. But "to proletarian Indians, including the intelligent Andreu, everything not immediately connected to a person was beyond their comprehension."

Now that Traven moved toward the inaccessible world of the logging camps, he introduced a number of errors into the books, none of which is serious in itself. One of these mistakes was that he made Celso Flores a Chamula Indian. The Chamula, in fact, were not contracted for the *monterías*. Accustomed to the cool highlands, they could not work in the steamy jungle; they would have died before they could have worked off their debts.[96] Traven's intention of rendering a truthful account of Indian exploitation in Chiapas was well recognized. Had he instead produced works of pure fiction, he would have provoked less anger by presenting Chiapans' misdeeds in multiple editions around the globe. It was his realism, his recognizable settings, the local gossip he inserted, and his implied intention of indicting the Chiapan landowners that sparked the angry reaction. The local *finqueros* were, therefore, highly amused when they heard about the presence of a Chamula in Traven's *monterías*, and the mistake was used by Traven's detractors as proof of his ignorance. Things worsened, moreover, when Traven, under the name of Hal Croves, assisted in the filming of *La rebelión de los colgados* in 1954. The film featured a scene in which a few dozen Chamula, dressed in their thick woolen tunics, labor on a mahogany trunk in the middle of the steamy jungle.[97]

Most of the time, however, Traven handled his data with great care. Aside from the scrupulous reconstruction of his own trip to Nuevo Filadelfia, the main camp of the Agua Azul concession, Traven made use of a true and well-known story that still forms part of local folklore.[98] He had heard about the labor contractor Pancho Celorio, whose face had been badly disfigured by a large scar from a machete blow. The son of Celorio, who had never heard of B. Traven or his novels, has retold the story of his father's scar in much the same way Traven did. While stopping at a river to drink his *pozol* on a trip to the San Quintín *montería* to deliver three workers, Celorio saw a reflection of light on the blade of a machete and ducked instinctively. Instead of severing his head from his shoulders, the blow landed across his face. With the impact he fell into the water, but managed to pull his revolver and shoot one of his attackers. The rest fled. Celorio then put salt into the cut, wound his bandana round his face, and rode back to the finca Tecojá where he was properly attended to. The son suspected that his father's attackers wanted to rob him and then regain their freedom, a very common occurrence at the time.[99]

In retelling this story, Traven merely changed the name from Pancho Celorio to Anselmo Espindola and added his own particular touch. The Bachajón Indians in Espindola's convoy, Traven wrote, start a successful mutiny against their overseer but throw away their victory just as the Chamula Indians had done during the siege of San Cristóbal de las Casas in 1869. The peons who attacked the real Celorio knew what they wanted and nearly achieved their purpose, but Traven explained the failure of the Indians who attack Espindola to follow up their victory in terms of an inherent ethnic weakness:

Indians lack talent for organization. Mexicans inherited this.
Therefore, they are merely the inhabitants of Mexico whereas
otherwise they could be the masters of both American continents.

And because the Bachajón did not show any talent for organization, the other [peons] . . . sat quietly on their seats and watched
the fight as if it was a comedy act in the circus.[100]

Traven's Bachajón Indians even help Espindola to dress his
wound, and he takes them to the *montería* as planned with his
authority restored.

The purposeful twist Traven had given to the story of
Celorio's scar was aimed directly at his German audience. Although Traven had now lived and worked in Mexico for nearly
ten years, he still wrote first and foremost for a German public,
and had become the most popular author of the Büchergilde
because what he wrote was clearly relevant to his readers. His
purpose, moreover, was not directed solely at increasing sales;
Marsch ins Reich der Caoba, published in the crucial year of
1933, was Traven's contribution to the fight against National
Socialism.

Traven and the Rise of the Nazi Movement

Regierung and *Marsch ins Reich der Caoba* both functioned as
commentaries on the great drama unfolding in Germany in the
early 1930s. Whether or not Traven was fully apprised of the
gathering force of the National Socialists cannot be shown from
independent evidence, but it is certain from his novels that he
had a darkening vision of Germany's future. His novels were
written with an increasing sense of urgency, one that culminated
in *Marsch ins Reich der Caoba*. In *Der Karren* there is no evidence
that Traven intended to do more than describe debt slavery and
the fate of agricultural peons in Chiapas. In *Regierung*, he began
to juxtapose two forms of government: the corrupt and greedy
rule of the ladinos, the representatives of the dictatorship,
alongside the fully democratic self-government of the Indians of
Pebvil, a village of Traven's invention. In between was Bachajón,
a self-sufficient, democratic community subverted by the impo-
sition of Gabriel. A dictatorship, once established, regenerates
itself, Traven warned, because "a dictatorship above makes a
dictatorship below unavoidable. . . . Those who did not grow fat
under this government could not vote."[101] At the time Traven

believed, with some justification, that Germany's fate could be decided at the ballot box.

Between the publication of *Regierung* in 1931 and *Marsch ins Reich der Caoba* in 1933, however, the political situation in Germany deteriorated to such a degree that the Socialist party, although still nominally in power, was in fact rendered ineffective. The strong Socialist vote had not prevented it from being maneuvered onto the political fringe, in part because the Great Depression had hit Germany harder than any other country and had taken the teeth out of the trade union movement. With half of all union members out of work, the strike had become a blunt weapon. The dismissal in 1932 of Chancellor Brüning and the Socialist government in Prussia completed the marginalization of Germany's strongest political party. Although the voters remained faithful and the organization continued to hold its annual party days and electoral assemblies, one historian has noted that "it all happened as if they were not really there, and the faithful were seized by a powerful feeling of isolation."[102] Hitler's National Socialists, in contrast, gained ground by leaps and bounds. By 1930, six and one-half million Germans voted for the Nazis, even though it was widely believed that Hitler's political program was a serious threat to all working-class organizations and that seizure of power by the National Socialists would mean the end of the Weimar Republic and likely lead to a dictatorship. The chances of defeating Hitler at the ballot box, it seemed, were fading.

Traven's line of argument in both *Regierung* and *Marsch ins Reich der Caoba* fits this situation too well to be accidental. In these two books, the author began to recommend his own remedies to the German situation. When it became clear that the strength of the working-class vote could not overcome the Socialists' virtual paralysis, he began to suggest the need for working-class action, independent of and even in opposition to party and trade union leadership. In *Regierung* he had already laid the groundwork for such action, showing that one of the most important elements in the Indians' weakness was the unquestioning obedience they demonstrated toward their leaders. In the novels, whenever the ladinos gain influence over Indian caciques and convert them into tools for their greedy manipulations, as happened in Bachajón, the whole Indian community has to bear the often bloody consequences. Traven's comment on the cacique Amelio's cooperation with the new *secretario* was strongly reminiscent of Marut's earlier warnings, and Traven now wrote that "whenever proletarians collaborate with capitalists and bourgeois parties, it has always meant for the last hundred years, the worker will pay the cost of the cooperation. It is the same with the Indians. Whenever they collaborate with officials, they will always carry their skin to market."[103]

The actual election ceremony of Pebvil dramatized in *Regierung* was entirely Traven's invention and takes literally the north German expression "to light a fire under one's bum." This, Traven stressed, was the essence of "the democratic and republican nature" of Pebvil and Bachajón. The fire under the chieftain's chair was meant to impress upon him the need to step down when his time in office ended, so as to "avoid life-long rule and dictatorship which does damage to the nation." The Bachajón Indians, Traven pointed out, obey their cacique Amelio in spite of evidence that he has betrayed them and collaborated with the new municipal secretary. It was unthinkable in Indian tradition, Traven stressed, to be disrespectful, even though there might be good grounds on which to refuse obedience. This incitement may be seen as a direct attack on the German Socialists' strong tradition of party discipline, and on the party's leadership, which had committed a long line of blunders and mistakes, the most unforgiveable of which, in Traven's experience, was the suppression of the revolution of 1918. Through all these events, Traven recognized, Socialist voters had remained faithful. In *Marsch ins Reich der Caoba* the author began to chip away systematically at the cherished discipline of the Socialist party, a tactic that would soon bring him into conflict with his German publisher.

Traven began increasingly to draw on the experience of Marut who, in Munich, had witnessed a number of glaring instances of the Socialist leadership failing to initiate and follow up revolutionary action when it had the political power to do so.[104] The twist Traven gave to the story of the labor contractor Celorio and his scar was a direct reference to events of 1918:

> It is the lack of an effective second offensive that distinguishes the proletarian from the non-proletarian. The proletarian enjoys his first victory. He is surprised that it was so easy to bring about his opponent's fall. And then he believes that the opponent will be afraid and acknowledge that he cannot recover. Because they lack toughness and untiring stamina for a second push, proletarians never win a lasting position.[105]

Traven also transformed his principal Indian characters. The further Andreu, Celso, and the other muchachos are removed from their home communities, the more they lose all specifically Indian characteristics and begin to resemble universal proletarians. By the time the rebellion of the hanged breaks out, they have no Indian features left except their skin color and hair. They become "the brother[s] of the European proletarian," as Traven had stressed in his introductory letter to *Regierung*. He knew very well that his readers had fully accepted the muchachos as their proletarian brothers. As one of his admirers put it: "Traven forced his readers to compare their own lives to those of the Indians of Chiapas."[106]

Traven deliberately called the march to the logging camp a "march to battle." The despised, the beasts of burden that created the wealth of their exploiters, the mute, illiterate, and powerless, slowly gain strength on the way to the very center of exploitation, the *montería*. Celso's native cunning and physical ability enable him to make a crucial breakthrough in the murder of the *coyotes*, which is the first seed that will blossom into the rebellion of the hanged. This message, taken together with Traven's repeated calls for proletarians to be wary of their leaders, amounted to sedition; the equivalent in the German context to Celso's action was sabotage. This was precisely what Marut had tried to incite in 1919 when he called for a second general strike to bring down the Ebert government in Berlin and was, as well, what the Wobblies had preached internationally.

The author had established an important principle. In the fight against capitalism and the threatened takeover by the Nazi movement, the working class would do better to ignore their elected leaders and take matters into their own hands in the style of the CGT workers, who had sent the new state governor of Tamaulipas packing. Traven's warning and advice came too late. Hitler came to power on 30 January 1933 without encountering significant opposition. Four months later the Büchergilde was exiled to Prague, leaving most of its readers behind. *Marsch ins Reich der Caoba* was the first book it published in exile.

The seditious content of *Regierung* and *Marsch ins Reich der Caoba* was not lost on the Büchergilde's editorial staff, which asked the author to modify his strong statements about trade union leadership. Traven's early enthusiasm for the Büchergilde's role as a cooperative, nonprofit trade union bookclub had already begun to wane when serious difficulties developed

between Traven and Bruno Dressler, the founder and managing
director of the club. Dressler, who was responsible for the financial well-being of the Büchergilde, "was a hard master, more
capitalistic than the capitalists," as the Danish author Andersen
Nexø characterized him. When Traven began to submit to the
Büchergilde the manuscripts of the Jungle Cycle, he was asked
repeatedly to alter them for political reasons and to "mollify and
beautify" his texts. His publisher objected strongly to such out-
spoken passages as Traven's comment on the Pebvil election
ceremony:

> I seriously advise proletarians to apply this well-tried Indian
> method, especially where the officials of their trade unions and
> political organizations are concerned. Not only in Russia where it
> is most needed, but in all European countries where Marx and
> Lenin have been put on a pedestal, the fighting proletariat could
> be more successful if they put a good fire under their officials'
> bums each year. No leader is irreplaceable; and the more fre-
> quently the new leader is put in a hot seat, the more alive will be
> his organization. Don't be afraid, proletarians, and much less be
> sentimental![107]

Traven's trusted friend and editor Ernst Preczang pleaded
with him in May 1933: "Most members of the Büchergilde belong
to Socialist or trade union organizations, and the Büchergilde
Gutenberg would be finished if it were to show a hostile attitude
towards those organizations. Such sentences are usually secondary. I would be grateful if you could consider it."[108] Preczang's
plea went straight to the heart of what Traven considered his
mission. The author regarded political education of his audience
as the essence of his work. Preczang now called it a secondary
activity. Traven was in fact being asked by his publisher to edify
instead of educate. How hurt Traven was by this suggestion
emerges from his reply:

> I cannot think of any act base or miserable enough which I would
> not trust a German labor leader capable of committing. Since 1914,
> the German labor leaders have constantly betrayed the German—
> and by implication the international—proletariat only in order to
> stick to their posts and to satisfy personal ambitions. They are
> capable of any kind of mean or unworthy action, I trust. Because
> of this I am quite prepared [to hear] that it is possible that certain
> people in the Büchergilde Gutenberg are ready to sell or barter
> away the organization.[109]

In fact, Traven was not far off the mark. With Hitler's rise to power, the Büchergilde, along with other proletarian organizations, tried to adapt to the new political conditions. Preczang's urgent appeal to Traven to censor his writings was part of the Büchergilde's new policy of retreating from the terrain of politics to that of entertainment in order to show a "high sense of duty toward the entire nation."[110]

The publisher's efforts, however, were to no avail; in May 1933 the Büchergilde, together with all other working-class organizations, was incorporated into the Nazi state. S. A. Sturmführer Otto Jamrowski was appointed as the new manager. The new editor was Max Barthel, whose career had begun with the Communist Press. Bruno Dressler was temporarily taken into custody. Together with Preczang, Dressler decided to leave Germany and to continue abroad. The censorship battle with Traven was over; the new Büchergilde Prague could now freely oppose the Hitler government, and *Marsch ins Reich der Caoba* was published without changes. As soon as Traven was informed of the occupation of the Büchergilde building in Berlin, he lodged a protest forbidding any further publication of his work under Nazi auspices. After a brief attempt to capitalize on Traven's fame, the new masters became aware of the author's subversiveness. Traven was blacklisted on 16 May 1933, in the distinguished company of such writers as the brothers Heinrich and Thomas Mann, Alfred Döblin, and Arnold and Stefan Zweig.

Had Traven complied with the wishes of his publisher, he would have betrayed those of his readers who were prepared to listen to him, to follow him, and to learn from him, especially the young people whom he had helped to politicize[111] and who learned "two things from Traven: compassion and resistance."[112] It was for them that his books were written in the first place, and some individual readers showed more courage than the Büchergilde management. One reader remembered his first acquaintance with Traven's writings at a time when reading or possessing one of the books could have meant banishment from school and any professional career for the seventeen year old. The young man was sold *Das Totenschiff* by an old bookdealer who kept Traven's books behind a row of Nazi-approved literature and who told his young customer: "After you have read this, my boy, you will throw away nine tenths of your so-called adventure stories. But don't throw them out. Bring them here and I'll sell them to those idiots who want to read 'John Kling' and all this fascist shit. And then I'll give you another Traven."[113] The young man was "left breathless" by what he read. Traven, he found, "is the son of the marriage of Egon Kisch and Jack London; Villon was his godfather and Grimmelshausen baptized him with tequila. [Such a mixture] had to be good." This was the kind of appreciation and lasting gratitude Traven wanted from his audience; this was the reason for his hard work between 1925 and 1933.

Despite the attempt to dictate to him the handling of his subjects, Traven remained faithful to his publisher, who now found himself in reduced circumstances in Prague. While it seems that there was never any formal contract between Traven and his publisher, the author stuck to his agreement with Preczang and the Büchergilde continued to enjoy first publishing rights for his books. Traven also kept supporting the book club wherever he could. During the annual advertising campaign, he promised prizes to readers who could recruit the most new members. Otherwise, he tried "to do everything I possibly can to promote the growth of the Büchergilde, be it under small or great sacrifices."[114] Nonetheless, the rift between author and publisher remained, and confidence had been broken. What was worse, Traven had lost most of his audience. He now began to look for a new audience and a new publisher.

In 1933 he began negotiations with Alfred A. Knopf in New York and Chatto and Windus in London. In 1934, *Das Totenschiff* was published both in London and in New York. *Der Schatz der Sierra Madre* followed in London in 1934 and in New York in 1935. *Die Brücke im Dschungel* was published in 1938 in New York. Knopf and Chatto and Windus, however, were both commercial publishers, which meant that Traven was no longer able to address a homogeneous audience imbued with a particular anticapitalist ideology. He was poised to address readers in the two largest capitalist nations in the world, but he was not about to make concessions. The only noticeable change was that he began eliminating references to German culture, history, and politics. In subsequent revisions of his earlier books Traven scrapped those references, not only because he began to try to brush over his tracks but also because the references meant little to his new audience. Traven did not need new readers for financial reasons, since such a motive was quite alien to a passionate and frugal man like him. He had very modest needs. The descriptions we have of Cashew Park, the first home Traven owned in Mexico, suggest that it was far from being a luxury establishment. Instead, he needed an audience to which he could talk, expound his ideas, and from which he could receive a response in the form of trust and admiration. Aside from this emotional need, Traven was also looking for a new cause to embrace. He found it in Spain.

In contrast with the collapse of the 1918 German Revolution and the apparent degeneration of the Mexican Revolution after 1928, a new dawn seemed to be breaking in Spain. Under the leadership of the anarchist Confederación Nacional de Trabajadores (National Confederation of Workers), an experiment in workers' self-management got under way in Catalonia. The reorganization of Barcelona and much of the Catalonian countryside developed considerably further than workers' power had in Tampico in 1925. Traven was delighted with the news from Spain.

When civil war broke out in 1936, as the republic came under siege from monarchist and fascist forces, Traven pledged his full support to the republican cause. He allowed his books to be printed in Spain, despite the danger that they might reach Mexico. He maintained regular correspondence with Pedro Herrera, editor of the anarcho-syndicalist monthly *Timón*, and he offered to send a collection of Spanish- and English-language newspapers as a present for the men and women in the trenches. But should he receive an invitation from the Spanish government to visit, he stressed, he would decline. Instead, he wrote, he would use the money to buy "cotton wool, condensed milk, coffee, and cigarettes." He hoped for a speedy and victorious conclusion to the war "against the enemies of civilization and progress under the command of Franco," concluding his letter with "Salud!"—the greeting of the Spanish anarchists.[115] His hopes were not realized, and after Francisco Franco's victory in 1939, Traven forbade immediately any further printing of his books in Spain. He also insisted that the positive description of the Spanish nation in *Das Totenschiff* be scrapped from a new edition, arguing that this would only mislead readers.[116] By 1939 all of Traven's bright political hopes were in tatters; he could only look back on three failed revolutions in Germany, Mexico, and Spain.

5 The *Monterías*: The Unknown Hell

An Introduction

Even before the publication of the first volume of the Jungle Cycle, Traven was aware of the danger that publication of the detailed and recognizable contents of his novels presented to him. In 1930, Traven bought the secluded property of Cashew Park in Acapulco, and after his return from Chiapas he settled there with the schoolteacher María de la Luz Martínez. The copyrights for his novels were transferred to de la Luz Martínez at about the same time. This proved after 1933 to be an auspicious move for the author, whose books were banned and had been burned in Germany. The new Nazi regime enjoyed growing support among the large German community in Mexico, and increasing numbers of Nazi agents infiltrated the country. After 1933, Traven, in addition to refusing to give information about his person, virtually disappeared from sight in Acapulco. His identity was, in fact, not made public until 1949, by the Mexican journalist Luis Spota.

The protests and threats issued by the Chiapan landowners against the author of *Die Rebellion der Gehenkten* must have been an additional reason for Traven's precautions. He did not expect a strong reaction to the books, because the mahogany logging industry, in the form Traven had described, had all but ceased operations when he published his work in 1936. By the time Traven began his inquiries into the timber business, all the large logging companies, including the Casa Romano, the Casa Bulnes (which became the Casa Vega in 1914), and the Casa Valenzuela, had gone out of business. Moreover, all three companies had worked in the depth of the Lacandon Forest for more than four decades, and yet little was known outside the immediate area about their operations. The activities of the Romano and Bulnes companies had continued largely undisturbed throughout the

turbulent years of the revolution with their primitive, even
archaic, production methods unchanged.

Traven's account of logging operations is drawn from the
viewpoint of a *montero*, and presents only such information as
an experienced worker would understand of the business in
which he was engaged. The owners or managers of the logging
companies were of interest to Traven solely in their role as
exploiters of labor. The author portrayed the principals as trapped
in the world capitalist system and in relation to the chief exploiter
Díaz, thus depriving them of any local or historical dimensions.
Mahogany logging itself, however, as did the families who
owned the logging companies, had a history of its own without
which the labor conditions prevailing in the different camps
cannot be understood.

The idea of exploiting the precious timbers of the jungles of
Tabasco and Chiapas is considerably older than is generally
accepted. As early as 1822, Cayetano Robles made an offer to the
Mexican government to explore the then uncharted jungle between Ocosingo and the Usumacinta River at his own cost, in
company with his friend Antonio Vives. In return, the government would grant him and his friend the exclusive right of
timber exploitation for six years and the right to run boats on the
Usumacinta.[1] His proposal indicates that Robles had a fair idea
of the wealth contained in the Lacandon Forest and the economic
future of the area. What is more, he suggested sending vagrants
("hombres bajos y mal entretenidos") to work in the jungle, thus
removing them from the cities. Many years later, President Díaz
took up this idea, creating one of the greatest nightmares of the
logging industry. Prisons were emptied, old loggers complained,
and their inmates began to arrive in the *monterías*, mixed in with
troops of recruited workers and creating major problems of
discipline and order.

Although permission was granted to Robles, no more was
heard of the enterprise. In fact, nothing more was heard of any
logging operations in Chiapas for the next sixty years, since
exploration of the Lacandon Forest proved more difficult than
don Cayetano had anticipated. After a number of unsuccessful
attempts, Juan Ballinas, a local from Ocosingo, established in
1877 that a direct waterway existed from the Lacantún River via
the Usumacinta River to the seaports of Tabasco and Campeche.[2]
The Casa Bulnes made immediate use of the discovery and
began logging operations in the Valley of San Quintín, named

after the patron saint of one of the Bulnes brothers. The Casa
Romano began logging at the confluence of the Tzendales and
Negro rivers in the early 1880s, on a *montería* they named San
Roman, variously known as San Roman Tzendales or Los
Tzendales. The administrative headquarters of all logging com-
panies remained in San Juan Bautista, later Villahermosa, in
Tabasco.

Logging was first introduced in Tabasco and was at one time
the most remunerative industry in that state. It was calculated
that the production and transport of a mahogany trunk cost the
logging company sixteen pesos. The price paid by the foreign
timber companies, however, was sixty pesos. The profit margin
was frequently further increased by evading the tax levied on
trunks by the Mexican government. Between 1887 and 1910,
timber prices rose by 74 percent, while labor costs remained the
same.[3] In that period, the timber trade rapidly expanded, and
the Tabascan forests were soon exhausted due to overexploitation, a condition that caused the major companies to
shift their operations to Chiapas. By 1899 there were three leading companies active in the two states, the Casa Valenzuela,
the Casa Bulnes, and the Casa Romano. Moreover, no additional logging concessions would become available; the
three giants had partitioned the greater part of the Lacandon
Forest among themselves.

The high profit margin of logging attracted many, but setting up a logging operation required significant capital resources
such as could not be found in Chiapas. In Tabasco, there was
only one man, Policarpo Valenzuela, with access to the necessary
funds. Valenzuela began logging at Aldama, in Tabasco, as
early as 1860. Said to be illiterate, he had begun to amass a huge
fortune with a fraudulent scheme in which he first insured his
coastal steamers and riverboats at a high premium and then
sank them.[4] Don Polo, as he was known, was not illiterate at all,
but this rumor fitted his image of crudeness. His speech was
accompanied by copious spitting, and his grandson estimated
that he had some two hundred illegitimate children throughout
Tabasco, many of whom were the fruit of the landlord's privilege
of the first night.[5] He was known and feared for his endless
lawsuits with the help of which, through a legal system at his
beck and call, he accumulated more and more land until he
owned a quarter of the state. Don Polo was not only the richest
man in the state, but he was also a friend of Porfirio Díaz, which

made him the uncrowned king of Tabasco.[6] In 1904, don Polo signed a contract with the Mexican government for 250,000 hectares of prime forest land in Chiapas, directly bordering the Usumacinta River. Half of this tract, called El Cayo, was later sold to the Agua Azul Mahogany Company to whose main *montería* Traven traveled in February 1930 with Paniagua. Valenzuela lost most of his property in Tabasco during the revolution, but his Chiapan landholdings were unaffected.

Valenzuela was the only Mexican among the owners in the logging industry; most of the capital invested at the time in the Lacandon Forest, with the exception of that of the Casa Bulnes, was foreign. The Bulnes family came from Asturias, in Spain, and had permanently settled in Mexico in the middle of the nineteenth century. Having started a successful trading business in Veracruz, its members had enough money twenty years later to help Porfirio Díaz finance his 1876 coup d'état. In return for their assistance, the Bulnes family was awarded vast stretches of forest land between the Jataté and Usumacinta rivers,[7] and with this base they induced friends and relatives from Spain to join their business. Their family names (Vela, Vega, Valle, Celorio, and Villanueva) appear again and again in the logging industry, where these Spanish immigrants worked as partners, contractors, overseers, managers, and timber fellers. The families intermarried, and many of the members bought land and farms in Tabasco and Chiapas, where their descendants still live today.

The Romano family also originated in Asturias. Although they accumulated considerable assets in Mexico, they never put down local roots and are not known to have married locally. In 1863, in conjunction with the Berreteaga family, they began an import business and department store in San Juan Bautista, and they subsequently operated steamships in the Gulf of Mexico. Timber felling was first introduced in the Barra de Chiltepec and at Tonalá as a sideline to their other investments, but with the discovery of the Lacantún-Usumacinta water route, the Casa Romano moved into timber felling on a grand scale. It acquired vast stretches of forest land through the Tierras Baldías Act, which was introduced in 1894 and designed to put state land and land without secure title on the market, prerequisites the Lacandon Forest fulfilled at the time.[8] The vast timber-felling concessions could not have been worked, however, without an adequate supply of manpower, and the act took care of that problem as well. By separating Indian communities and small farmers from their land, a vast army of vagrants and unemployed was created in Tabasco. Between 1895 and 1900 the number of available farmhands was increased by 361 percent.[9] These men without choice formed the stock of the Casa Romano labor force until even this supply dried up and the company had to look further afield for laborers.[10] It was the Casa Romano, under the management of Mijares Escandón, that developed a system of labor and resource exploitation unparalleled in Chiapas or Tabasco.

The Casa Romano was essentially a family enterprise. While its owner, Manuel Romano, remained in Spain, the Casa's representative in Mexico, Pedro Romano, lived at San Juan Bautista and died there at the age of eighty-six. In 1924, Mijares Escandón, a relative of the Romano family, a partner in the business, and its economic pillar, was murdered in prison in Villahermosa. On 10 December 1925, the Calles government annulled most of the land titles of the Romano holdings in the Lacandon Forest despite the fact that the government of President Carranza had confirmed them. The annulment came at a time when—due to overexploitation—most of the Romano forest lands had become worthless. In 1929 the sons and heirs of Pedro Romano contrived to get a loan from the Mexican national bank, offering as collateral 66,000 hectares of forest land for which they still held secure title, plus other rural and urban properties in Tabasco, Chiapas, and Campeche. They received a loan of more than 415,000 pesos. In February 1930, they obtained another loan of US $201,373. With these substantial sums they disappeared to Spain, leaving behind considerably less in rural and urban real estate, machinery, and forest land.[11] The sudden departure of the Romanos was an added bonus to Traven, who did not then need to fear reprisals from that powerful and well-connected clan.

The protests by the Chiapan landowners were most often directed against *Die Rebellion der Gehenkten*, which became the most famous of Traven's Jungle Novels. The landowners principally objected to the author's choice of data on the *monterías*, arguing that Traven had chosen the worst evidence he could find concerning the most notorious logging camp, San Roman Tzendales. The novel, the landowners charged, presented this evidence as if it were the norm rather than the exception in Chiapas. In fact, Traven took great care to avoid implicating his friends, the Bulnes family, or the Casa Bulnes/Vega by differentiating between the various types of management and labor systems active at the time. It was clear to insiders like Duby or Cordan that Traven described the operations of the Casa Romano and not those of any other company. Later commentators and historians lumped the *monterías* together and cited Traven as supporting evidence for their claims. In this, they did a great injustice to Traven, as well as to *montería* owners such as the Vega family, who were never guilty of the excesses committed by Mijares Escandón.

One of the reasons for these misunderstandings can be found in the publication history of Traven's books. *Die Troza* and *Die Rebellion der Gehenkten* have to be read together in order to see just how carefully Traven made his distinctions. The former, however, has never been translated; reading *Die Rebellion der Gehenkten* alone indeed gives the impression that Traven generalized and thus damaged the reputation of the Chiapan elite, and since he was the first investigator into the logging industry, there is no other record against which his claims could be measured. Before the discovery of the Mayan ruins at Palenque, Yaxchilán, and Piedras Negras began to attract outsiders such as Blom, Palacios, Tannenbaum, Robert Morley, and Traven, only men connected to the logging industry had any business traveling through the Lacandon Forest. Employees, managers, contractors, and traders, all had an interest in not having their business disturbed. Their good relations with local officials were such that it took until Cárdenas came to power in 1934 for the government of Chiapas to finally establish some degree of control over the signing and supervision of work contracts.[12]

During the Porfiriato, reports on life in the logging camps were subject to strict press censorship. Even in Chiapas and Tabasco itself knowledge of the *monterías* was vague. The seventeen-year-old Trinidad Malpica had heard stories that life was tough and survival difficult, but he dismissed them as old wives' tales and entered the San Pedro *montería* in 1916. He learned the truth soon enough and only a daring escape saved him.[13] With the advent of the Madero government in 1911, a few accounts of survivors from San Roman Tzendales appeared in the national press. At the time, so many similar reports about abuse, exploitation, and cruelty were published that the sporadic accounts of Los Tzendales made no particular impact. What is more, the Lacandon Forest was the most remote and inaccessible part of Mexico, and relations between the government of Chiapas and the new revolutionary governments in Mexico City were slow to develop. San Roman Tzendales was far from being the nation's principal news item during the turbulent early years of the revolution.

Just how careful one had to be about what was said concerning the *monterías* during the Porfiriato was demonstrated by a geological expedition into the Lacandon Forest in 1908. The geologists Jorge Engerrand and Fernando Urbina led the expedition partly by boat, partly on foot, all the way to the Usumacinta River and the Guatemalan border. The group must have stopped at several logging camps, for these were the only places in the Lacandon Forest where food supplies could be replenished. In their expedition report, the two geologists carefully avoided mention of the logging camps and what they had seen and heard there and merely wrote: "It is noteworthy that almost all inhabited places are situated at the border with Guatemala and that they are purely Mexican."[14] Among the "inhabited places" along the border with Guatemala were La Constancia of the Casa Romano, San Nicolás of the Casa Valenzuela, and Egipto, owned by the Casa Torruco. The expedition used canoes and boats that conveyed food and other goods to *monterías*. They "were treated nicely by the owners of the estates who allowed us to use their boats without payment." Engerrand and Urbina, like other travelers to the region, must have heard stories about the brutality at Los Tzendales. Yet, they failed even to take note of the harshness of timber felling and never used the word *montería*.

Strict press censorship assisted the Díaz government in its attempt to attract foreign investment to Mexico, for which the principal lure was a cheap and plentiful labor supply. In 1895, one year after the promulgation of the Tierras Baldías Act, the Chiapas Information Bureau published a booklet listing the advantages of investing in the state. In the districts of Las Casas, Simojovel, Palenque, and Chilón, the booklet pointed out, "the low wage of 20 centavos a day" was current.[15] These districts also happened to have the greatest concentration of Indians in the state. Land was available cheaply there thanks to the Tierras Baldías Act, which despoiled Tzeltal communities such as Bachajón, Oxchúc, and Cancúc of all their village land.[16] Such land was offered at 2 to 5 pesos per hectare and had the added advantage, the booklet stressed, of being located near a village. Thus the indispensable labor force of impoverished Indians was ready at hand. Buying land under the provisions of the act could prove wonderfully economical for logging companies, a similar propaganda production for Tabasco pointed out: "Some companies buy the forest land from the state. It often happens that in a plot of one hundred hectares costing three hundred pesos, there are so many trees that, had the company rented the lands, they would have had to pay six hundred pesos alone in taxes."[17]

With the onset of the revolution a few outsiders entered the *monterías* by cunning or by force, but the reports of these events reveal little about what the intruders found. Alfonso Taracena, a historian from Tabasco, found evidence that in 1911 Licenciado Emilio Vázquez Gómez, who had been vice-president of the de la Barra government earlier in that year, had covertly sent political agents from New Orleans and Texas through Guatemala to Tabasco. In 1912 the agents, Taracena wrote, infiltrated the Romano *monterías* and incited a rebellion there.[18] Taracena never disclosed his sources. Most historians dealing with the subject have repeated Taracena's information without further commentary, and the primary source on which the historian had drawn has still not been located. José Toriello Bulnes never heard of such an event, although he stressed that there were continuing minor troubles at Los Tzendales throughout the early years of the revolution.

The only solid evidence of the revolutionary message reaching Los Tzendales comes from a source dated two years later and quite unconnected to agents of Vázquez Gómez. Revolutionary troops from the area known as Los Ríos, under the leadership of General Luis Felipe Domínguez, entered the jungle in search of soldiers and supplies. They came as far as Los Tzendales. General Domínguez, however, had no time to sit down and write a lengthy report about what he had seen and merely drafted the first decree for the liberation of the serfs at his base camp at El Ceibo.[19] Taken all together, existing information on working conditions in the logging camps of Chiapas, aside from Traven's accounts, is often uncertain, frequently highly emotional, and always patchy. The following section collects the available evidence from the San Roman Tzendales and San Quintín *monterías* in order to show the way in which Traven selected from the evidence at his disposal.

San Roman and San Quintín

The evidence Traven and subsequent investigators into *montería* life employed came primarily from oral sources, because most timber fellers were illiterate. *Monteros*, however, could only tell their stories if they returned from the jungle, and many never did. The death rate was not only high due to harsh treatment and hunger, but the climate, as well, was deadly and the work hazardous. Tuberculosis, malaria, and intestinal disorders were rampant. Snake bites and accidents due to unsafe working conditions were frequent causes of death. Traven's description of the death of the peon Eulalio in *Die Troza* was only too realistic. Medical attention was nonexistent; at San Quintín, medical supplies were limited to a small chest of elementary drugs and bandages in the possession of one of the managers. Men who suffered an accident while working and who could not be cured by the simple medical means available were left in the jungle to die.[20]

Thus most of the accounts we have of working conditions in the industry come from survivors. These fall into two categories. The first consists of men who considered themselves "macho" because they were able to survive in the harsh climate of a logging camp and who consequently were proud of their profession and fiercely loyal to their bosses. These men prevailed at San Quintín, and many of their testimonies distinctly voice contempt for those who did not make it in the *monterías*.[21] The second is comprised of men who were liberated from San Roman Tzendales in March 1914 by General Domínguez. These men had been forced to enlist due to hunger, misery, or the manipulations of the Porfirian authorities. Once the Casa Romano operations came under the management of Mijares Escandón, few peons volunteered to go to Los Tzendales. In fact, the camp's reputation was so bad that it was said in Tabasco that any peon could be scared into submission by the threat of being "sold" to Los Tzendales.[22] The few surviving testimonies of these men are pitiful.

The bulk of the more recent testimony concerning San Quintín comes from Pedro Vega, son of the owner of the Casa Vega, from José Toriello Bulnes, manager of San Quintín from 1913 until it closed in 1924, and from Professor Prudencio Moscoso Pastrana, who published a book on life at San Quintín based on a series of interviews with a former *montero* named Villanueva. By themselves these three men do not seem ideal witnesses on which the historian can draw to evaluate either Traven's accounts or accusations concerning Traven's untruthfulness. There are, fortunately, accounts from other sources that corroborate their versions. A former worker at San Quintín, Rubén Navarro, later a journalist in Tuxtla Gutiérrez, has recorded his memories of life at the camp, reaching back as far as 1916. Some patchy information about San Quintín has also come from Gertrude Duby, who came to San Cristóbal de las Casas in 1942 and was a good friend of the Bulnes family of El Real and the Vega family of Tecojá. The archeologist Cordan, who traveled the length and the breadth of the Lacandon Forest in the 1950s, has also supplied information. He, too, was a friend of the Bulnes and Vega families. Both Cordan and Duby responded to the interest in *monterías* aroused by Traven's work. The accounts of San Quintín and the Romano camps differ so greatly not because the surviving witnesses are apologetic for their associations with the Bulnes and Vega families. Rather, the differences must be explained by the organization of each company, which resulted in vastly different styles of management. Thus the testimonies of the former workers of San Quintín and the survivors of Los Tzendales vary greatly, although the work processes they carried out were the same. The prevailing working conditions in each camp allow us to distinguish between them.

The camp of San Quintín consisted of simple wooden buildings with thatched roofs, housing some fifty or sixty settled families. Residents not directly involved in logging were engaged in services such as bookkeeping, cooking, mending, washing, and storekeeping. Access was free and unlimited, except for restrictions on unlicensed itinerant traders who smuggled liquor into the camp. A priest came once a year from Ocosingo to baptize and marry the inhabitants, and the mail arrived once a month. The mule caravans that supplied the camp with foodstuffs rested for a week in the camp before returning on the six-day trek to Tecojá where the San Quintín trail started.[23] There was a constant coming and going, and between San Quintín and Tenosique there was even a telephone line, which was used to communicate the number of trunks to be expected downriver.

Conditions were markedly different at San Roman Tzendales. Visitors were not welcome and the camp was guarded. Rodulfo Brito Foucher, a lawyer involved in the revolutionary movement in Tabasco, once tried to visit Los Tzendales after he and his party had heard whisperings from indiscreet personnel about "a famous administrator." Mijares Escandón made sure that Brito Foucher and his traveling party had no opportunity to speak to workers. He furnished the party with a competent guide who saw to it that they did not get anywhere near a logging camp.[24] San Roman Tzendales itself was a place well worth seeing. Although it took twelve days to reach it from Ocosingo, the remote camp featured elegant brick buildings. Rubén Navarro, who had seen San Roman in its prime, reported:

> This building of which some ruins should still remain, had two stories. Upstairs was the bedroom of the managers and the employees [of the administration] and the archive; downstairs was the dining room and a study. But at the highest level there was a rain meter, a barometer and other measuring instruments, finishing off at the top of the cupola with a weathervane. To the left, a long brick building followed with kitchen, bread oven, store rooms and sickbay. Since the beginning of the century the general administrator don Fernando lived here.[25]

During the early years of the revolution, a number of visitors entered Los Tzendales by force of arms and were shocked at what they saw. General Domínguez maintained that the cruelty and misery he saw there moved him to issue the first decree for the liberation of the serfs in Tabasco. At San Quintín, however, life went on undisturbed. When the liberation of the serfs was decreed in Chiapas by Colonel Castro in 1914, only a few workers left San Quintín, and nobody prevented their leaving.[26]

Of all logging companies, the Casa Romano had the largest landholdings, which were divided into three different *zonas Romano* comprising a total of some 200,000 hectares of forest. The Romano heartland lay tucked into a remote corner formed by the Guatemalan border to the south, the Bulnes holdings to the west, and the Usumacinta River to the east. At the center of this territory lies the Tzendales River, tributary to the Lacantún, which in turn flows into the Usumacinta, thus ensuring direct communication with the ports of Frontera and Ciudad del Carmen. The first *zona Romano* had a total surface of about 100,000 hectares. The second formed an extension of the first and covered an additional 49,000 hectares. The *central* San Roman, the camp from which harvesting of the area was directed, was established at the confluence of the Tzendales and Negro rivers, because from that point the Tzendales becomes navigable. San

Roman Tzendales was the most remote logging camp on Mexican territory, and so it is all the more astounding to see its brick buildings in the jungle landscape. All the materials to construct them had to be brought in by boat and mule caravan. Typically, everything about a *montería* was makeshift and temporary, but Los Tzendales, it seems, was built to last.

The third *zona Romano* comprised some 51,000 hectares of forest near Boca del Cerro close to Tenosique on Tabascan territory. Its *central* was called Santa Margarita after a tract of that name. It also featured a brick building, which today forms part of the finca Santa Margarita, property of Pedro Vega. Little is known about the operations, working conditions, or staffing of this large holding, but it is clear that Santa Margarita was an important way station for the transport of workers to San Roman Tzendales. The men arrived by boat via the Usumacinta River, having stopped overnight at Montecristo, today Emiliano Zapata. The men contracted nearby were lodged in the town's jail and in the morning herded in chains to the boat. Eliecér Mendoza Cambrano, the longtime official historian of Emiliano Zapata, watched these men when he was a little boy. He recalled that there were always women crying when the boat left because they knew their husbands, sons, and brothers might not return.[27] The Casa Romano lost most of the third *zona* during the revolution. In addition, it rented about 100,000 hectares in the old concession "Marqués de Comillas," a low-lying terrain with an unhealthy climate. By the time that the Calles government annulled the Romano land titles in 1925, the forest land was not only exhausted due to forty-five years of overexploitation but the Casa Romano was bankrupt as well. That year their American trading partner had refused to buy the Casa's entire crop because the trunks, it seems, were not up to the usual standard.[28] The drop in quality was likely due to the removal of the iron fist of Mijares Escandón, who had died the previous year.

Mijares Escandón, a large, bearded Spaniard, had ruled over the first and second *zonas Romano* for a quarter of a century. A man totally devoid of respect for humanity, he not only exploited his labor force mercilessly but also took clever advantage of the corruption of Chiapan and Tabascan government officials. During a drinking bout at Ocosingo, he once declared: "Everything can be fixed with money, everything is made of money, and 10,000 pesos are nothing to me."[29] During his long career, Mijares Escandón only seems to have encountered one politician whom he could not buy. This was Garrido Canabal, governor of Tabasco, who eventually called him to justice and had him killed. Ironically, Mijares Escandón was not arrested for the countless murders of defenseless workers. He was instead charged with responsibility in the death of a Spaniard by the name of Rivera, murdered near Tenosique,[30] and was imprisoned in Villahermosa, where thirty buckets of ice-cold water were poured over him. Some say that he was then bundled off to Spain. According to one version of his death, Mijares Escandón died of pneumonia on the boat. Others say he "died of shame and fury" in prison. But these are the parlor versions of his death; he was, rather, clearly mistreated, including being repeatedly submerged in excrement. He contracted pneumonia, died in prison, and is buried at Villahermosa.[31]

The Casa Romano depended for much of its labor supply on official cooperation, and one important source of labor deriving from such relationships was the prisons. At the beginning of the Porfiriato, there was no jail in Tabasco; at the end there were seventeen.[32] The Casa Romano's administrator also had other connections that provided Indian labor virtually without cost. Mario Domínguez Vidal, son of General Domínguez, referred to a system of forced recruitment financed by the Casa Romano: "The authorities rounded up the Indians of the area and picked out among them the youngest and forced them to serve the company, cheating them with illusory salaries which the unfortunates never received. In this manner four hundred to five hundred Indians were contracted yearly."[33] This practice only succeeded because Indian caciques collaborated "to procure laborers and maintain discipline."[34] They were handsomely paid for their efforts. The work of rounding up Indians was probably organized by Joaquín Peña, the powerful *jefe político* of San Cristóbal de las Casas who, at the same time, was the authorized agent of the Casa Romano in Chiapas.[35]

This cozy arrangement was very much in the style of Mijares Escandón, whose recruiting practices were all of a kind. He paid nothing to his actual labor force; whatever was paid went instead to the procurement of labor. Substantial sums greased the palms of state and village authorities. The idea of paying his workers properly and treating them well, thus creating a skilled and faithful labor force, does not seem to have occurred to him. The only employees he—presumably—paid well were the police who were needed to enforce his reign of terror. Mijares Escandón employed a small army of men whose only function was to prevent workers from leaving and to bring him back should one manage to escape.[36] A former worker at Los Tzendales, when asked why he did not leave such a horrible place, replied: "We could not. There were armed guards that prevented us. Don Fernando only let us go when he felt like it."[37]

Fleeing from Los Tzendales was a hopeless undertaking. The fugitive had to cross three hundred kilometers of hostile terrain without food, water, or compass, keeping off the established tracks to avoid pursuers. Many men seem to have tried, but the fate of a worker who failed in his attempt was gruesome. In April 1911, *El País* reported the case of an Indian who had tried to escape. After his capture, he "was led into the presence of the administrator who ordered the man's legs to be cut off and then had him buried up to the waist. Two days later the victim died."[38] This was not an isolated instance. A former worker remembered: "One day I witnessed a horrible scene. Some men who had attempted to escape had been captured. The foreman, Maximiliano T., tied them up and cut their feet off. Then he released them and told them: 'Now you can go.' "[39] The normal punishment for attempted escape in Tabasco and Chiapas consisted of the fugitive being "sent back in chains . . . [to the estate] where he will receive an extensive lashing and will have to watch how the expenditure for his capture is being charged to his account at a fabulous price."[40] Mijares Escandón himself far exceeded this norm. Even after the pursuit of fugitives was outlawed in 1914, he kept up the practice.[41]

Mijares Escandón secured the profitability of his company by exploiting a system of forced labor, especially in Tabasco, not seen in any other logging company. Apart from buying workers who were justly or unjustly imprisoned, he employed *enganchadores* who deceived illiterate peons with promises and generous advances on their future salaries. Attracting applicants was not difficult in a state where 79 percent of the population were miserably paid farmers or farm laborers and 78 percent of the population were illiterate.[42] Workers who did deliver the workload expected by Mijares Escandón were an asset to the company, and they were prevented from leaving Los Tzendales when their contracts expired, even if they had no debts with the company. This fate befell Joaquín Chacón, who was detained at Los Tzendales for nine years and who told his story after his liberation:

I was twenty-five years old, married, and I had five sons. How did I get to cut wood in the fincas of Tabasco? . . . You see, sir, my life has always been of the countryside. There was no work where I lived and I had to go to Tabasco, precisely to these *monterías* administered by Mijares. My contract ran, exactly like that of other peons, for one year. After one year I was not allowed to leave the finca but was recontracted like all the others. My contract stipulated that I would earn 5.50 pesos per cut and prepared ton of wood, that I would have enough to eat, especially fat and meat which was distributed on Sundays. At the same time, I would receive rice, sugar, coffee, salt, half a bottle of petrol, and lime to make bread in order to feed myself. But these offers were merely a bait. Once the contract was finished—which was fulfilled as long as it lasted—we were forced to be something meaner than slaves. All those who wanted to return home after their term received the answer that they could go when it pleased Mijares.

And here the infernal life started. There was no alternative but to stay at the *montería* and to keep working at the mercy of Mijares. From then on, we were not paid for our work. There was no more fat, coffee, everything we received before. The only food we received were beans and rice and a measure of corncobs to feed ourselves all week. We were only given forty pesos in cash when the contract ended, but this payment was not in Mexican currency that is valid everywhere. We were paid in Guatemalan money which would only be accepted in the company store where everything was sold at phenomenal prices and where all the goods were very bad. Thus we left the store without a centavo.

When a man fell ill, there was nothing for him, not even human consideration. . . . Mijares flew into a rage and ordered the man whipped. There was once a comrade who was burning with fever. He asked permission to cure himself. The foreman, a Spaniard, replied: "You are sick? Then go to the forest to die!" and he administered heavy blows to the unhappy man which caused him to faint for a while. Still unconscious, he [the foreman] dragged him by the arms to a stream and kept his head under water.

Only in some rare cases when a sick man was really already in agony, was he given as the only remedy for his illness a dose of quinine or as a purge some Epsom salt. This was paid for in gold. Most of the time, they charged us twelve reales or two pesos for each dose of salt because, they said, it was very expensive medicine.[43]

Since the hand of the law did not reach Los Tzendales, Mijares Escandón's wishes and whims were the law. He also used his absolute power for purposes unrelated to the profitability of the Casa Romano. Rubén Navarro recalled:

At some time, two young men eloped with their brides, two pretty girls from Chiapa de Corzo, and they went to the Romano *montería* to work. Don Fernando Mijares liked one of the girls and so he ordered his pistoleros to liquidate the husband. Immediately, the widow was brought to work in the kitchen.

His orders were followed. But when he tried to make the girl his own, she clawed her fingernails into his face. In revenge, don Fernando had her stripped naked and hung from a tree. One of the scoundrels [meaning one of the overseers] of the *montería* gave her lashes with a whip until the girl fainted from pain. Later he ordered her to be taken care of and to advise him when she was restored. When this happened, he tried once again to possess her but she responded in the same way as before; so did don Fernando. The girl was whipped until unconscious and cured once more. This was repeated four times until he could enforce his whim. But then the girl left off food, she slowly dried up until she died. And there she was buried.[44]

Embodying the law in the first and second *zonas Romano*, Mijares Escandón reacted fiercely to any form of insubordination, which to him included not reaching the expected production levels, attempting escape, and refusing his amorous advances. Insubordination was generally punished in Tabasco and Chiapas with shackling and whipping. Mijares Escandón, however, went to extremes here as well. A number of punishments were designed to cause extreme discomfort and pain without disabling a worker. One such punishment was El Grillete. A chain, some 1.5 meters long, was attached to a man's ankles and wrists. The victim was then left lying on the ground among the red ants and other jungle insects. In El Torito a man had his arms and legs tied behind his back and was then exposed to the sun.[45] El Cepo was a particularly cruel form of shackling. The victim had a pole pushed through his knees and elbows in a squatting position. The pole was then connected to a short chain round his neck. This form of shackling was still employed in Los Tzendales well after the revolution; Mijares Escandón even charged one peso per day for the "hire" of the chain.[46] Various forms of hanging, often by the thumbs and by the feet, were also used; few survived this ordeal. Hanging, however, the way Traven described it did not seem to be practiced at all.

Former workers of San Roman Tzendales claim that Mijares Escandón took pleasure in whipping them.[47] Although a streak of sadism was certainly present in the man, many of his actions seem due to an obsession with discipline. He ran Los Tzendales like a military camp, requiring workers to stand at attention in the morning as he passed review like a general. "The unfortunates trembled under the eye of the ferocious administrator, more than any soldier ever trembled before the most cruel instructor in the army."[48] The brutality with which the administrator enforced discipline is often attributed to the difficulties he had controlling criminal elements that came to Los Tzendales to hide from justice. It was true that a man who voluntarily ventured into the jungle likely had a criminal or violent past. Sometimes, he was persona non grata from a village, but, more frequently, the man was a fugitive from justice like Traven's character Santiago Rocha "who had to flee after he had killed the seducer of his wife . . . with a brandy bottle."[49] Often, these men were political agitators like Traven's character Martin Trinidad. Pedro Vega has commented on this situation:

> The bosses had to be men used to everything and able to wield a machete as well as the best. Above all at Los Tzendales where, when the Islas Marías [Mexico's penal islands] did not exist, the influence of the bosses variously caused criminals to be sent there for punishment and hard labor when they became too dangerous to be kept in prison. In Mexico they were not allowed to carry weapons, but when they arrived at the *montería*, they were given a machete and an axe. Their bosses would not have survived long if they had carried a rosary instead of a pistol.[50]

Such dangerous characters were often deliberately allowed to escape so that they would not "break discipline, incite rebellion or keep robbing and murdering."[51] Whatever the magnitude of this problem, however, the surviving evidence from San Roman Tzendales indicates that the victims of Mijares Escandón's brutality were most often defenseless and sick men and women, most of whom were cheaply contracted Indians rather than vicious criminals.

Indians were employed in *monterías* mainly for the badly paid jobs of fetching and carrying, clearing of lanes, and, with the Casa Romano in particular, for growing foodstuffs and looking after the bullocks. Domínguez Vidal witnessed a mass whipping of what seemed to be primarily Indians at San Roman:

> We went closer, and with deep astonishment did I see an Indian woman tied by the feet and hands, bent over the boat, receiving terrible lashes from the overseer. I counted them, they were twenty-five. After the lashing was over, she was untied and since she had fainted, she was dragged away by one foot and then dropped.

And there she remained on the ground, not like a human being but like a thing. Right after that a young Indian of some eighteen years of age came up to the execution block. He looked sick, pale and yellowish. He was tied up in the same manner in which the Indian woman had been tied up and he started to lash him. I did not count the lashes. I fled from that cruel place where another thirty or so sick looking and cadaverous men waited their turn. . . .

All of these unfortunates groaned under the slow fire of malaria, typhoid or dysentery.[52]

A former worker at San Roman confirmed the systematic whippings of workers unable to complete their tasks:

I knew the *monterías* of San Roman before the revolution. Much has changed now but that was a hell difficult to describe. If a man did not fulfill his task, he was lashed with a whip until his skin cracked and thick marks formed. When he fainted, water was poured over him so he would recover and [the process] could go on. He was whipped for days until he died. No, I am not lying. A man who could not fulfill his task because he was sick or because it was excessive, was good for nothing.[53]

Men unable to complete their set tasks became expendable because they no longer represented the possibility of profit. Indeed, the guiding principle behind the organization of the Casa Romano was a concern to maximize its income. This characteristic can also be seen in the way Mijares Escandón addressed the company's overhead. No independent contractor made money from the Casa Romano. The Casa Bulnes/Vega had independent contractors to supply their logging camps with food. Such was not the case with the Casa Romano, which owned large agricultural estates throughout Tabasco and Chiapas on which all the foodstuffs for its camps were produced.[54] This self-sufficiency further enhanced the company's considerable profits. One commentator has noted:

One of the secrets of the economic success of the [Romano] *monterías* was that they produced everything that was consumed. They had a captive clientele for their agricultural products in their own workers. In San Vicente [an abandoned *montería* where the forest had been cleared] the Romanos kept a considerable quantity of cattle which were used for the traction of logs, as well as extensive fields that had been cut from the forest. In those fields their peons sowed for low wages what would later be consumed in their *monterías*. The "secret" then was the intensive utilization of the labor force, of the land, and a price fixing system for agricultural products as well as their labor force.[55]

The total profit extracted by the Casa Romano from its Mexican operations is not known, but it must have been substantial. The only time the Casa Romano suffered considerable losses under the management of Mijares Escandón was in 1914 when General Domínguez sacked Los Tzendales and released all its workers. The administrator escaped capture; instead, the general took some of the overseers. One of them, Tacho Gil, "died on the boat," which presumably means that, before going on board, he was treated in the same manner he had previously treated workers.[56]

Most of the horror stories recounted in this study were related by men liberated by the intervention of General Domínguez. After this event, silence once again descended on San Roman Tzendales. Mijares Escandón resumed work and lost none of his touch; physical punishment and forcible retention were practiced in the camp until his death. The guide who accompanied Brito Foucher told him without hesitation that two months before their meeting in 1924 a worker had asked to leave. "He was taken to the main camp. . . . There the employees hit him with sticks and then, lying on a stretcher, he was taken from the main building and sent downstream in a canoe."[57] Nothing had changed at San Roman Tzendales. When Mijares Escandón was finally arrested, it seems that discipline completely collapsed in the first and second *zonas*, and all hell broke loose. People who passed the site years later reported that it bore all the signs of sudden abandonment. Work tools were scattered everywhere, as were shackles.[58] Whatever was left of San Roman Tzendales was transferred to the Pico de Oro *montería*, the location Traven proposed to visit in order to meet Sergio Mijares. The abandoned site of San Romano Tzendales was avoided in later years by chicle gatherers. They would not go near the place because, they said, it was cursed.[59]

When the Tabascan territories of the Casa Romano were confiscated in 1914 and 1915, evidence of brutality on the scale of San Roman was not uncovered. In fact, no other logging company produced a comparable history of cruelty. There were individual and isolated acts, but cruelty was not elevated in the other camps to the level of company policy. Other Romano camps such as La Constancia, which was not under the immediate rule of Mijares Escandón, did not produce such a crop of horror stories either, indicating that conditions were such that nobody found them worth noting. It is quite possible that the labor conditions of San Roman Tzendales were unique even within the Casa Romano, at the same time that its evil reputation, which Traven related in his novels, was not a figment of the author's "sadistic" Germanic imagination, as Vega believed, nor untrue, nor ludicrous. Indications are that Traven stuck to the truth very closely, even understating at times. In the final analysis, however, the evidence he used related only to the actions of one man who ruled despotically over one *montería* for a quarter of a century. Still, Traven did not create the *monterías'* evil reputation; it existed long before his arrival in Chiapas. It originates in the surviving *montería* lore consisting chiefly of horror stories concerning San Roman Tzendales. It is doubtful whether Traven would have taken note of the *monterías* had they all been like San Quintín.

The distinctions between Mijares Escandón and the other administrators are based on the manner in which each exploited the existing system of forced labor. In Tabasco and Chiapas, this system was supported by the twin pillars of extremely low pay rates and a scarcity of labor. The daily wage of a peon in Tabasco was thirty-seven centavos, while one kilo of meat cost twenty-eight centavos, a kilo of rice twenty-two centavos, and a kilo of beans nineteen centavos.[60] In this situation a wage of 5.50 pesos for one ton of cut and prepared mahogany, such as that received by Chacón, constituted good money indeed. It was, however, the custom on most estates for the worker to pay for his work tools just as Traven described in *Die Troza*. The tools had to be bought at the company store at inflated prices and an increasing and crushing debt for the peon was therefore unavoidable. General José Domingo Ramírez Garrido related the case of a peon who entered a finca with a debt of a few hundred pesos. After sixteen years of labor and helped by his wife and children, he had accumulated a debit account of over one thousand pesos. When he went to complain to the authorities, he was first whipped and then returned to the estate, where he eventually died.[61] Still, the Porfirian authorities in Tabasco, together with the landowners, maintained that the social problems of the state were solely attributable to the indolence and ignorance of the lower classes.[62] When the revolution finally put a stop to physical punishment, debt slavery, and dependence, many peons in Tabasco felt lost. They even came to believe that the revolution, instead of helping them, worked against them. Their habits of dependence and the tutelage of their masters had disenfranchised them physically and mentally. Traven became acutely aware of this problem and began dealing with it in his last novel, *Ein General kommt aus dem Dschungel.*

In contrast to the slow and somnolent life of the traditional fincas, the *monterías* were harsh workplaces, where a merciless environment combined with backbreaking labor to cut short many lives. If, however, San Roman Tzendales had the very worst reputation, then San Quintín had the best. This point is well illustrated by an incident related by Duby. In 1913 or 1914 a woman called Filiberta Ramírez decided to flee from Los Tzendales. The only guidance she had was the knowledge "that somewhere to the west there is a *montería* where people are treated well." That camp was San Quintín. After three weeks in the jungle, half-crazy with hunger and fear, she managed to reach San Quintín, where some workers found her in one of the lanes. She eventually recovered and settled there. When San Quintín closed in 1927, she moved to Tecojá to stay with the Vega family. There she lived out the rest of her life.[63]

San Quintín lay at the center of the Bulnes landholdings, some ten kilometers southwest of the Laguna Miramar at the confluence of the Perlas and Jataté rivers. The *montería* was comprised of 48,000 hectares of forest land, lying at an altitude of between five hundred to seven hundred meters, making the climate at the camp agreeable, even cool at times. The Casa Vega did not employ *enganchadores.* Most of their workers came from Huimanguillo and Comalcalco in Tabasco, and Ocosingo in Chiapas.[64] These men, most of whom came back every year, were proud and experienced in their work. The atmosphere at San Quintín, therefore, was quite different from that at San Roman Tzendales. Its men could not be ordered around and "patroncito," the humble address of Indians to their masters, was not heard. The workers took pride in their work, and one of the oxdrivers is reported to have exclaimed about his oxen that they would be flowers in other places. The fearful drinking bouts at Tenosique and Ocosingo were part of the macho self-image of these *monteros*, but this was part of their life as much as the hard work in the *montería.*[65]

The men at San Quintín, we are told, worked *with* their bosses, not *under* them as at San Roman Tzendales. When things became rough, they all suffered together. "Boss, employee, and simple worker, all struggled in the same mud, they ate when there was food and if there was none, they all went hungry."[66]

There was no physical punishment at San Quintín. This was impossible for quite simple reasons: "If one night it might have occurred to a new foreman who did not know these people—an impossibility because the foreman was selected among the ablest and toughest of them—to hang a *montero*, the following day when he was free again, he would have gone after the foreman with shots, machete blows, or bites and made him rest, but not in his bed."[67] All men, bosses, foremen, and workers, depended on each other, especially in difficult and dangerous situations. Even before the laws against physical punishment of workers were passed, there were no beatings or lashings at San Quintín.[68]

At the time when Navarro entered San Quintín in 1916, the administrators of the camp were Julián Celorio Valle and his brother. At their first meeting, don Julián informed the newly arrived Navarro in his curt way: "He who does not acclimatize here, dies." However, his despotic statement was soon belied when the new arrival was freed from work the first day in order to rest from his journey, an unheard-of act of humanity in a *montería*. After a while at San Quintín, Navarro came to the conclusion that "studying the Celorio brothers psychologically, they were not what they appeared. Deep down they were decent people and understanding to the limit of what the times allowed."[69] Indeed, if discipline at San Roman Tzendales was enforced with the whip, at San Quintín it was fostered by example. At the Tecojá finca there were no hammocks strung across the verandahs as was the custom in Tabasco and Chiapas. Their absence removed all temptation for the bosses to lounge and so set a bad example for the workers. It was the rule of the Casa Vega that the bosses had to work harder and better than the employees.[70] There was no alcohol available at San Quintín, except for small quantities that were distributed free by the managers when it was particularly cold.

Before the revolution, when debt slavery was legal, no one was allowed to leave the camp if he had not paid up. Workers who fled were pursued. Pancho Celorio received the cut across his face while returning Bachajón Indians who had escaped from San Quintín. Once debt slavery was abolished, however, nobody was detained against his will. The reasons for this are not at all clear. It would have been as easy to break the law at San Quintín as it was at San Roman Tzendales. It seems that human decency and the mutual respect among bosses and workers were responsible. By the same token, when the eight-hour workday was introduced in Mexico in 1917, it was also introduced at San Quintín.[71] This acceptance, however, was largely symbolic; a task once commenced had to be finished. No log could be left lying in a lane, nor could a tree be left half-felled or the oxen unattended. Sundays were celebrated as holidays, and workers from the outlying camps came on that day to San Quintín to draw supplies. Otherwise, these days off were used for *fajina*, domestic chores such as collecting firewood and mending. Contractors had the day free and could go hunting or collect wild cocoa.[72] In San Quintín, payments were only made at the end of the season. In effect, timber fellers could take away all at once between two thousand and three thousand pesos, from which only the costs of equipment were deducted. If the *montero* did not spend all his money in the bars and dance halls of Tenosique and Ocosingo, he could save enough to buy a house. An oxdriver could even grow rich if he protected his earnings.[73]

The demise of the Casa Vega bears an uncanny resemblance to that of the Casa Romano. When its owner, Pedro Vega Villanueva, fell ill, an unfortunate decision was made. Logging was begun in an area where access to the nearest waterway was remote and led over sharp stones that injured men and beasts and damaged the logs.[74] After this miscalculation and in the face of a contracting world timber market, the Casa Vega cut its losses and closed San Quintín. Despite this similarity, and the fact that San Roman Tzendales and San Quintín were neighbors and operated simultaneously, their styles of management could not have been more different. Ultimately, the tone in both camps was set by the managers, and it was their personalities that differed so sharply. Pedro Vega maintained that his father "could not have hurt a fly, let alone one of his men who worked with him and on whom he depended." And indeed, there is nobody in Tabasco or Chiapas who would give Pedro Vega Villanueva a bad name. Those who knew Vega speak of him with great respect, whereas Mijares Escandón is uniformly referred to as *cabrón*.

Traven's decision to disregard what he had heard about San Quintín and to concentrate on the horror stories from San Roman Tzendales was not made from bias or because the author wanted to give the *monterías* a worse name than they already had. During his investigations, he believed that he had come across an account of a massive uprising of Indian laborers at San Roman

Tzendales, in the course of which the camp was destroyed. This uprising, so the story went, was the immediate outcome of the cruelty and oppression practiced by Fernando Mijares Escandón. The story of the rebellion, however, was pure fiction. Had Traven made his intended trip to Pico de Oro and talked to Sergio Mijares, he might not have made this mistake; the Bulnes brothers would also have set him right had Traven only asked. The product of the author's acceptance of this misinformation was *Die Rebellion der Gehenkten*, Traven's strongest and most controversial book. He thought he had produced a case study of how exploitation leads to rebellion, a warning to capitalists and exploiters; in reality, he was derailed in his work both by his distrust of capitalists and his disregard of history.

Work in a Montería

Much of Traven's two *montería* novels is taken up by accounts of work processes so primitive, dangerous, and strenuous that it is hard to believe that they were still in use at the beginning of the twentieth century. All felling was done with axes; the chain saw was an innovation that reached the Lacandon Forest only after the Second World War.[75] The operations in every *montería*, irrespective of who owned or managed it, had not altered over the four decades of logging. Some specialized jobs were developed, but the five essential roles saw little change: there was the scout who located and assessed the clumps of trees, the timber feller, the oxdriver, the Indian peon who cleared the lanes, and the *balsero*, or *boga*, whose job it was to guide the trunks in the river to assure a smooth passage as far as Boca del Cerro near Tenosique. All these jobs relied on cheap human or animal labor rather than on technology. The Canadian Agua Azul company did at one time attempt to replace oxen with tractors, but it was soon found that transporting the fuel from Tenosique by mule caravan was financially prohibitive. By 1945 oxen operated again at Agua Azul's Nuevo Filadelfia camp, because they were both more economical and more manageable. Traven, who visited Nuevo Filadelfia just at the time when tractors had been introduced, never witnessed the spectacle of a mahogany log being dragged through the jungle lanes by up to fifty oxen. His account of this work process, therefore, is riddled with inaccuracies and improbabilities.

Traven limited the focus of his description to the immediate logging camp. Presumably, he knew little about the work processes beyond the *montería*, such as the dangerous job of the *balsero*, which would have offered him great dramatic possibilities. He proved most knowledgeable about the process of timber felling, which he described in such detail and with such accuracy as to make his account the most complete one we have. This information, no doubt, he derived from his guide Paniagua, a former timber feller on the Bulnes estates.

Traven, however, was aware of the difficulties of setting up a logging operation. His most knowledgeable character, Andreu, explains to his helper Vicente how costly a business this can be:

> It is not so easy to set up a *montería*. There might be enough trees, but if there are no riverbeds, or if the riverbeds run in the wrong direction and do not connect to the [Usumacinta] river, then the *montería* is worth nothing. . . . If a *troza* has to be dragged more than five leagues, that is twenty kilometers [*sic*], then it is no longer worthwhile. . . . The work of the *contratista* [contractor] is not as easy as you think. Frequently, they have to look for one, two, even three weeks for riverbeds that will lead to the river with certainty after the rains. The *contratista* then has to walk the entire length of the riverbed with a few muchachos with machetes, to be certain where it leads. These riverbeds are often fifty, perhaps even one hundred kilometers long before they reach the river. Then the riverbeds have to be cleaned of trees and bushes so that the *trozas* will not get entangled while they float [down river]. . . . The work of surveying alone takes months, and while it is done, not a single *troza* of *caoba* is being produced.[76]

The importance of this exploration work was highlighted in 1880 when the Casa Bulnes sent out independent surveyors to map the area around the Tzendales River. The surveyors chose to sell their knowledge to the Casa Romano instead, which was then looking for profitable logging terrains in Chiapas. This double cross enabled the Casa Romano to start its highly lucrative logging operations in competition with the other company.[77] After the land was acquired, the Casa Romano began construction of San Roman. It was not, however, enough to erect the buildings that formed the camp. A track had to be cut through the jungle from Santa Margarita to Nuevo Filadelfia to bypass that stretch of the Usumacinta River that is not navigable. All provisions for San Roman had to be carried by mule to Nuevo Filadelfia and there transferred to riverboats. What is more, huge tracts of jungle around San Roman had to be clear-cut to make way for pasture land for the *montería's* six hundred oxen.[78]

The relationship of total capital outlay to borrowed money determined the interest rate a logging company had to pay. In *Die Troza* the sale of the *montería* by the Company to the Montellano brothers, and the subsequent tightening of its administration, is due directly to the interest the brothers have to pay on borrowed capital. Acquisition of capital was a real problem for small-timers in the Lacandon Forest, many of whom, like Traven's Montellanos, had risen from being contractors to owning a logging operation outright. The problem was first documented by José Coffin, a Protestant preacher from Tabasco and the biographer of General Ignacio Gutiérrez, the first revolutionary general of Tabasco. Ignacio Gutiérrez had grown up in the first *montería* set up by Polo Valenzuela near Aldama in Tabasco. When the operation was sold a few years later to a Spaniard by the name of Pancho Rubí, the Gutiérrez family experienced what economists later termed "superexploitation." Quirino Gutiérrez, Ignacio's father, was persuaded with the help of great promises to keep working for Rubí, but he soon realized that the Spaniard's capital was much tighter than he had led his workers to believe. Rubí began to drive his workers mercilessly. Quirino managed to keep his family out of debt until his wife fell ill and a doctor's visit was required. Rubí advanced the money for the doctor's fee on condition that young Ignacio enter the *montería* as a *gañán*, an assistant to the oxdriver.[79]

The cost of labor was the only element in the large bill of expenses open to manipulation by the owners. Consequently, Rubí, the Casa Romano, the hemp planters of Yucatán, and the tobacco planters of the Valle Nacional looked toward the superexploitation of the workforce as they began to squeeze for larger profits. Working conditions became more onerous, salaries sank below subsistence level, reinforcing the permanent debt that, together with *"tiendas de raya* and more than twelve working hours daily,"[80] tied the worker to the estate.

One key element of this superexploitation was the foreign investors' failure to modernize or mechanize their operations. Coffin has described how the old *montería* at Aldama functioned in the 1860s. It is clear from his report that the jobs and work processes did not undergo any changes in the following forty years; only the status of workers was modified from free and voluntary collaborators with Valenzuela to the miserable wretches of the likes of Joaquín Chacón. Quirino Gutiérrez, Coffin writes, had joined the new *montería* because the pay was good. The logging camp itself was a pleasant little village in the virgin forest, from which the *monteros* left in the mornings to join their foreman "with jokes and songs generally too liberal." The timber fellers usually had a "basic knowledge of medicine. They cut trees well, they know how to handle a plummet line, they work to set jobs and rest and eat at specific hours. They get time off to do their home jobs, to pay visits . . . [and] to sing with their sons. They know enough of numbers so as not to be robbed of their gains." The impression is of timber fellers living a normal life with their families within a rural community. The work consisted of felling trees, some of them two meters wide, the wood as hard as iron, with the help of two axes. Coffin does not describe in detail the daily tasks of a timber feller, but there is no indication in his account that superhuman efforts were demanded of them.

Once the timber feller's job was finished, and the tree cleared of branches and tapered at one end to fit the chains, the oxdrivers moved in. To enable the oxen to drag the heavy trunk, lanes were cut into the forest that led to the *tumbo* (dump). Once the logs had reached the *tumbo*, they remained there until the rainy season started and the swollen rivers could float them into the Usumacinta River. This majestic waterway would then carry the logs to Boca del Cerro near Tenosique where they would be formed into large rafts and floated to the Gulf port of Frontera or Ciudad del Carmen.

The actual *montería* work ended at the *tumbo*, but the floating of logs was just as difficult as the felling or dragging. It required as much skill, and the work of the *balsero* was even more perilous than the other tasks. In order for the logs to travel safely on the swollen rivers, to prevent blockages and to negotiate the turbulences, waterfalls, and narrow tracts, the *balseros* traveled along with the logs in order to set them afloat again should they get stuck:

> Day and night [these men] work with the rudder, the pole, the hook, and chains in their hands in order to guide their trunks in the river bends, in the bays, and through treacherous waters. They are always ready to throw themselves into the water between the poisonous river creatures and the whirls. They are wet day and night and take their food cold, often fermented. The *balseros* suffer from malaria and rheumatism.

> Their terror is to be surprised by a thunderstorm in a bay. When that happens, the rafts are destroyed and their unlucky conductors almost always drown.[81]

Malaria, tuberculosis, and rheumatism were professional hazards for anyone living in the jungle for any length of time, but the *balseros* were exposed to more than the usual perils. Apart from the ever present danger of drowning or being crushed between two logs, the *balseros* were often incapacitated because the soles of their feet lifted off due to prolonged immersion in water. What is more, scorpions, poisonous ants, and nahuyacas, the most deadly snake of the Central American jungles, frequently nested in the trunks stored at the *tumbo*.

If, according to Coffin, the *balsero* was the hero, the *gañán* was the "martyr of the profession." *Gañanes* were usually young boys who, like Ignacio Gutiérrez, had to work in the *montería* because of debts incurred by their parents. In *Die Troza*, Traven described the fate of one such boy in the character of Vicente, *gañán* to Andreu. Vicente is "sold" to the company because his family cannot pay the funeral expenses of his father. It was not unusual, in fact, for boys aged eight or nine to earn their own living, as was the case with Juan Celorio, illegitimate son of the contractor Pancho Celorio. When his mother could not support him any longer, eight-year-old Juan went out to work on the farms of the neighborhood. In the *monterías*, these young boys, according to Coffin, were at the bottom of the pecking order:

> In a *montería* there is no dog, no bullock, as badly treated as the *gañán*.
> In every inch of his body he displays the traces of thorns, stocks, lashes from whips, marks from bullocks' horns, and kicks from feet. The foreman, the oxdrivers, and even the women insult and beat him because generally he is a defenseless and weak boy.
> His job is to hold the bridle of the bullock leading the team. Mud is his element, he works in it, eats, drinks, and suffers in it every day eighteen to twenty hours. He has no free Sundays nor any other day of rest or holiday.
> His fever is cured with cold water thrown over him. His errors or inattentions are punished with twenty to fifty lashes of the whip while tied to a tree, post, or trunk.
> The worst thing that can happen to a *gañán* is to lose a bullock. Frequently, this is the first link in a chain leading to slavery, [a chain] he will drag all his life. After being punished, the cost of [the bullock] is charged to his account at a fabulous price. Poor lads![82]

Gutiérrez, after serving for eight years as a *gañán*, rose to the most prestigious job a *montería* had to offer: the *monteador*. The job of these scouts was to roam the forest and discover new clusters of mahogany trees, to explore riverbeds, to guide workers through the forest, and to be able to make independent estimates. On the findings of the scout depended the income of the entire logging operation; it was his work that determined the amount of cubic meters of timber the company could sell. The Casa Romano had its own employees for this job, "men of confidence," loyal to Mijares Escandón. The guide who accompanied Brito Foucher was such a person, faithful, reliable, and familiar with every nook and cranny of the Romano logging zones.

Gutiérrez managed to earn enough money in the *montería* to become independent and to set up a logging company of his own, and so he was a wealthy man by the time he took up arms in the name of Madero in 1910. Such a career became increasingly unlikely, however, as more and more capital was required to set up a logging operation. By the time the large logging companies moved from Tabasco to Chiapas in the early 1880s, the idyllic living conditions of the timber fellers as described by Coffin had thoroughly disappeared. Provisioning a logging camp with food became ever more costly and complicated because of the increasing distance between the towns of Ocosingo and Tenosique and the logging camps. Most camps, especially those of the Casa Romano, no longer allowed women and children unless they worked for the *montería*. Thus the camps gradually grew into a brutalized world inhabited and run solely by men. Women became chattels. If a man brought his wife to the camp and he proved weak (*flojo* in the *monteros'* terms), then his wife was taken away from him and awarded to a stronger man.[83]

Due to the increasing shortage of women in the forest, prostitution became a thriving business. Traven pointed out in *Die Troza* that women who could not possibly have made a living anywhere else as prostitutes, because they were old or ugly, came to the *monterías* under the pretext of being cooks.[84] They were generally known as "jungle whores."[85] These cooks moved from one camp to the next and many of them suffered from venereal diseases. A Mexican anthropologist traveling in the Lacandon Forest in 1928 noted: "During my tour I followed one woman's trail clearly marked in the whole region through the confessions of her 'victims' of how and from whom they had contracted a certain disease. Given the isolation in which they live and the total absence of adequate medication, these diseases develop virulently and are followed by all sorts of pathological complications."[86]

Illicit bars, gambling, and whoring such as Traven described in *Die Troza* was one method of depriving workers of their hard-earned income. Only in *monterías* such as San Quintín, where no alcohol was available and gambling was strictly prohibited, did men have a chance of taking money home at the end of the season. On the other hand, the reason why the *monteros* of San Quintín were known and feared when they came down to Ocosingo and Tenosique once a year was because of their orgies of drinking, dancing, and whoring. This was the immediate consequence of life in the jungle. The hard work, the brooding heat, the constant danger of accidents, made worse by the loneliness in the greenish twilight, often made men depressed and melancholic. Juan Celorio at one stage was so affected that he seriously considered shooting himself.[87] Traven, who remarked about the strange greenish twilight in his travel notes, had also become aware of its depressing effect. In *Die Troza* he wrote of men who suddenly, after returning from a ride through the jungle, had "their health ruined and their bodies filled with fever, their souls affected by chronic dislike of work and a general apathy toward thought and achievement," the symptoms of severe depression.[88]

If counteracting depression by drinking, whoring, and gambling failed, men frequently resorted to violence. Murder was a common event in all logging camps. The men did not "reckon an occasional murder as any crime: It's just proof of manhood." Hacking somebody to pieces in a drunken brawl was nothing extraordinary.[89] Old *monteros* maintain that it was this form of violence that Mijares Escandón tried to control with his remorseless discipline. Violence and beastliness, however, were also balanced by acts of great heroism and sacrifice. Pepe Tárano Vega, known as the Bull, once carried a fellow worker, who had been blinded by a forest fly, on his back from one of the remotest logging stations on the far side of the Colorado Creek on Guatemalan territory, over steep mountains and difficult terrain, all the way to Nuevo Filadelfia.[90]

Loneliness affected primarily the timber fellers, who worked either alone or in pairs and lived for prolonged periods of time in small makeshift camps away from the main camp. In order to log a terrain the size of the Romano holdings, the logging zone was divided into districts with smaller camps at their center. From here the so-called *semaneos* were established. As the name indicates, these smallest subdivisions were moved frequently, even weekly, from one cluster of trees to the next. In a logging zone the size of the first or second *zona Romano*, or those of Traven's Montellano brothers, these logging districts, Traven pointed out, "were often two, three, even five hours away from the *oficina*, the center. The center, in turn, was one or two days' ride away from the headquarters of the *montería*, the *ciudad* or city of the *montería*."[91]

Provisioning a *semaneo* was often a logistic problem. The men had to take all their food for one week, plus their tools and equipment. If they were lucky, a cook was sent along. Otherwise, like Traven's muchachos or Joaquín Chacón, they had to cook their own meals after a heavy day. Every corncob, every kilo of beans, chili, or dried meat had to be carried. The weekly food rations of the Casa Romano in the 1920s amounted to 15 kilos of corn, 2.4 kilos of beans, 0.5 kilos of rice, and 2.5 kilos of fat, sugar, and salt for a husband and wife team.[92] Food in the *semaneo*, therefore, was even more monotonous than in the larger camps. Manager and common worker, Traven pointed out, "received exactly the same rations." It was expensive to transport such quantities of food by mule and in boats all the way to San Roman Tzendales. Therefore, food rations were cut down as soon as the workers' contracts expired. For Mijares Escandón, this was effective cost cutting. Since the men remained against their will, the quality of their work would drop and malnutrition would do the rest. Camps the size of San Roman Tzendales also needed large quantities of axes, machetes, tools, chains, saddles, and hardware. This cargo had to be transported in the same costly manner as the food. Although the equipment itself was worth little, the cost of the transport added to its value and inflated the prices at the *tienda de raya*. If a logging company was sold, Traven pointed out, its equipment, if not taken over by the buyer, would be given to him for free or left behind in the forest.

The *tienda de raya* was the clearinghouse of the *montería*. The company ledgers were kept there as were the store records and workers' accounts. Once a year the books were balanced and the profits of the company distributed. In the year 1914–15, the last year of the Casa Bulnes operations, four members of the Bulnes family received 110,101 pesos profit each. Three members of the Celorio family, working as administrators, received 24,905 pesos each. The remainder of the work force had a total of 213 pesos and 18 centavos distributed among them. This pathetic sum was the immediate impact of the *tienda de raya* on workers' salaries.[93] Juan Celorio left logging after twenty years of back-breaking labor as a timber feller without a centavo. His brother, the legitimate son of Pancho Celorio, left logging with a total profit of 20,000 pesos, because he had inherited a little capital from his father that enabled him to set up as a contractor.[94]

A contractor confronted the same problems as a logging company, only on a smaller scale. He needed some initial capital for the *enganche*, an advance on his workers' wages. Even today it is impossible to hire an agricultural laborer in Chiapas or Tabasco without offering a substantial *enganche*, despite the fact that the practice has been illegal in Mexico since the revolution. With his crew of men, the contractor could offer his services to a logging company for any of the work processes. He worked for a set sum of which he received 15 to 20 percent upon signature of the contract. After that his expenses were covered each month, the total credit amounting to 50 percent of the contracted sum.[95] The contractor decided the wages of his men, but like everywhere else in the world, he had to pay good wages for good workers. San Quintín engaged many independent contractors every year, whereas the Casa Romano had ceased reliance on them as much as possible in order to pocket the contractors' profit.

Many *enganchadores* were independent contractors, similar to Traven's character Gabriel, who were not choosy whom they sold for money. Brito Foucher had an encounter with such a contractor who led three Indian children, the oldest of whom was about fourteen, the youngest ten years of age, to a logging camp. None of them, including the *enganchador*, knew a word of Spanish. Some old *monteros* in Ocosingo maintain that before the revolution, all three logging companies, Romano, Bulnes, and Valenzuela, had *enganchadores* "who contracted vagabonds and hoodlums who had never worked before [in their lives]. The treatment they soon received showed this up, and that is how the black fame of the *monterías* was created."[96] Even the job of the *enganchador* was fraught with danger. It frequently happened that the contracted men, once they woke up to what they had let themselves in for, attacked the *enganchador* on the way to the *montería*. Pancho Celorio was lucky; he only received a deep scar. His relative Gabriel Celorio was killed on the banks of the

Usumacinta River below Santa Margarita where the workgang stopped for the night. He was hacked to pieces.[97]

Enganchadores worked according to set patterns. When there was a holiday in the small villages of northern Chiapas or southern Tabasco, a labor contractor was usually present. He sat down in a bar, well provided with large quantities of strong liquor. He then began to offer drinks to easily seducible individuals. "Once they are drunk," an observer noted, "he paints a paradisical picture of life in the *montería*. . . . The chosen victim, animated by alcohol and under the influence of the *enganchador*, asks for and receives thirty to forty pesos with which to go on celebrating the fiesta." By this time it was too late and the contractor knew that he had caught his bird. Although nothing was signed, the recruit was incapable of repaying the first loan. Instead, he usually came for a second loan. "Four or five days later a large number of inhabitants of that village find themselves in a situation where they have accepted one or two hundred pesos and have signed before witnesses and accepted a work contract for a certain *montería* for one year." By the time they were ready to leave the village, they needed another loan to provision themselves and to leave some money behind for their families. In total, "it could be said that [the recruits] received nearly all their salaries in advance for one year's contract."[98] Since the worker would have to make some purchases from the company store throughout the year, an additional debt was secured, and the contract would certainly have to be extended.

One of the principal centers of *enganche* was Ocosingo during the celebrations of San Jacinto's Day in August and Candelaria in February. Great numbers of Indians gathered every year for these fiestas, and many came with the intention of finding work in a logging camp. It seems, however, that there were never enough applicants, and so contractors and town authorities collaborated to mutual benefit. One of their favorite tricks was similar to the maneuver that brought Traven's character Celso back to the *montería*. An old *montero* related:

> There was a lonely and dark lane where the Indians went for their physical necessities. A pair of policemen usually was hiding there. As soon as the Indian appeared, they blocked his path and fined him. Even today, this lane is still called "money lane" because of the harvest the authorities collected during every holiday. The moment the [Indian signed a contract in exchange for the money

the *enganchador* had advanced] his freedom was limited. He had to sleep, together with his family, tied up in a court yard and under police supervision. They never tried to flee because they knew wherever they went they would be captured.[99]

Traven must have heard about this practice, because his character Cándido and his young sons are subjected to much the same treatment.

It would be wrong, however, to assume that all contracted *montería* workers were tricked into signing. Many individuals, attracted by the promise of high wages, traveled long distances to meet a labor contractor, as did Traven's character Celso in *Die Troza*. The truth was that an Indian had only a minimal chance of earning pay above the rate of an agricultural laborer unless he was a Bachajón, who were known as superb timber fellers, dexterous, skilled, and very strong. Tzotzil Indians, such as the highland Chamula, were not accepted in any *montería* because they could neither wield an axe nor a machete with skill.[100] The Tzeltal contracted were rarely accepted in the high-paying jobs. An old *montero* explained: "Generally, the Indians were used as *callejoneros* [who cut and maintained the lanes] and in a few cases as timber fellers. But since among the contractors were those that provided corn, these Indians were employed to tend the fields. But in these jobs the pay was only fifty to seventy centavos a day, from sunrise to sunset."[101] The reason for such selective employment had to do with the Indians' physical characteristics. Their strength, it was argued, is in their thighs and their necks. Therefore, one commentator remarked, an Indian "can carry fifty kilos by means of a wide forehead strap . . . and cover immense distances in a day. . . . He has no strength in his arms. . . . Tzeltal Indians from the *tierra caliente* fetch and carry in the *montería*, light fires, fetch water from the river, slaughter oxen and pigs."[102] "Sinewy mestizos" were allegedly much better suited to wielding a heavy axe. The surviving evidence from Los Tzendales suggests that it was mainly cheaply contracted workers, weakened by disease and malnutrition, who were whipped to death. There is no story indicating that Mijares Escandón ever treated an able-bodied man in a comparable manner. Even he could not afford to wantonly waste an experienced timber feller or oxdriver because he did not fulfill his set task one day. This point became crucial in the evaluation of Traven's work by his critics, who denounced his ignorance about how a logging operation functioned.

The daily workload of a timber feller was one tree of about eighty centimeters across, weighing up to one ton. Timber fellers primarily worked in pairs and felled two trees between them. This included erecting the work platform around the trunk two meters above the ground. Traven explained why: "Many trees of the tropical forest have their main roots growing upwards along the trunk. These roots form strong ribs, two inches thick at the ends. The closer they are to the trunk, the thicker they are, until they merge with the trunk. Some trees have seven or even nine such ribs radiating from the trunk. These ribs . . . are made of wood much harder than that of the trunk."[103] The work platform was constructed from branches at such a level that the timber feller made the cut where all the roots had blended into the tree. Using an axe while standing on such an unsteady surface required great skill, and the timber fellers used their long lassos slung around the trunk to prevent falling off of it. After the tree was felled, it was stripped of branches and bark and tapered at the top. If a trunk was too thick and heavy, it was honed into a square shape, all by the use of axes. The timber fellers worked from sunrise to sunset with a lunch break during the hottest hours of the day. Before the revolution, there was no holiday. As Traven put it: "Sundays or holidays don't exist. The jungle does not know holidays either. Mahogany trees grow every day."

The men in charge of the lanes, the *callejoneros*, had to clear sixty to seventy meters of track to a width of six to eight meters, for which they were paid fifty to seventy centavos a day. The clearing involved making sure that no obstacles, including roots, remained on the ground. Unevennesses had to be bridged and a number of small logs had to be cut on which the trunks could be rolled whenever possible. The smaller lanes, connecting the principal routes with the locations of trees, were only four meters wide, and the daily quota was to clear one hundred meters. Traven considerably underestimated the difficulty of this work when he wrote that the lanes were only superficially cleaned out, to the extent that "some trunks and shrubs forming obstacles had been cut away."[104] The heavy trunks could not be dragged over such an obstacle course. When the rainy season started in September, the lanes became quagmires of mud and could not be used at all, and frequently the oxen were sent "on holiday" until January. This was the time when the timber fellers and the *callejoneros* worked hardest. This is not to say that for every work process there was a different set of men. Many of the old *montería* hands were experienced in all aspects of the work and could fell trees, and lead oxen, as well as guide the trunks downstream.

The oxdrivers' task was five kilometers of traction a night and they received three pesos. The distance of five kilometers is a fair indication of how difficult it was to move a mahogany log through the jungle. Traven, who had only a vague idea of the job of the *boyero* (oxdriver), wrote that Andreu, together with his little *gañán* Vicente and two oxen, managed to drag one log one kilometer in twenty-five minutes.[105] A pedestrian can hardly do better. It was mistakes like this that gave ammunition to Traven's critics.

Just how much Traven's account of *montería* life and work depended on information from workers rather than managers becomes apparent when he deals with organizational problems. In Traven's version, the daily task of a timber feller is two tons of mahogany, whereas in reality it was difficult for a pair of axemen to achieve two tons between them. When the Montellanos take over in *Die Troza*, this expectation is doubled. Even if this quota was indeed realizable, there would still remain the problem of how to remove this great quantity of logs. Traven allowed only about twenty oxdrivers for the whole camp. One pair of oxen with one *boyero* and one *gañán* could not handle a mahogany log of the usual size; it would have been impossible for the few oxdrivers to cope with the increased production. Furthermore, according to Traven, "three to four timber fellers worked with one *boyero*. The Montellanos had managed to increase this figure to six timber fellers to one *boyero* and one *gañán*. During the working hours of the *boyero*, the district assigned to him had to be cleared of *trozas*."[106] There was no need for such haste. Logs were left lying where they had fallen for months, because the work of the timber fellers and the oxdrivers was not coordinated.

Traven not only misconstrued the coordination of work processes, but he also ignored the most difficult of all the organizational problems: the supplying of food. The author's ignorance on this point surfaces in *Die Rebellion der Gehenkten* as he maintained that an army of five hundred mahogany workers traveling for three months from the La Armonía camp to Ocosingo did so without organized food supplies. Traven never thought how such an army of men could carry supplies for three months in a climate where foodstuffs deteriorated rapidly. The organization of food was, in fact, so crucial to the establishment of a logging camp that it, rather than the availability of mahogany, determined the size of the operation. San Quintín, considered one of the larger installations, had only about eighty to one hundred men, a third of whom were timber fellers. The camp had three dependencies, operated by twenty to thirty men each, out of whom six to eight were timber fellers, another six or eight worked with the oxen, and eight to ten looked after the lanes. The terrain worked by these men measured roughly sixty to seventy thousand hectares. The Casa Vega sent many of their workers home for two or three months a year during the rainy season, because this was the time when the likelihood of the food caravans getting stuck in the mud was greatest and famine threatened.

The workers from San Quintín returned every year because logging was their profession, and it would have been difficult for them to find another less hazardous job for the same pay. Many wanted to come back because their work made them feel "one hundred percent men."[107] After the closure of San Quintín its men settled all over Tabasco and Chiapas, and they looked back on their lives in the jungle with the pride of old soldiers looking back on a successful campaign. Tárano Vega, "the Bull," never loathe to discuss the horrors of logging with journalists and visitors who stopped at El Real, used to say to them: "Give me two hundred thousand pesos, and I'll go with them to Ocosingo. Next day there won't be a man left to ring the bells and not an Indian in El Real Valley to plant the milpas. They'll all be off to San Quintín as fast as they can go."[108]

Traven intentionally disregarded this side of *montería* life: men perceiving themselves as being "a type of *bohémien* whose highest honor was to be considered macho and whose relaxation was work."[109] Such men did not fit into Traven's vision and he overlooked them. In all probability, the old *monteros* of San Quintín would have shrugged off the considerable mistakes Traven made about the organization and work processes of a *montería*. After all, it required a good inside knowledge to understand the complexity of such operations, and Traven, a mere tourist, had done rather well. But he overlooked that dimension of *montería* life that to them was at the heart of their working lives, that is, their manliness and their loyalty. Traven had deeply insulted them by portraying them as defenseless Indians, victims of sadism and cruelty, or as perpetrators of cruelties on Indians. It is not surprising that they threatened him with a most unfriendly reception should he ever show his face again at Ocosingo or Tenosique, and that Traven stayed out of their way for the rest of his days.

Die Troza

Die Troza, published early in 1936, was quickly overshadowed by the powerful and stirring *Die Rebellion der Gehenkten*, published a few months later. We can only guess the reasons why *Die Troza* was never translated into either Spanish or English. Clearly, the novel contained a number of crude mistakes in the description of work processes. Perhaps by the time Traven became aware of his errors, he had lost interest in the work, and from then on was content to impede translations in the same way as he did with *Land des Frühlings*. As mentioned earlier, the two novels were meant to form a sequence, and, read together, they demonstrate that Traven had a better understanding of the Chiapan logging industry than many of the later investigators. More importantly, the author placed a number of clues in the text of *Die Troza* to signal to his friends, and the Bulnes family in particular, that he had no intention of insulting them and that he understood the differences between the logging companies that deserved his criticism and those that did not.

Die Troza opens with the description of the *central*—Traven called it the *ciudad*—of what he simply termed the Company. This *central* was an assembly of ramshackle buildings with basic and rough furniture, little better than Indian huts. Workers' accommodations consisted of merely a roof held up by four poles—no walls, no doors. Traven made his *ciudad* far shabbier than anything he had seen with his own eyes. In fact, his model, Nuevo Filadelfia (also often referred to as Agua Azul, after the name of the concession), which Traven visited in 1930, was a far more luxurious place. The Agua Azul concession had been acquired in 1920 by the Canadian John Buchanan. Compared to the giants of the business, the Casa Romano and the Casa Bulnes, the Agua Azul Mahogany Company was a modest enterprise that only cut about five hundred trees a year, compared to four thousand five hundred produced by the Casa Romano and four thousand by the Casa Bulnes. Yet, Buchanan, unlike his Spanish and Mexican competitors, had made considerable capital investments at Agua Azul. Apart from substituting tractors for oxen, he had greatly improved the administration building, a long bungalow built of mahogany, high above the banks of the Usumacinta River, with a superb view and a wide verandah running all around.[110] The house had electricity, a shower, a library, and, luxury of luxuries, "an English toilet."[111] Agua Azul had an airstrip that still serves the nearby ruins of Yaxchilán. "These gringos liked to live comfortably," a Mexican contractor rightly observed.[112]

None of these comforts appeared in the description of Traven's *ciudad*. His main camp was built in the typical jungle style, makeshift and temporary, that in reality was used only in the dependencies and burned every year, or in the *semaneos* that were abandoned after a week or so. Even San Quintín, which was primitive by the standards of Agua Azul and San Roman, was more luxurious than Traven's *ciudad*. There were other features of Agua Azul, however, that Traven did incorporate into his novel. While the camp was in Canadian hands, it had a string of Canadian and American administrators. "Juan Staf . . . He was a *gringo* and lasted only a short while. He was replaced by Gerardo Somer who was a drunkard and a hard worker. But he drank a lot. He died from too much drink. He was replaced by Juanito Buchanan," John Buchanan's son.[113] Although alcohol was not available to the workers of Agua Azul, many members of the administrative staff developed alcohol problems and were renowned as *"borrachales"* (drunkards).[114] It seems that one (not many, as Traven wrote) Lebanese trader who ran mule caravans to Agua Azul not only provided the illicit alcohol but also, being an avid gambler himself, organized gambling sessions whereby he stripped the administrative staff of all their savings.[115]

Traven must have closely observed the drinking and gambling habits of the Agua Azul administrative staff, for he reproduced them accurately in *Die Troza*. In the novel, the camp is run by don Leobardo, the manager, and don Remigio, the principal contractor. Leobardo, forever entangled with a woman, is just as much a commonplace sinner as Remigio, but it is known of the La Armonía camp under his management, we are told, that conditions there are less cruel than elsewhere. Both men are rough but not brutal. The easygoing, lazy atmosphere of the *ciudad*, and the continuous "wetting of throats" after the smallest effort, is led by those two and duly imitated by the whole camp. What they demand of their workers is the norm of the logging industry and therefore possible for a man to achieve. Each proves finally to be influenced by his conscience, as when together they refuse to have anything to do with the Montellanos after the sale of the *montería* because of the brothers' fearful reputation as cruel exploiters.

By dwelling so long and with so much careful detail on the laxity of the Company's administration, and on the drinking and gambling habits of its personnel, Traven signaled to potential readers in Chiapas that he was describing the well-known conditions of Agua Azul. But at the same time, he laid the groundwork for an important transition. By means of the sale of the logging operation to the Montellano brothers, Traven clearly established that the social climate of any logging camp was determined by the character of its administrator, a fact borne out by the surviving evidence about Mijares Escandón and Vega Villanueva. The changes under the Montellano brothers are enacted through a tightening of the administration and a rationalization of the work force, and are imposed with brutality and upheld by a crew of vicious overseers. Traven's model was clearly the San Roman camp under Mijares Escandón.

In addition, Traven inserted a number of identifiable references into his text that were designed to signal to an insider that the Montellano administration was closely modelled on San Roman Tzendales. Quite abruptly, for example, Traven introduced a change of distance. According to his own travel notes, it had taken him ten days to reach Agua Azul; don Gabriel and his convoy in *Marsch ins Reich der Caoba* take the same amount of time to reach the camp. After the takeover by the Montellanos, however, Traven wrote, "a ride of three weeks through the jungle" is required to pass from the camp to the nearest town. There was only one logging camp on Mexican soil that took three weeks to reach; San Roman Tzendales was located at the end of the *camino de Tzendales*, which ran nearly the whole length of the Lacandon Forest. Furthermore, Traven pointed out that it took four days on horseback to reach the smaller camps of La Estancia and La Piedra. This was, we know, roughly the time it took to reach the Romano dependencies in the first and second *zona Romano*. Traven even used the name La Constancia, one of the smaller Romano camps, and, in case there were lingering doubts about what the author described, he added that La

Armonía was situated "on a peninsula at the confluence of two jungle rivers." This location matches the superb position of San Roman at the confluence of the Tzendales and Negro rivers.

The treatment of workers that Traven attributed to the Montellano brothers was also unique to San Roman under Mijares Escandón. Evidence of women being whipped has not come from any other logging company, but there are two separate cases reported from San Roman Tzendales. Traven expressly pointed out that a girl who twice failed to deliver the share of her income from drinks in the cantina "would be handed to the foreman of the office to be whipped," just as was the unfortunate woman who refused Mijares Escandón's amorous advances. Similarly, only the Casa Romano was known to have systematically killed incapacitated workers. In Traven's novel, the Montellanos enforce their doubled work loads with the help of whippings and hangings. The Montellanos also begin to shackle their men overnight when working away from the main camp, a practice also known from Los Tzendales. Finally, the Montellanos, like the Casa Romano, exploit their forest land ruthlessly down to the last tree. Traven even created the triumvirate of the three Montellano brothers in imitation of Mijares Escandón's arrangement with his nephews Fernando and Sergio. With these details the author firmly established that he was describing the Casa Romano and no other company. He had provided an unequivocal and historically correct analysis, although the implications of it would have been discernible only by insiders of the logging industry. These details, however, never became known to these insiders for lack of a Spanish translation. Thus Traven indeed created the impression that the Montellano *montería*, the full horrors of which he developed in *Die Rebellion der Gehenkten*, was a model for *all* logging camps. It is no wonder that the economic historian Moisés de la Peña, for instance, judged the novel as "awesome and full of lies."[116]

The most dramatic organizational difference between San Quintín and San Roman Tzendales concerned the employment of contractors. One commentator explained: "The companies had two different systems to organize work. One operated through work centers [*centrales*], and the other through contractors. In the work centers of the jungle the administrator supervised the entire work process and sometimes participated. Under his command were overseers who directed every single operation, but he [the administrator] held [ultimate] control over each work process."[117] This was the arrangement Mijares Escandón chose for San Roman Tzendales, in order to deploy his fearful crew of overseers to greatest advantage. The terrain of the Casa Romano, however, some three thousand square kilometers, was far too large to rule from one *central*, and the outlying areas were, therefore, operated by contractors. In the isolation of the *semaneo*, it was impossible for a contractor to rule through terror or to whip a worker to death, for the contractor needed the cooperation of his men and would not be foolish enough to disable a worker. Should one or several of his men be unable or unwilling to work, it could take months to replace them, and the contractor would jeopardize both his contract with the logging company and his reputation in general. The available evidence on punishments in the Casa Romano clearly indicates that whippings and beatings occurred only in the main camp. The prospective victims were on occasion purposely brought to the *central* for punishment.[118] Mijares Escandón was a seasoned administrator who could see with a glance among the new workers who was fit for *montería* work and who was not. He would allot work accordingly, and would certainly not whip a man he expected to rely on later.

Traven took great pains in *Die Troza* to explain to his readers what the elimination of *contratistas* (contractors) and their substitution with *capataces* (foremen) signified. One of the Company's contractors explains to a colleague:

> Each one of them [foremen] is going to eat at least thirty muchachos alive within the next twelve months. But they will produce *caoba*, that is certain. Together with the *capataces* who remain and do not leave with the *contratistas*, the Montellanos have good and reliable personnel. They pay the *capataces* one peso fifty a day, and then they have a chief *capatáz* in every *semaneo* who they pay fifty centavos per delivered ton of *caoba*, and the second *capatáz* receives one *real* per ton. They will see to it that *caoba* is being produced, rest assured, gentlemen. They would have had to pay ten pesos per ton to the *contratistas*. They pay four reales to the first *capatáz* and one real to the second [*capatáz*]. That makes sixty-two centavos per ton instead of ten pesos. And the *capataces* will kiss the dirt off their necks for this tiny dividend and they will be subservient and obedient, whereas the *contratistas* have their own will and won't be ordered around.[119]

Being experienced *enganchadores* themselves, the Montellanos bypass the middlemen and contract workers directly. Since they maintain discipline by terror and eliminate anybody who does not fit into their system, the consumption of labor soon rises sharply. "When a new troop arrived," Traven wrote, "half of the previous consignment . . . was already rotting in the ground."[120]

The labor policy of the Montellanos raises the issue of the cost represented by the continuous flow of workers, each having received a substantial sum as *enganche*. The same question also hangs over the discussion of Mijares Escandón's wasteful labor policies. Traven answered it, however, with a simple explanation. Every worker, he wrote, had a guarantor for his debt. Should the worker die, then the guarantor would have to take over the debt and replace the deceased in the *montería*.[121] This is the recipe for an unending labor supply costing little more than the initial *enganche*. There is no indication in the surviving evidence about the Casa Romano that the Indian laborers in particular had to have a guarantor for their debt, but since debts were passed on from father to son on every farm in Chiapas and Tabasco during the Porfiriato, there is no reason to believe that the Casa Romano did not take advantage of such a legal provision. If this was indeed so, then Traven provided the answer to the puzzle posed by the *monterías'* alleged wastefulness.

Once the Company's contractors are eliminated and the Montellanos and their overseers have assumed their duties, a new division of labor is devised. Felix Montellano is to run the *ciudad* and to look after the administration and the paperwork. Severo Montellano is put in charge of producing timber at La Armonía, and the youngest, Acacio, takes over production in the two dependencies. The ten or so *capataces* assume the jobs of foremen. With this arrangement the Montellanos spread themselves and their staff thinly but effectively over their large terrain. As the process of restaffing and reorganization gets under way, Traven's muchachos begin a campaign of "bucking the system" under the careful guidance of Celso. This campaign, as Traven characterized it, however, strikes a false chord, because the author allowed his antiauthoritarian and anarchist beliefs to substitute for the realities of the role of respect and authority in the work environment.

At the end of *Marsch ins Reich der Caoba*, Andreu and Celso are traveling in the convoy of the *enganchador* Gabriel. Immediately after their arrival, chronicled in *Die Troza*, at the *montería*, Celso begins the education of his companions by warning everybody not to buy alcohol because it contributes to their growing debt. After a few weeks in camp, Celso provokes a more volatile incident when he sings in the darkness, predicting the overseer El Gusano's death. El Gusano responds to this unprecedented act of insubordination by blindly firing a few shots in the direction of the voice, yet is answered by a shrill laugh that "was not the laugh of a discouraged man. It was the sound, shrill laugh of a man who knows what he wants and why he wants it."[122] The effect of this laughter is instantaneous; El Gusano feels threatened and Andreu is not slow to perceive this. "He has shit in his pants, that's what it is," he comments to another oxdriver, confirming that the muchachos have a realistic estimate of the overseers, El Gusano and El Pícaro, and that they recognize that the two bunglers are incapable of inventing a method of punishment such as the systematic hangings. In effect, even with the severe punishments introduced by the Montellanos, the muchachos know how to turn the tables on their superiors. Andreu encourages his *gañán* Vicente after the boy's first whipping by telling him that "it makes you tough and you will generate the necessary wrath we need. Next time when he deals with you, you won't feel a thing and you'll spit right into his face. No whimpering! Perhaps the day of revenge will come."

When the work loads are doubled and the muchachos realize that the alternatives are either to comply or to die a horrible death, they also realize that the only escape from that hell is "to kill them all, not only El Pícaro and El Gusano, but also all the *capataces* in the other camps and the goddamned Montellanos as well." All the muchachos are waiting for, Traven stressed, is "the day of revenge," an opportunity to get back at their tormentors. Opportunities, however, arise every day. The overseers are always alone when they come on their inspections. It would be easy for the assembled *boyeros* to snatch them off their horses and club them to death. Traven acknowledged the overseers' vulnerability when he wrote that "like all *capataces* and like all whiphands and torturers, El Pícaro was careful not to overdo it. He knew he was outnumbered and in an environment that he could not control once it started moving." But Traven failed to heed his own warning. Instead, he initiated a process in which the two overseers systematically undermine their own authority and jeopardize the respect that supports their strength. At one point, the workers are sitting around the fire exhausted and El Pícaro comes along, wishing to be saluted. Celso later informs them that, had anybody gotten up to salute the boss, "I swear to you . . . I would have smashed his teeth in tonight." The workers' respect for their overseers is eventually so diminished that they shove one of them about during a funeral.

The muchachos test the two overseers on several occasions and find that both back down easily each time their position of command is challenged. El Pícaro, in particular, makes an ass of himself in front of the oxdrivers, as when he tries to leap with his horse across one of the muddy lanes and sinks into the quagmire up to the saddle. Ultimately, every time one of the overseers appears on the scene, Traven chips another piece off of his authority. Since neither of the two earns the respect of his subordinates, the question arises in the reader's mind as to why the workers do not get rid of their torturers. The staff, it is clear, is outnumbered; the workers could have defeated El Pícaro, El Gusano, and "all the *capataces* in the other camps and the goddamned Montellanos" on the first day. The workers' revolt that is called the rebellion of the hanged in Traven's narrative is the explosion of the muchachos' pent-up frustration and wrath that finally enables them to break through the barrier of respect that the Indian feels for the ladino and the worker for his boss. Traven, however, had dismantled that barrier in the course of *Die Troza*, and so had made the dynamic unbelievable for his readers.

Mijares Escandón, however, did not run San Roman Tzendales on a skeleton staff of the likes of El Gusano and El Pícaro. The job of his well-trained police force was to maintain discipline and to guard against premeditated or spontaneous murder, committed, in fact, for far less reason than Traven gave his Indian workers. When Pedro Vega dismissed Traven's scenario as ludicrous, he was not denying that horrible punishments were carried out in some logging camps. Rather, he was noting that such punishments were impossible under the conditions described by Traven. Only San Quintín, under the control of the Casa Vega, was run with a comparable skeleton staff; extreme physical punishment did not and could not exist there.

Traven so entangled himself in his attempt to show the shoddiness of authority that he began to disregard the realities of *montería* life. In the macho atmosphere of the jungle, working relationships were based on respect of one man for another. Riding about the forest, passing on orders, and occasionally in the style of his fictional overseers, "marking trees," was not enough. What the author dismissed so lightly as marking trees was in reality the important and arduous work of the scout. El Gusano and El Pícaro, as they appear in the novel, are incapable of carrying out such responsible work. Merely "whiphands and hangmen," they are propped up by the dictatorial management of the Montellanos. Mijares Escandón did not run his empire using such men. He needed overseers who were both more capable and also more loyal. Loyalty, moreover, was not one-sided; in 1924, Mijares Escandón began a lawsuit in Villahermosa on behalf of his collaborators against the Casa Romano because the sons of Pedro Romano had apparently begun to disadvantage them.[123] Traven clearly underestimated the influence of machismo on the workers in the *monterías* when he stipulated profit as the only motive for the Spaniards and ladinos who worked there, and thus experienced *monteros* like Toriello Bulnes dismissed Traven's accounts of *montería* life with a wave of the hand. The question, however, is left open as to whether the punishments meted out by Mijares Escandón and his crew were not tacitly accepted by many workers, including perhaps some of the victims.

Celso's last wish in *Die Troza*, to smash the spade he used to dig a peon's grave over the head of a *coyote*, is only Traven's dramatic device to build up tension before the outbreak of the massive rebellion of the hanged in the next volume. In *montería* life, such incompetents as El Gusano and El Pícaro would never have risen to the position of overseers; more likely, they would have been dismissed like Uncle Fulge or become the victims of someone like Celso with his spade. The artificiality of Traven's scenario and his failure to understand the dynamics of work are presumably due to his own lack of work experience. The author, however, made other mistakes on the technical level, mistakes so crude that his critics felt free to dismiss him and his *montería* accounts outright. His worst error concerns the work of the oxdrivers. It has already been noted that he never had a chance to witness the spectacle of a huge mahogany log being dragged through the lanes of Agua Azul; Traven, who according to his own testimony was unable to "chew anything out of his pencil," also proved unable to make sense of the complicated process about which he had only heard reports.

In the novel, Andreu, having worked as a *carretero* and immediately assigned to the oxdrivers, explains to his assistant Vicente that most logs weigh about one ton, "many weigh two tons." To move a one-ton log required a team of oxen, that is ten animals and not two, as Traven wrote. Thus, a five-ton log, a not uncommon occurrence, required fifty animals. Logs heavier than five tons were rarely cut, because the two-and-one-half-inch chains could not withstand the weight.[124] We have one eyewitness description of a mahogany log being dragged through the lanes of Nuevo Filadelfia:

> The dragging is the most emotional and dangerous stage. Frequently, the mahogany log gets caught in a deep furrow, and to get it moving again does not only require enormous strength from the oxen but also exact coordination of the yokes of oxen. This can only be achieved with oxdrivers who know their business well. Each team has its own oxdriver and a *gañán*. The whole [show] is directed by the *caporal de bueyes* [overseer of the oxen] who is something like a general, a mature man with lots of experience. The spectacle of a three-ton mahogany log being dragged is unique. It requires three teams of oxen, that is thirty animals. This is a veritable strategic maneuver and like in the army, each animal has its place.[125]

Traven's description indicates that he had not understood that the work of oxdrivers was team work and that they had a hierarchical order of their own. This misunderstanding was the source of many subsequent mistakes. Traven's *boyeros*, for example, have no overseer; El Pícaro and El Gusano visit them occasionally to check whether or not they are working. Given the delicate cooperation between up to twenty-five pairs of oxen and thirty to forty men, the weakening of one team member by whipping or hanging would have jeopardized the whole work process.

The incident that triggers the rebellion of the hanged is a mass punishment of the oxdrivers, who are hanged by their feet and hands and "whipped mercilessly." "Pieces of bloody flesh," Traven wrote, "flew around and they could taste their neighbor's skin when they opened their mouths to groan with pain."[126] As arresting as this particular scene and its buildup are, in historical terms it is untenable. Oxdrivers were the best-paid workers in Chiapas. Frequently, they owned their own oxen with which they worked for a logging company.[127] Oxdrivers, therefore, were not proletarians in the sense in which Traven used the term. In fact, the chief *boyero* was the most respected and skilled man in the *montería*, and no vital decision could be made without consulting him.[128] He was the one who decided what was humanly possible for the men and the animals in his charge. The idea of punishing an oxdriver by stringing him up was outrageous and offensive to old *monteros*. On a practical level, moreover, Traven was misinformed about the hours of the oxdrivers and noted that they stopped work at ten in the morning. Those were the hours, however, of the timber fellers, who began shortly before sunrise, stopped between ten and eleven in the morning, and then worked until sunset. The oxdrivers worked at night, start-ing at five in the afternoon and ending with the first light of the day, as the timber fellers began. Only a few petroleum lamps and candles lit the oxdrivers' way. These hours were on account of the oxen, which could not work during the heat of the day.

Ultimately, Traven was also mistaken about the distances the heavy logs were dragged. He claimed that Andreu had to transport a log for eight kilometers to the nearest dump. "Some-times," he wrote, "the distance between where the tree had been felled to the dump is ten kilometers." The maximum a log would be moved is "five leagues, that is twenty kilometers." Given the slow speed of progress and the investment of man and animal labor, this would have been very costly. Logging companies tried to avoid transports longer than five kilometers because this was the daily maximum of a bullock. Otherwise, an extra camp had to be established at the five-kilometer mark where the oxen could rest and where another set of oxen was ready to take over. Every company tried to avoid such additional expense unless the area was particularly promising. Most im-portant to Traven's plot, the oxdrivers and timber fellers had much less contact with each other than the author assumed. Not only did they have different working hours, but they also lived in different camps. The oxdrivers lived in the *montería*, whereas the timber fellers moved from *semaneo* to *semaneo*. The *montería*, not to be confused with the *central*, was usually situated close to the dump where the work of the oxen ended. Thus Traven's idea of a combined rebellion of timber fellers and oxdrivers was not really feasible.

To understand how the logging industry functioned for an outsider was a difficult business. Traven was a passerby, some-one who had arrived at the camp "by accident" and who was "uninitiated." One had to spend many weeks in a logging camp, he wrote, to understand how it functioned.[129] Traven was, how-ever, the only traveler who made a serious effort to understand what he saw. Thus, that he failed in some details cannot be held against him, except that this failure prevented what Traven most desired: instead of stimulating debate and calling attention to the dismal socio-economic conditions of the Chiapan Indians, he exposed himself to justified criticism on technicalities. The unevenness of his account of *montería* life ultimately prevented him from being taken seriously as the chronicler of the Chiapan logging industry by those who could judge what he wrote. Traven undermined his own case by delivering into the hands of those he accused the weapons with which to attack him. The fact that he and his critics actually agreed that the black fame of the *monterías* was created by "las pendejadas de este cabrón" Fernando Mijares Escandón, the victims of one cruel overseer, remained obscured.[130]

Die Rebellion der Gehenkten

"You have to take your freedom,
it is never given to you."
Der Ziegelbrenner[131]

Between 1933 and 1936 the style of Traven's writing changed markedly; he no longer addressed a German audience. The first fifty pages of *Die Troza* were written in the spirit of *Marsch ins Reich der Caoba*, full of pointed remarks about the origins and impact of dictatorship, but in subsequent pages all references to German life, customs, and history are absent. Instead, in the opening pages of *Die Rebellion der Gehenkten*, Traven began to address a prospective American audience. In that book, he cited the case of an American slave who was asked after liberation whether she had not lived better under slavery. Her reply, he reported, was: "I certainly lived better then, but today I am much happier because, you see, sir, it is the feeling and not the stomach which makes men happy." This quote set the tone for Traven's new novel, and the author even began to flatter this audience. When an axe breaks, one of the overseers at La Armonía comments: "Naturally . . . I thought so. Made in Germany. That is a German axe. Cheap as dog shit and as worthless as a matchbox. There, take this one. It is not exactly new but it is an American axe. This one will not bend."[132] In the course of this transition, the role played by a dictatorship in the exploitation of the working class moved into the background. In the later writing the profit motive and capitalism torture the muchachos to the point where their only way out is a bloody rebellion. Traven had even rethought the role of the press, Marut's archenemy, and now spoke favorably of investigative journalism, even muckraking.[133]

Die Rebellion der Gehenkten was such a powerful work that pirated editions, necessary because the author refused permission for a Spanish translation, appeared soon after its publication.[134] Traven was writing at the height of his dramatic powers, and yet the self-appointed defender of the Chiapan Indians proved unable to show what motivated the actions of the indigenous peoples. During his fact-finding tours of Chiapas, the author had uncovered the story of an Indian uprising in 1908 in the *monterías* of the Tzendales region. According to this story, the rebels destroyed the logging camp and left the jungle, conquered half of Chiapas, and then settled somewhere near Ocosingo. The only changes Traven introduced in his reproduction of this superficially plausible story were a few names.

Bloody mutinies were not rare in the logging camps. In fact, old *monteros* maintain that they were quite commonplace although few were ever reported. In one uprising, occurring in 1904, "the peons of the *montería* Las Tinieblas organized a rebellion and almost managed to gain control."[135] In 1912 another uprising seems to have broken out at Los Tzendales:

> In mid-July 1912, fifty federal soldiers left from San Juan Bautista to fight some mutinous peons in the so-called *monterías*. . . . Fifty of those peons were sent to the capital, accused of attempting to start a rebellion which was suffocated by the federal forces. . . . In order to save themselves, they [the peons] alleged that they were victims of slavery in the *monterías* owned by the Spaniards Romano.[136]

The mutinies cited above had one thing in common: they achieved little and failed to bring more than momentary relief to the mahogany workers. The only report of a successful rebellion was the one Traven utilized, but this event was in fact a fiction, which he further adapted for his own purposes. By making use of this story the way it came to him, Traven demonstrated that he had understood very little of the recent history of Chiapas.

Traven remained ignorant, it seems, about the Mapache War and military preparations in Chiapas. A genuine rebellion was largely impossible in the *monterías* because Alberto Pineda, leader of the *Brigada Las Casas* and an ally of Felix Díaz, nephew of the former dictator, guarded the access trails from Ocosingo into the Lacandon Forest for most of the war. The *camino de Tzendales*, the main highway of the Lacandon Forest, was under his authority, and so Mijares Escandón was protected by troops whose avowed goal was to reverse the reforms brought about by the Constitutionalist government. Had a major rebellion erupted at Los Tzendales, it would never have been able to spread beyond the confines of the camp before, during, or after the revolution. The labor conditions of San Roman Tzendales were, in fact, never abolished, either through legislation or rebellion; they simply ceased to exist when the Casa Romano went out of business. Moreover, the bankruptcy of the Casa Romano was caused by forces within the capitalist commodity market and not by outrage against the way the commodities were produced. In the final analysis, Mijares Escandón operated with the connivance both of revolutionaries and of opponents of the revolution, and was a source of money for them rather than an occasion for outrage.

Confidently relying on the—fictitious—story of a successful Indian uprising at Los Tzendales, Traven made it the point of convergence of the entire Jungle Cycle, blithely disregarding such elemental facts as a language barrier between the Tzotzil and Tzeltal Indians who mixed in his *montería*. All the preceding volumes of the Jungle Cycle led up to this climax by showing that the oppressed condition of the Indians in Chiapas was only rectifiable through the total destruction of the system that created and maintained it. Traven had detailed these conditions in many different scenes in which Indians, unlucky enough to come in contact with ladinos, would lose their money and at times their freedom as well. The rebellion of the hanged was meant, by the author, to embody bloody revenge for these injustices and cruelties. The muchachos, however, who conspire and finally carry out the rebellion in Traven's novel are hardly recognizable as Indians. Traven had systematically divested them of all their indigenousness in order to help his readers to identify with the characters. He achieved his goal, as the response of his readers showed, but the price was that the rebellion of the hanged failed to make sense in the context in which the author placed it.

The hangings that the Montellanos introduce in order to squeeze more work out of the muchachos are designed to instill such fear in the victims that they will do anything to prevent a repetition. The hanging consists of a man being strung up on a branch, his hands and feet tied together, like a piece of game. Traven acknowledged that more than two overseers would be required to hang a strong man like Celso in this manner. El Pícaro complains to don Severo: "It is only two of us here. . . . It is not so easy to hang half a dozen men. The older muchachos resist. We need at least three men to subdue one of them." Furthermore, El Pícaro's revolver, symbol of his power, does not impress the workers. When threatened with it, they laugh and mock the man, calling him "Picarote." Even whipping no longer has the desired effect, El Pícaro complains: "What else could I do, *jefe*? I whipped them like biting dogs, so that they hardly had a piece of pelt left on their backs. But they soon got used to it. The more I whipped, the less they worked."[137] Eventually, even the effect of the hangings wore off. Traven explained: "Celso was the first who no longer cared. But now it is half a dozen. The trick is: men can become like mules and oxen that do not move when poked and whipped once they have interned the proper sense of rebellion."[138] This last point raises the question of why Celso would agree to be hanged by the two bungling overseers who, between them, could not even subdue him.

The hangings in Traven's account are not carried out individually but are instead collective punishments of either oxdrivers or timber fellers. One such scene occurs just when a troop of workers arrives at La Armonía. The new men receive a fitting introduction to *montería* life under Montellano rule, "to hell and all devils," as the oxdriver Santiago puts it. While sitting at the camp fire, they hear sounds of human groaning coming from the jungle. The old oxdrivers explain to the newcomers that these are the timber fellers being punished by hanging for insufficient work. One of the new men asks innocently whether the workers defend themselves against this treatment. The oxdriver Prócoro explains to him: "Even pigs struggle when you try to slaughter them . . . but what can you do if there are three or four torturers to hold you down? They club you over the head and when you come to, you are hanging on a branch with red ants crawling up your nostrils and your ears." The oxdrivers claim they are "unable to help their brothers," and remain unmoved by the suffering, even taunting the newly arrived workers with descriptions of the cruelties awaiting them. Traven had made the point earlier that hanging was not enforced by a power that made its acceptance compelling, and in this scene there are on hand only five overseers, who are drunk and spending their time in the office with some women. There is, in effect, no one to watch the hanged timber fellers, and so, it appears, disinterest alone prevents the assembled oxdrivers from going to the aid of their comrades.

In his previous books, Traven had frequently given biting examples of the failure of proletarian cooperation. Traven's Indians, however, are made to seem an exception, acting cooperatively at all times. Generally, Indians are not shown failing one another or betraying their comrades; such things happen only in the world of the ladinos. "The overseers," Traven wrote, "knew that the muchachos would help their comrades. It was not the duty of the *capataces* to look after the well-being of the hanged." Sure enough, the muchachos are there when the hanged are cut down, to treat their wounds, to feed them, and to carry them to their sleeping quarters. Traven made an attempt to explain why it was particularly cruel to Indians to be hanged in Montellano fashion and why nobody went near the hanged:

> Nobody knows better than the Indians from the districts close to the jungle what horrors are contained in the jungle. Hanging and the defenselessness of the hanged in the middle of the night was so unspeakably and mysteriously horrible to the Indian because of his irrepressible fear of ghosts and spirits, his superstition and his belief in the return of the dead which, alone in the night, he thinks he sees everywhere. . . . If they had hanged the lads somewhere deep in the jungle, far from the camp, none of them would have been alive in the morning. They would have been strangled by ghosts and spirits. Some would even have shown marks of strangulation on their necks. Of course not caused by ghosts but by the uncommonly strong power of imagination of these natural and unlettered people.[139]

None of Traven's muchachos suffers from a trace of such superstition, and the hanged feel only the torture and the sheer discomfort it produces. The workers, in fact, are perfectly rational in the way Traven was rational. Celso, in a manner quite unlike an Indian, pronounces what the atheist writer had learned long before: "Why wait for the savior? Save yourself, brother, and your savior will come!" The workers consciously build up their wrath against their tormentors, and they understand their economic value to the logging company much as industrial workers would who were trained in the teachings of Marx. They watch the deterioration of their lives as if they know that they have to reach a certain depth of degradation before they will have the courage and power to hit back. One of the oxdrivers confides to the newly arrived workers: "Just wait. . . . The day will come when we hang and cut loose and when we shall go where blows fall, but not to receive but to distribute them. Those sons-of-bitches always forget that you cannot whip a man forever. One day he will learn how to whip and who to whip in order to have peace in his soul."[140] And Celso sings in defiance amidst the groans of the hanged: "It does not cost us anything to kill our hangman. If we no longer act like human beings, then those who hang us are to blame." These comments display the political rhetoric of Marut and the insights of Traven, not the fruits of experience of an unlettered Tzotzil Indian, half dead from malnutrition, overwork, and ill-treatment.

In the characterization of the muchachos, Traven's voice is ever present. The men never take on complete personalities of their own but instead remain facets of Traven's political ideology. Moreover, the insights that the author gave to his Indians are not those of fearful, befuddled men, afraid of priests, spirits, and ladinos, with no other choice but to subject themselves to any form of punishment meted out to them by town authorities, labor agents, *finqueros*, and shopkeepers. Armed with a new rationality, Traven's workers cease to be the kind of Indians he had observed in 1926 during the Fiesta de San Juan in Chamula or at El Real farm in later years, Indians steeped in ceremony, religious beliefs, and a worldview in which spirit forces shape their destiny. By divesting his Indians of their Indianness, Traven had undermined his own argument: The barrier of respect between Indian and ladino never became real. By creating a set of proletarians, brothers to all workers, the Indians of Chiapas had ceased to be the focus and the heroes of Traven's novels in all but name, and the particular setting of the Romano *montería* had become a universal framework of labor exploitation.

The novels demonstrate that the most humiliated and the poorest of proletarians were capable of starting and carrying through a successful revolution. If, however, Traven had created credible Indian characters and made them rebel, the outcome would have been a *guerra de castas* with its limited goals of independence for the Indian communities to conduct their affairs as they chose, without interference from town authorities and the church. As it is, Traven only retained the outward trappings of such a war by pitting his pure Indian workforce against the ladino overseers and the Spanish proprietors. By converting his Indians into a heterogeneous, interchangeable set of proletarians, the rebellion of the hanged became a class war, a notion that many of Traven's readers understood but which was alien to the Chiapan Indians after whom he modeled his characters.

Traven provided two different schemata for the rebellion, one based on the actions of individuals and the other of the group. Both appeal to the understanding of his readers rather than explore the mentality of Chiapan Indians. What triggers the rebellion is the unplanned act of a single Bachajón, Urbano, who, having hit Acacio Montellano in the face, recognizes that his life from that point on is worthless. He can only go ahead and kill Acacio, he thinks; otherwise "he would be hanged to death under the most horrible torture for this blow." His desperation enables him to suddenly break with his habits and customs of respect and turn on his master. Urbano proves unable to cope with this break, and he goes to drown himself in the river. His solitary act destroys his life; the muchachos, however, later succeed because they act as a group.

The individualist-anarchist legacy of Marut, carried on by Traven and revised under the twin impact of the IWW and the union strength of the CGT in Tampico, was finally laid to rest in *Die Rebellion der Gehenkten*. The book is the most personal statement Traven made in novel form. He had begun to settle his score with Marut and his experiences of revolution, and the voice of the German anarchist can be heard loud and clear through the events at La Armonía. Almost twenty years after the uprising at Munich, Traven produced an anarchist's handbook on how to make a successful revolution. He achieved this point at a time when the German Revolution of 1918 was a distant and suppressed memory, the Mexican Revolution had lost its impetus, and the Spanish Republic had come under siege from fascist and conservative forces.

The *montería* workers, under Traven's direction, do considerably better than did the followers in Bavaria of Kurt Eisner and Gustav Landauer. Celso realizes long before the outbreak of the rebellion that "an individual can do nothing and change nothing. We all have to do it, at the same time, or leave it altogether."[141] Only a concerted action of all the muchachos can prevent the artisans and employees, the bourgeois element of the *montería*, from betraying the rebellion at the first opportunity. The workers do not fall into the traps into which Marut and his

comrades from Munich had fallen. Describing the muchachos'
first war council, Traven reminisced: "The sad fate of all revolutions and their parliaments was not in evidence here. There
were no endless debates and discussions. And when a decision
was finally taken, the debating starts all over again about how to
execute the decision. It is always the sessions of the revolutionary parliaments that lay waste to the revolution and defeat it."[142]
While irrelevant points of order and procedure are being debated
by the revolutionaries, Traven commented, the enemy begins to
rally and appears "downstairs at the door of the hall where the
revolutionaries debate." This was the lesson from Munich where
the Bavarian revolutionaries proved unable to consolidate their
new power, and while they sat debating "points of order,"
White Guards appeared where the Council of Soviets was in
session. Few escaped capture. This is why Celso shouts at the
debating muchachos: "We are in a rebellion, and a rebellion
means fighting and not talking!"

Traven, who had first observed in Munich that "the proletariat instinctively always acts correctly," retained this belief.
His muchachos, model revolutionaries, "all possessed a good
and natural instinct which taught them: if you have weapons
and your opponent has none, then you will win the revolution
or the rebellion or the mutiny or the strike or whatever you will
call what assures justice to the proletarian."[143] The sound revolutionary instincts are the direct consequence of the ignorance of
the muchachos. The illiterate Indians who had "never rebelled
before nor contradicted their masters," who "had never in their
lives read a revolutionary article in a paper or studied the
history of a revolution," understand that they can only succeed
if they disregard their own wishes. Their rebellion started as an
act of revenge; all they wanted was to return to their villages.
Soon, however, "the thought of going home was forgotten; the
fight for the whole emerged ever clearer." Their "local mutiny"
can only grow into a revolution if it sweeps along even "the
most phlegmatic and fearful revolutionary and rebellious group
in the land."[144]

Likewise, the rebels have no concept of what will happen
once their revolution succeeds. Their instincts tell them that first
they have to eliminate the enemy in order to be free to start
remodeling society. Traven invested his muchachos with the
conclusion he had drawn from the events in Munich in 1919,
and the workers carry out a thorough spring cleaning, eliminating

the bourgeoisie, destroying all records and papers so that there is nothing that can be used against them in the future. They also abolish all hierarchical order. Martín Trinidad, El Profesor, explains that "there are no more *jefes* and no more *patrones*. I am your *camarada*." The new proletarian society will be composed of equals, because only equality can prevent new forms of exploitation. Lack of planning for the future, moreover, prevents the muchachos from falling into the traps set by revolutionary dreams and utopias; their lack of any concept of their future is in fact their strength. The revolution itself, Traven explained, must be a spontaneous act because "a revolution that needs explanations and even justifications, is no revolution but a quarrel for property and offices." The revolutionary "sacrifices himself and dies in order to shake the foundations and realize his ideas." This, then, was Marut's political testament, expressed in the guise of a rebellion in a logging camp in the remotest corner of Mexico.

Die Rebellion der Gehenkten was also Traven's farewell to his lifelong dreams of revolution in a world gradually overrun by fascism. One last flicker of hope for his political ideals seemed to arrive with the coming of the presidency of Lázaro Cárdenas in 1934, but soon Traven saw that Cárdenas did not live up to the hopes of *Land des Frühlings*, and he began to reject the new president's revolutionary radicalism. The world in which Traven's political ideals were viable had disappeared, and the aging author, bitter and sad, perceived that this was so. His disillusionment became apparent in his next volume, *Ein General kommt aus dem Dschungel*.

6 The End of a Great Vision

Ein General kommt aus dem Dschungel

The story of the Indian rebellion at Los Tzendales that inspired *Die Rebellion der Gehenkten* seems to have originated in the district of Montecristo in Tabasco, a district traditionally associated with the logging industry. A version of the story paralleling the one used by Traven has been told by Eliecér Mendoza Cambrano, the chronicler of the township of Emiliano Zapata, Tabasco, where he was born in 1902.

> Land reform in Chiapas began in June of 1908 [not in 1910, as the official record states] in the logging camps of the region of the Zendales River with the cry "Justice, land and freedom!" shouted by the slaves, to the tune of a thousand Indians who rebelled against the owners of the *monterías* which exploited mahogany, and against the tyrant Porfirio Díaz who permitted such ignominy.
>
> This army of Tzotzil and Tzeltal Indians was led by ex-Sergeant Juan Méndez, who was called General. Lucio Ortiz held the rank of colonel, and Celso Cruz became the chief-of-staff. Professor Pilar Ramírez, the brains of the rebels, was named *comisario*. They made their headquarters in the finca Sta. Margarita to get food, cattle, horses, and mules. From there they left to occupy the cities of Balún, Ocozingo, Jovel, and Alhumal in the state of Chiapas.
>
> Division General Patronio Bringas headed his federal troops and a body of *rurales* to attack and exterminate the rebels. There were four battles with the rebels but they were beaten by the rebel General Juan Méndez. The federals lost great quantities of arms, ammunition, and four machine guns, and General Bringas and his Lieutenant Bailleres fell prisoners and were executed.
>
> The victorious rebels then looked for land on which to found their first village. They named [their own] municipal agent and built a town hall. This historical fact of the initiation of land reform

in Chiapas in the *monterías* of Zendales is quite unknown and therefore, I make it known because this is the truth of the beginning of land reform in Chiapas.[1]

More details, disagreeing at times with Traven's version, of this alleged beginning of land reform subsequently emerged in an interview with the historian. Mendoza Cambrano claimed that Celso Cruz, whom Traven called Celso Flores, was not a Tzotzil Indian but a Tzeltal half-caste who came from near Ocosingo. He and his brother, a sergeant, served with the rurales and they had traveled as far as Campeche. When Cruz was nearly drowned by one of his superiors, his brother killed the officer, and the two brothers decided to flee to Los Tzendales where they met Juan Méndez. Traven, who used all these details, attached them to the biography of Méndez rather than his Chamula, Celso. Cruz, together with his brother and the former sergeant Méndez, Mendoza Cambrano argued, initiated the rebellion in December 1908. They killed all the overseers at Los Tzendales with machete blows and then burnt the *montería*. The army of workers then came down to the Santa Margarita finca in search of Mijares Escandón, but failed to find him.

Meanwhile, according to Mendoza Cambrano, General Bringas was dispatched from Tuxtla Gutiérrez (not Comitán, as Traven wrote), to attack the rebels at Santa Margarita. Close to the village of San José, between El Real and Ocosingo, the rebels encountered the regulars, surprised them during the night, and removed all their arms. Cruz was put in charge of the machine guns because he had a military background—unlike Traven's Celso, who first had to learn how to operate the complicated piece of weaponry. When General Bringas and Lieutenant Bailleres fell into the hands of the rebels, they were drowned—not hanged, as in Traven's version.

The conquest of half of Chiapas and four fierce battles with regular troops took, according to Mendoza Cambrano, from December 1908 "until Madero was already in power" (therefore, sometime after May 1911). The historian did not know exactly where the rebels founded their village, nor could he say whether any remains still existed, but he was sure that he had heard the story "in his youth," and "so did everybody else hereabouts." This story apparently has formed part of the folklore of Montecristo and enjoyed a life independent of Traven's rendering of it in *Ein General kommt aus dem Dschungel*. Mendoza

Cambrano, however, was proud of Traven's use of this story, which, although he had no doubt, further confirmed for him its authenticity. Traven repeated it with few alterations, most notably to relocate the battle scenes thirty kilometers farther south. He even used most of the names as they came to him, presumably in an attempt to show his Chiapan readers, whom he thought familiar with the contents of the story, that he relied firmly on factual information.

Not a single element in the story, however, as told by Traven and Mendoza Cambrano, is in fact true. There was no Division General Patronio Bringas, or Petronio Bringas as Traven called him, stationed at Tuxtla Gutiérrez or Comitán. A momentous occasion such as the departure from a garrison of a division general, accompanied by a large troop of soldiers and rurales to fight a band of a thousand rebellious Indians, would no doubt have been reported in the local newspapers, since every minor troop movement was described and commented on at length. The actions of an army of Indian rebels conquering important cities such as Comitán, San Cristóbal de las Casas, Ocosingo, and San Carlos would have been mentioned in the metropolitan press. There was no mention of these events in the newspapers of the time.

José Toriello Bulnes, who arrived at San Quintín in 1913, stressed that news of an event of such magnitude would have reached his ears, but says he heard nothing of it. Pedro Vega, today's owner of the finca Santa Margarita, has pointed out that he no doubt would have heard from one of his older workers of the arrival of a rebel army of a thousand Indians ransacking the farm, but nobody has mentioned such an event. What is more, the area between Santa Margarita and El Real is thinly settled and mostly flat pasture land, offering no strategic advantage to an army. No competent general would attempt to fight a battle in such terrain when both sides in the conflict had machine guns. Nor could an army of a thousand men have found food in the area for more than a week. Finally, in disagreement with Traven's assumption, the historical record indicates that the impact of the revolution on the *montería* system was, as we have seen, minimal. Traven's portrayal of the new revolutionaries' commitment to destroy the profiteers of the old system was not only simplistic but wholly fictitious. In reality, the development of the revolutionary struggle in Tabasco and Chiapas is full of ambiguities and divided loyalties, and concern for the degraded condition of the peons was often a matter of political expediency. General Domínguez, who is known for having sacked Los Tzendales, is a case in point.

Domínguez rose in arms in August 1913 in the area called Los Ríos, which included Tenosique, Montecristo, Balancán, and the Tabascan access routes to the Lacandon Forest. Little can be ascertained about his visit to Los Tzendales, but the evidence that exists indicates that, despite later protestations to the contrary, the fate of the workers of Los Tzendales was not uppermost in his mind. His history is of interest here because the story Traven used in *Ein General kommt aus dem Dschungel* may well be connected to a smear campaign against the general during his political struggle against General Ramírez Garrido and General Carlos Greene for the governorship of Tabasco, and to the dispute surrounding the authorship of the decree for the liberation of the serfs. The story, as retold by Mendoza Cambrano, may well have survived *because* Traven utilized it, for the historian has placed supreme trust in the authenticity of all of Traven's *montería* material which, he has stressed, exactly described the conditions of Los Tzendales. To Mendoza Cambrano, Traven was a man of great courage and integrity, the champion of the victims of Los Tzendales, many of whom had been the historian's childhood friends.

General Domínguez was a rich landowner with chicle, rubber, and timber interests in Belize and Tabasco. He was introduced to the cause of the Maderistas by his cousin, José María Pino Súarez, Madero's vice-president. It appears that the general visited Los Tzendales in March 1914 and that he afterwards decreed the liberation of the serfs at his base camp at El Ceibo. This latter event was later vehemently but unsuccessfully disputed by his political rivals. Why the general went to Los Tzendales and what exactly he did there, however, have never been clarified. The existing evidence indicates that he went there to requisition money, food, weapons, and men for his continuing war against Victoriano Huerta. He went as far as San Roman Tzendales, it appears, because only the Romano operations were large enough to guarantee substantial amounts of cash, arms, ammunition, and food. How he laid hands on large sums of money has been described in a booklet written obviously in an effort to defame Domínguez:

Francisco Castellanos D., contractor of the Casa Romano and Co., accompanied Domínguez when he went around levying large sums from the Casa Romano, to give him a receipt for the 35,000 pesos which he [the contractor] owed the company, by way of commission. He only got this receipt when Sr. Mijares, manager of the company, was threatened with being transported to a better life and he had to give in. After that, General Domínguez took all the workers, oxen, foodstuffs etc. and only returned part of it when the Casa Romano offered him a large sum of money. This can be proven from the ledger of the Company.[2]

Had the general really had any intention of destroying Los Tzendales, he would have left it inoperative by removing all its animals, men, equipment, and foodstuffs. As it was, he seems to have wanted a ransom. With the money gained, according to the malicious but well-informed author of the booklet, Domínguez went on to Belize to buy arms.

If this report is correct, General Domínguez made personal contact with Mijares Escandón but did not take him along to be punished, as happened to the overseer Tacho Gil who, we remember, "died on the boat." General Domínguez, it appears, never intended to punish the Casa Romano's administrator for his cruelty, which, the general claimed, had moved him to decree the liberation of the serfs; in fact, he had set out on a money-raising tour and not a punitive expedition at all. If indeed General Domínguez let the villain go free and instead bargained with him for money in return for men and animals, then it is quite likely that his famous decree was no more than a propaganda gesture, exaggerated later for political purposes.

Indications are that Los Tzendales recommenced operations as soon as Domínguez left the area and that this continuation of the status quo was guaranteed by the survival of Mijares Escandón. The author of the booklet cited above claimed that, during his short military governorship of Tabasco, General Domínguez worked hand in glove with the large mahogany-exporting companies and helped them make substantial profits. Whatever the truth of this accusation, there is no evidence to suggest that the logging business suffered from the activity of revolutionary armies. General Ramírez Garrido later claimed that the actual decree liberating the serfs, which was issued in September 1914 after the conquest of San Juan Bautista, was signed under duress by General Domínguez.[3] His previous decree penned at El Ceibo, Ramírez Garrido rightly pointed out, was only effective in the area occupied by the general's troops at the time. This opinion is certainly consistent with the immediate resumption of the old work patterns at San Roman Tzendales.

It is quite likely that the story that Traven used as the basis for *Ein General kommt aus dem Dschungel* was part of the defamation campaign directed against General Domínguez. General Ramírez Garrido's argument against Domínguez hinged on the claim that he himself was the true author of the decree. It was, he argued, his lobbying at San Juan Bautista in September 1914 and his moving speech about the fate of the workers of Los Tzendales that caused the law to be passed, and not Domínguez's ineffectual and unofficial decree. With the Constitutionalist government in power in Mexico City and Carranza in the presidency, the question of the authorship of this state law became a matter of great political prestige.

General Domínguez lost the 1915 election for governor of Tabasco to Carlos Greene. After the defeat, the new state governor, with the help of Ramón Sosa Torres and Ramírez Garrido, embarked on a systematic character assassination of his rival Domínguez.[4] The anonymous booklet quoted above is part of this campaign and gives an indication of the maliciousness with which it was conducted. The history of this defamation has not yet been explored, but there is every indication that Greene was not particular in his choice of ways to discredit his political rival. Releasing disinformation about Domínguez seems to have been a tactic used. As a result, none of the actions, motives, and purposes of General Domínguez is beyond question today.

The superficially plausible story that Traven took as fact would have fitted nicely into a propaganda war against General Domínguez. Had there been a successful rebellion at Los Tzendales in 1908, one in which the *montería* was destroyed and an army of workers created strong enough to conquer half the state, then the general's claims to have initiated the liberation of Los Tzendales would have been severely undermined. If a group of humble Indians could free themselves from the grip of Los Tzendales, then the general's decree loses a good deal of its importance. Domínguez, in fact, has not become a legend in his home district, but he is remembered in neighboring Chiapas as the liberator of Los Tzendales.[5] A story, however, directed at devaluing his reputation has survived for seventy years in his home territory, and it has never occurred to Mendoza Cambrano, for one, to make the simple inquiries necessary to ascertain its factuality. The survival may be attributable to the fact that Traven immortalized it and so endowed it with a respectability that it does not deserve.

The extent of Traven's belief in the veracity of the story of the rebellion at Los Tzendales emerges when the geography of *Ein General kommt aus dem Dschungel* is considered. The story as recounted by Mendoza Cambrano has a specific geographic setting, with the army of rebels marching from Los Tzendales via the *camino de Tzendales* to Santa Margarita where the *camino* ends. From there, they go to San José near El Real, where they fight their great battle against federal troops and finally settle "somewhere near Ocosingo." Traven, however, who had become careful to avoid offending certain people, transferred the site of the battle from near El Real, the home of his friends, the Bulnes family, to an equally recognizable location some thirty kilometers farther south. In *Marsch ins Reich der Caoba*, don Gabriel's convoy takes the conventional route from Ocosingo via El Paraíso and El Real (which Traven renamed La Condesa) to Agua Azul. In contrast, the rebels of *Ein General kommt aus dem Dschungel* return over a different track for no apparent reason. They emerge from the jungle nowhere near El Real, but close to the finca Santo Domingo.[6] Traven on this point began to confuse his readers, who were unfamiliar with the geography of Chiapas, by making out that Santo Domingo was indeed La Condesa, "where we stayed for one day and two nights on our way to the *montería*."[7] From Santo Domingo, he wrote, the muchachos proceed to Las Delicias on the road to Achumal, which is the Indian name for San Carlos. The Santa Cecilia finca, however, was Traven's own invention. With this little maneuver he signaled to his friends, the Bulnes family, that he did not attribute to them what was being perpetrated at Santa Cecilia.

It is at the fictitious location of Santa Cecilia that the *finqueros* show their true faces. It is they who persuade the army officers to leave the rebel prisoners in their hands to punish them and they who have the idea for the prisoners' execution. First, the muchachos' ears are cut off; the men are then buried up to the shoulders in the ground, and their heads are smashed by galloping horses. Traven, it seems, had taken this fearful image straight from Sergei Eisenstein's recently completed film *Que Viva México!* The author may have become acquainted with Eisenstein during the shooting of the film and have been shown some of the images the Russian director had taken.[8] Traven must also have known, however, that the mode of punishment he had described was not feasible in the part of Chiapas where he located Santa Cecilia; the bedrock in that area is covered only with a thin layer of topsoil. He was, indeed, familiar with the area, and he knew it would be recognizable to at least some of his readers. While staying at El Real and Ocosingo in 1929 and 1930, Traven spent much of his time exploring the tributaries of the Jataté River,[9] the area in which he placed Santa Cecilia. In effect, Traven had once more inserted a landmark into his text for his Chiapan friends, having seen the need for such manipulation of geography because the scene at the *finca* was entirely his own invention. He had never before presented *finquero* cruelty as anything other than the product of habit and thoughtlessness, but the *finqueros* at Santa Cecilia, he made clear, want blood.

Traven must have believed in the veracity of his story, otherwise he would not have felt the need to protect his friends from any suspicion that might fall on them should he have retold the story of the rebellion exactly as he had heard it. Traven made sure that none of his readers could think that members of the Bulnes family were associated with any event before, during, or after the rebellion. His concern for his friends' reputation, as it turns out, was unnecessary: They knew that Traven's general from the jungle had never existed.

It appears that Traven, at the same time as he was finishing the last of the Jungle Novels, was once more asked by his publisher to "sweeten" his texts.[10] After his experiences in 1933, and equipped with his new publishing contracts in Britain and the United States, the author finally initiated the break with the Büchergilde. *Ein General kommt aus dem Dschungel* first appeared in a Swedish translation in Stockholm in 1939; the Allert de Lange publishing house in Amsterdam produced a German version in 1940.[11] The break with the Büchergilde was the end of an era for Traven, and it certainly contributed to his disillusionment. But his disappointment by political developments in Mexico after 1925 seems to have played the leading role in his decision to stop writing.

Traven and the Presidency of Lázaro Cárdenas

Although *Ein General kommt aus dem Dschungel* appears on the surface to be a success story full of victory and optimism, underlying the book is a deeply pessimistic statement about how revolutionary goals deteriorate once military victory is complete. Traven's last novel bears clear signs of resignation and disillusionment, as well as a heightened understanding of the complex problems associated with the restructuring of a society along revolutionary lines. Such a message coming from Traven at that time was particularly surprising given the nature of the Cárdenas presidency, which brought a massive revival of land reform, collectivization of agriculture, experiments in worker administration of key industries, and the nationalization of the oil industry. All of these measures should have delighted Traven, but there is no indication of any such response in his last novel. Rather, the author indicated that he had changed his opinions concerning a number of crucial ideas that he had earlier supported. He retracted completely, for example, his praise of the Indian "sense of community." Ten years after *Land des Frühlings* he wrote: "Nobody had taught them [the peons] how to organize their work, how to form cooperatives. Their sense of community was so underdeveloped, or had been so destroyed, *providing it ever existed* [emphasis added], that a cooperative would not have helped them because jealousy, envy, and eternal quarreling about predominance would have destroyed it slowly."[12]

The muchachos of *Ein General kommt aus den Dschungel*, although cooperative and helpful at all times, learn to adapt themselves to political realities as they encounter them during their campaign. They set out from La Armonía with the simple program of eliminating everything and everybody standing in the way of *tierra y libertad*. In the process of implementing their simple plan, however, they end up being destructive rather than constructive, "because all that was not part of them was the cause of their slavery, [and] they had to destroy [it]. They no longer cared for tomorrow, they only cared for yesterday when they were tormented. . . . They now only knew revenge."[13] These gloomy words in the first pages of the novel introduce the change that the muchachos undergo between the destruction of the *montería* and their first battle with regular troops. On the way, they learn how to plunder, murder, and pillage in the name of their revolution.

Wherever they go, the rebels assure the peons on the farms that all ranks have been abolished and that they are all *amigos* and *camaradas*. Among themselves, however, they maintain a strict hierarchy cemented by military rank. Their command structure is indisputable, and El General declares coolly that he will kick in the teeth of anyone who disagrees with him. Yet, Celso, still filled with the spirit of the rebellion in the *montería*, enthusiastically declares: "We are always right! We are always right because we are rebels." The gap between ideology and practice widens slowly.

As time goes on, the original goal of the rebellion is abandoned and the revolution peters out. The rebels' initial goal was to free the state and to rule it, but after their victorious battle against General Bringas and his troops, they decide to build a village and sow a crop of corn and beans on the land around the camp. They begin to become complacent, content with their victories, despite having liberated less than one tenth of Chiapas. Only later do they have the justification of having heard that the old dictator Díaz has left the country. After their settlement at Solipaz, the rebels limit their activities to small sorties, attacking military posts and small detachments of rurales. The muchachos have, in fact, begun to settle down in the midst of the system that they have vowed to destroy. The overall impact of their actions on the state is minimal; the former rebels limit themselves in the end to securing *tierra y libertad* for themselves.

It was, apparently, difficult for Traven to work out what happened between 1911, when the Indian army had supposedly conquered half the state, and 1930, when he found the Indians back in their humble and exploited condition. His explanation for the decline was one he had used before. In *Land des Frühlings* he had wondered about the Chamula Indians' failure to exploit their victory at San Cristóbal de las Casas in 1869, and he had fictionalized this failure in *Marsch ins Reich der Caoba*. The muchachos of *Ein General kommt aus dem Dschungel* are caught in the same dilemma, and they content themselves with becoming dirt farmers, just as they had been before entering the hell of the *montería*. Despite all the upheaval and bloodshed, nothing has really changed, and the rebels prove unable to break with their own past. This situation, in fact, carries the germ of its own destruction, and the cycle of oppression and exploitation erupting in rebellion will, the novel implies, repeat itself many times.

At the same time that Traven was addressing the failure of revolutionary ideals, he made an attempt to come to terms with rural poverty and the impact of the revolution's land reform program on the social and economic conditions of rural Chiapas. One of the reasons why the rebels give up their erstwhile revolutionary goals is the realization that their simple program has little relevance to the needs of the peons they encounter. At the first ranch that they reach after leaving the jungle, neither *tierra* nor *libertad* makes much sense. The "manor house" is an adobe building of the simplest construction and without windows; "the only object in the house which reminded [the viewer] that the inhabitants did not live in the fourth century . . . was an American sewing machine." The manor house is surrounded by a few thatched huts occupied by the peons. Although there is sufficient land for all, the quality of the land is low, and only one tenth of it is worth cultivating. "During the dry season it was rock hard; during the rainy season it was boggy and knotty. If the rainy season lasted too long, then all the inhabitants . . . including the ranchero, were close to starvation."[14]

The poverty of the land and the marginality of the economy keep the ranch perpetually on the brink of catastrophe, so that the question of labor exploitation generating wealth for the landowner never arises. Had the ranch been "liberated" and its land distributed to its peons, Traven clearly realized, the former laborers would not profit at all. Instead, "the freedom they would receive from a revolution would have rendered these peons poorer and more helpless by half than what they were before." Being as poor and marginal as they are, "nobody would give them seed because they lived too far from the centers of distribution, if those existed at all."[15] This ranch is a far cry from the idyllic, carefree, and patriarchally ruled White Rose farm owned by the Huastecan Indian Hacinto and his numerous clan.

The muchachos, as they move through the countryside, encounter other faces of rural poverty. They come to an Indian village consisting of ten huts: "The revolution could not improve here either. The revolution would have to bring fertile soil, cattle, and grass to feed the cattle, plus a few sacks of rags so that these poor peasants and their families had the most necessary clothing."[16] In the whole village there are only three machetes, the basic tool of Indian peasants. Traven put his finger on the sorest spot of the Mexican land reform program: What could a peon do with land he received through land reform, if he had neither the knowledge nor the tools, seeds, or credit to cultivate it? Indeed, none of the villagers understands the rhetoric accompanying the rebels' program of *tierra y libertad*, nor is it relevant to their lives. "Their problems were so simple that the most beautiful revolution . . . freeing the country from the dictator, passed their lives [without touching them] and they did not pay any attention." The only change a revolution would ever bring to their lives, Traven wrote, would be a rise in market taxes "to build a rural school which would never materialize." The rebels soon give up trying to convince any of them; the difficulties they encounter are simply overwhelming.

Problems of rural poverty and ignorance had accompanied and affected the Mexican land reform program from the first, and Traven had already acknowledged some of them in *Land des Frühlings*. In 1933, on the eve of Cárdenas's rise to power, there were still over 2 million landless peasants, day laborers, and sharecroppers in Mexico. Only 4,090 ejidos had been created nationwide, and they consisted mainly of "bad land with little water."[17] Their inhabitants had only minimal access to credit facilities, reinforcing their marginality. Most of the operations were inefficient, and the plots were rarely able to satisfy the needs of a rural family.[18] It looked as if the ejido program was a failure, and Traven, who had praised the communal idea so highly in 1926, was unable or unwilling to look for the reasons for its shortcomings in the implementation of agrarian policies. Rather, he pointed to the continuing ignorance and helplessness of the Indian peasants and implied that the failure was due to some inherent weakness in the concept itself.

The development of state policy toward agriculture since the times of Obregón had one clear goal: to thwart the development of what was considered an inefficient ejidal sector and to prevent the break-up of profitable capitalist estates producing for export-oriented agroindustry. Land reform, one historian has noted, became "one of the greatest myths of governments emerging from the Revolution,"[19] an opinion Traven appears to have shared during the mid-1930s. However, opposition of the political parties in favor of land redistribution (the *agraristas*) to former President Calles—now called *el jefe máximo*, because of his dominant role behind the scenes—grew until in January 1934 an autonomous Department of Agriculture was created to direct and regulate land reform. Cárdenas was the presidential candidate of the *agraristas*, and their program became government policy. These important events were accompanied by a lively public debate over the merits and demerits of different forms of land reform. Given Traven's commitment to the agricultural workers of Chiapas, one might expect that he followed this debate with deep interest and reflected some of its arguments. In *Ein General kommt aus dem Dschungel*, however, there are no signs of such engagement.

With Cárdenas's rise to power, Mexico entered the most progressive phase of its postrevolutionary development. The ejido, the stepchild of earlier land reform programs, finally came into its own with increased acreage and credit facilities for *ejidos colectivos*. In consequence, production on the communal farms rose sharply.[20] After 1935, in his effort to promote land reform, Cárdenas, *el presidente errante*, began to crisscross the country for months on end, familiarizing himself with the problems of landless peasants and the rural population. He appeared in the smallest villages, often unannounced, listening to the complaints of peasants; the visits were usually followed by a presidential initiative for a land grant, an irrigation canal, a school, or another improvement required by the community. This populist approach cemented the president's support among the rural population, who referred to him as "*tata* Cárdenas." The land reform program instituted by the Cárdenas administration mirrored the cooperative model Traven had praised so highly in 1926. He had, at that time, envisioned that Mexico's glorious future would be based on such cooperatives. Now, however, he remained mute.

In 1936, Cárdenas gave orders to keep telegraph offices open for one hour per day to receive complaints from peasants and workers, free of charge. Such measures not only profoundly enhanced the president's credibility, but they also served as a check on bureaucratic performance.[21] All of this should have been highly attractive to Traven, yet he chose to ignore it. Indeed, all he reported were the—very real—abuses of land reform officials in Chiapas before the advent of the Cárdenas administration:

> The peons, for centuries used to lords, tyrants, oppressors and dictators, were not freed by the revolution, not even where the

feudal domains were broken up among the families of the peons as ejidos. They remained slaves, with the only difference that they had changed their overlords, that skilful revolutionary leaders now became rich, and that the politicians now used seemingly liberated peons of small property to enrich themselves no end, to strengthen their political influence and with the help of murder and bestialities to terrorize them and to commit any kind of lawlessness in existence in order to become *diputado* or *gobernador* with no other intention than to fill their coffers.[22]

When workers and landowners in the fertile and irrigated cotton-growing lands of the Laguna area of Coahuila and Durango became embroiled in a massive conflict in 1936, Cárdenas, a believer in workers' ability to administer their own affairs, decided to expropriate the prime cotton estates and grant collective ejidos. Even these echoes of Tampico's heyday failed to move Traven.

It is not known exactly when *Ein General kommt aus dem Dschungel* was written. If it was written about 1937, as the publication date suggests, then Traven deliberately disregarded the new impetus of the Cardenista land reform. Instead, he perpetuated a vision of land reform that was outdated and negative. If the book was already written before 1936, then Traven failed to revise it and to bring its information up to date. Whichever was the case: Traven indicated that he wanted no part of Cárdenas's Mexico.

Traven, who had always been a great admirer of the rural schoolteachers and who had sung their praises in *Land des Frühlings*, introduced an "itinerant rural school teacher" in his novel. Gabino Villalva shares the muchachos' ideology. Therefore, the rebels take to him immediately, and he agrees to stay at Solipaz to act as the village teacher. By staying, however, Villalva opts out of national affairs and joins a small, self-regulating, independent community of Indian dirt farmers who have disassociated themselves from the greater Mexican nation. Villalva realizes that a greater Mexico has nothing to offer him—a complete reversal of Traven's optimistic ending of *Die weisse Rose*. At the same time, Gabino Villalva is the first ladino in Traven's work who is not bloody-minded toward Indians. He is, in fact, polite and easygoing, "an intelligent looking ladino, moderately well dressed but unshaven for days."

Despite the manifold attractions that the Cárdenas administration's political program and the president's personal style should have had for Traven, it is obvious that he objected to the new form of government. Cárdenas renewed emphasis on the central position of the state in national politics. In his inaugural address, the new president stressed that "the state alone embodies the general interest. . . . The state must continually broaden, increase, and deepen its intervention."[23] This involvement was the prime reason for the former anarchist's rejection of Cárdenas's revived revolutionary policies. As far as Traven was concerned, the revolution as he had known it in Tampico in 1924 and 1925 was dead.

Cárdenas took steps to concentrate control over workers and peasant movements fully in his own hands. His first move was to use the PNR apparatus to organize peasant leagues nationwide. The president then began to dispense patronage liberally to individual villages, thus creating a personal following independent of other power brokers such as local caudillos and *agrarista* groups. Control over land reform, and consequently over peasant movements, now rested firmly in the hands of the president and the bureaucracy of the Department of Agriculture. It was impossible for Traven to applaud such a development, even though it was designed to eliminate the political and economic domination of the landed classes and of quasi-feudal relations of production such as debt slavery.

Traven also lost all interest in the trade union organization, his first love in Mexico. The reason was obvious, in that the Mexican labor movement had also taken a course the aging anarchist could not welcome. Although 1935 and 1936 were years of great worker and peasant mobilization under the leadership of Lombardo Toledano and the Marxist-oriented Confederación General de Obreros y Campesinos Mexicanos (General Confederation of Mexican Workers and Peasants), the CGOCM, the anarcho-syndicalist traditions of the CGT had disappeared. In 1936 the CGOCM, the Mexican Communist Party, and various craft unions united in the Confederación de Trabajadores Mexicanos (Confederation of Mexican Workers). This federation, the CTM, was not as much a creation of the government as had been the CROM, but the unification of the labor movement in the CTM and Cárdenas's strong support of it gave the impression that the emergence of the CTM was the exclusive work of the state. CTM ideology was directed at improving the economic and moral conditions of the working class *within* the capitalist system. When the federation became part of the sectoral organization of the newly founded Partido Revolucionario Mexicano (Mexican Revolutionary Party) in 1938, the labor movement was subordinated to the Mexican state and was thus institutionalized. This was anathema to Traven, who rejected both government leadership of the workers' movement and accommodation within the capitalist system.

Traven's argument in *Ein General kommt aus dem Dschungel* revolves precisely around this development: the muchachos turned rebels begin to forget their initial revolutionary fervor. Their program shrinks the further they move away from the place of its inception. They are, in short, able to handle the military side of their struggle but not the creation of a new society. This was the bleakest and most unjust commentary Traven could have produced on the outcome of the Mexican Revolution, the only revolution he was privileged to witness that was not nipped in the bud. Traven's commentary, however, no longer reflected the state of Mexican politics but rather his own inflexible perception of the rights and wrongs of Mexico's postrevolutionary development.

Shortly after his arrival in Mexico, the enthusiastic Traven had sung about his newly adopted homeland: "All is green, the land of eternal summer. Oh, you beautiful, wonderful old country of Mexico, full of legends and songs! I had to sing . . . [and] I sang from a joyful heart." Now he saw Mexico very differently. In one of his concluding remarks in *Ein General kommt aus dem Dschungel* he wrote: "They knew their country, their beautiful, pitiful, and sorrowful country. They were born in this country and grew up in it. The revolver is not a piece of decoration. It is worn to be used at any opportunity and as in the case of war, if there was no opportunity, one would be created."[24] In the fifteen years that elapsed between Traven's arrival at Tampico and the publication of his last Jungle Novel, his vision of Mexico had radically changed. From being a dreamland it had become a wasteland where violence begets violence in an unchanging cycle. Traven was condemned to live with his disappointment for another thirty years.

Conclusion

By the standards Traven had set for himself as a writer, he had become redundant by 1940. His social and political ideals no longer fitted into the world in which he lived; he no longer had an adoring audience to instruct, nor was he any longer a political reporter. His later history demonstrates that he became aware of his own failing. He retired to his Cashew Park property near Acapulco, where he had the opportunity to realize Marut's dream of "placing a seed into the ground and making it sprout": he became an *agricultor*.[1] But he did not seem happy. He occupied most of his time revising his books, burned out and unable to produce anything new.

Traven formed part of a generation of leftist writers that viewed the Mexican Revolution as representing a deep and lasting break with old traditions and a movement of renewal and emancipation in the social, political, and economic fields. Many of his fellow writers were no less disappointed at the turn Mexican politics took after the halcyon days of the early Calles presidency. Where they did not stop writing on Mexico altogether, they observed the changes and commented on them.[2] Traven, however, lacked such flexibility and coolness. His work is characterized by great moral energy, which gave edge and vigor to his descriptions of Mexico and endeared him to his readers. He was passionate in his condemnations, in his affections, in his prejudices.

Yet, Traven loved to pretend that he worked scientifically. His travel notes, obviously written with a view to publication, paraded as those of a meteorologist cum geologist, although the writer Traven never made use of more than the anecdotal or gossipy from them. He lacked scientific training. *Land des Frühlings* was his only attempt to work in that mode, that is, to interpret his discoveries in Chiapas in light of "scientific" theories. Ultimately, he neither understood those theories, nor could he recognize the weakness of their scientific foundations. On the other hand, Traven was one of the first writers who, by 1929, had understood clearly that there were strong continuities between Mexico's prerevolutionary and postrevolutionary periods. Traven's Jungle Cycle is a record of these continuities. He no longer blamed outside forces, such as those originating in the United States, for the country's ills. Instead, he began to examine the part Mexican politicians and state authorities played in the failure of revolutionary ideals. Writing and publishing the Jungle Cycle was an act of great courage for Traven; it was also an act of ideological despair.

Traven's compassion and commitment to the proletarian cause was always tempered by a dogged single-mindedness and self-righteousness. When he realized in 1928 that his perception of Mexican politics of 1925 had been shallow and naïve, he never questioned the beliefs that induced his mistake. Even after three resounding failures of his ideological principles in Munich, Mexico, and Spain, his opinions never wavered. Instead, he preferred to reject a world that no longer accommodated his principles, even turning away from the Mexican Indians,[3] who, as he saw it, had failed to live up to his expectations. The erstwhile *indigenista*, who had sung the praises of Indian anticapitalism, never blamed his wrong perception of Indian customs and organization. When he was approached in 1938 to authorize a Spanish translation of *Die Rebellion der Gehenkten*, he refused. This would be understandable in light of the author's fears for his security, but the reason Traven gave—that "the Mexican proletariat has more important problems than reading novels"—was a most cavalier answer for a man who had dedicated his life's work to the struggle for Indian literacy.[4]

After World War II, Traven's political position, "so far to the left of the radical parties that his breath could not even touch them," as Marut had written, became unacceptable in the atmosphere of the Cold War. His anticapitalist and anti-imperialist analysis of the problems of a Third World country became unpopular. A critic of an American edition of *The Rebellion of the Hanged* (1952) wrote that "the novel has a wonderful opening, a dreadful and horrifying middle, and a flat and rhetorical ending."[5] Traven's books did not sell well in the United States.[6] In Germany, his books were sold at railway station kiosks next to penny dreadfuls, until Traven, together with other proletarian writers of the Weimar Republic, enjoyed a revival in the 1970s.

By the time his books became available in Mexico after the war,[7] the author had long reached the conclusion that his principal theme, Mexico, was no longer worth writing about. Although he no longer needed to fear extradition to Nazi Germany, nor persecution by the Mexican government, he had replaced his political convictions and his deep commitment to his adopted country with the empty gesticulations of an egocentric whose compulsive secrecy had become the most prominent aspect of his image. In the end, he abrogated responsibility for his work on Mexico, and the man who became obsessed with hiding his identity turned his back on everything his literary career had stood for. The gray-haired figure who appeared in John Huston's hotel room at dawn was only the shell of the writer who had created *Der Schatz der Sierra Madre.*

Notes

Introduction

1. A list of works by B. Traven appears in the Bibliography. After 1940 Traven did not cease writing. However, his literary output was very small. More importantly, the quality of his writing dropped to such low levels that it led to the suspicion that the author of *Aslan Norval* (1960) could not be the same man who wrote the Traven books. See Oskar Maria Graf, "Gelächter," in Johannes Beck et al., eds., *Das B. Traven Buch* (Hamburg, 1976), 110. The only exception to this suspicion was the novella *Macario* (Vienna: Büchergilde Gutenberg, 1950), which, however, might have been a fragment written much earlier.

2. Hans Jörg Martin, "Eine Trommel für Traven," in Beck, *Das B. Traven Buch*, 10.

3. Will Wyatt, *The Man Who Was B. Traven* (London, 1980), 40–41.

4. Quoted in Beck, *Das B. Traven Buch*, 26.

5. Quoted in Rolf Recknagel, *Beiträge zur Biographie des B. Traven* (Berlin, 1977), 32.

6. See the Traven biography, constructed by Charles H. Miller from allegedly autobiographical remarks, in "B. Traven: An American Author," *Texas Quarterly* 6 (Winter 1963): 162.

7. Karl Guthke, *B. Traven: Biographie eines Rätsels* (Frankfurt am Main, 1988).

8. Wyatt's *The Man Who Was B. Traven* is the account of the search for Traven's parents and also the history of the BBC program about Traven.

9. Michael Baumann, *B. Traven, An Introduction* (Albuquerque, 1976).

10. Hubert Jannach, "B. Traven: An American or German Author," *German Quarterly* 36 (1963): 359–468.

11. Rolf Recknagel, "Marut-Traven: Ein Stilvergleich," *Die andere Zeitung* (12 July 1962): 13. An expanded version of the documentation appears in idem, "Geheimnis und Geschäft: Zu B. Traven," *Neue Deutsche Literatur* 9 (1961): 86–109, 10:132–48.

12. Charlot Strasser, *Vier neue amerikanische Dichter* (Zurich, 1930).

13. Ronald G. Walker, *Infernal Paradise: Mexico and the Modern English Novel* (Berkeley, 1978). See also George Woodcock, "Mexico and the English Novelist," *Western Review* 21 (Autumn 1956): 22–32.

14. See D. H. Lawrence, *The Plumed Serpent* (1926; reprint, Harmondsworth, 1975). See also Graham Greene, *The Lawless Roads* (1939; reprint, Harmondsworth, 1979).

15. *Der Ziegelbrenner*, 18–19 (3 December 1918): 10.

16. Ibid., 35–40 (21 December 1921): 11.

17. The short-lived Munich Soviet Republic was one of the more radical manifestations of the centrifugal forces unleashed in Germany after the defeat of 1918. It was founded by leftist intellectuals after the assassination of the Bavarian prime minister Kurt Eisner. The new republic failed to create order out of chaos—a point Traven was to recognize clearly twenty years after the events—and was crushed by troops sent by the recently elected Socialist president of Germany, Friedrich Ebert.

18. *Der Ziegelbrenner*, 35–40 (21 December 1921): 11.

19. Traven, *Die Troza*, 186.

20. Letter written in 1919 by Ret Marut to his friend Götz Öhly's fiancée. Quoted in Recknagel, *Beiträge*, 109.

Chapter 1

1. Quoted in Wyatt, *The Man Who Was B. Traven*, 111.

2. It is most likely that Irene Mermet, Marut's associate from his Munich days who had legally emigrated to the United States, organized the letter, as she also used the same channel to send money to Marut in London.

3. Wyatt, *The Man Who Was B. Traven*, 240, 250, 251.

4. Unnumbered document, Traven Archives, Mexico City.

5. Tampico Post Records, letter dated 16 November 1923, Record Group 84, "General Correspondence," National Archives, Washington, DC (hereafter cited as RG 84, NA). I am indebted to Dr. Lief Adleson for allowing me access to this information. Consul Stewart's initials do not appear in the correspondence.

6. Quoted in Melvyn Dubofsky, *We Shall Be All* (New York, 1969), 155.

7. Barry Carr, *El movimiento obrero y la política en México, 1910–1929* (Mexico City, 1981), 155.

8. Lief Adleson, "Coyuntura y conciencia: Factores convergentes en la fundación de los sindicatos petroleros de Tampico durante la

década de 1920," in E. C. Frost et al., eds., *El trabajo y los trabajadores en la historia de México* (Mexico City, 1979), 632–33.

9. Another report on this strike informed the State Department in Washington that "it is interesting to note that the governor of the state encouraged the men in their unlawful procedure and actually congratulated the syndicate on the orderly . . . methods they had pursued." Undated and unsigned document, RG 84, NA.

10. Letter dated 24 March 1924, RG 84, NA.

11. Adleson, "Coyuntura," 656.

12. Letter by Consul Stewart, 22 April 1924, RG 84, NA.

13. Undated letter, RG 84, NA.

14. "Manifiesto anarquista del grupo Luz of 1912," quoted in John M. Hart, "The Urban Working Class and the Mexican Revolution: The Case of the Casa del Obrero Mundial," *Hispanic American Historical Review* 58, no. 1 (February 1978): 5.

15. Carr, *El movimiento obrero*, 95.

16. Irwin Granich, "One Big Union in Mexico," *One Big Union* 2, no. 1 (January 1920): 36.

17. Letter dated 8 May 1925, RG 84, NA.

18. Carr, *El movimiento obrero*, 82.

19. José Rivera Castro, *La clase obrera en la historia de México: La presidencia de Plutarco Elías Calles (1924–1928)* (Mexico City, 1983), 117.

20. Undated letter, RG 84, NA.

21. See Tzvi Medin, *El minimato presidencial: Historia política del maximato, 1928–1935* (Mexico City, 1982), 20–21.

22. Adleson, "Coyuntura," 633.

23. Ibid., 201.

24. Traven, *Die Baumwollpflücker* (Hamburg, 1962), 143.

25. Recknagel, *Beiträge*, 13.

26. Unnumbered document, Traven Archives.

27. This was one of the reasons why Harvey S. Leach's action in 1921 made him so unpopular in Tampico.

28. Such a union had actually been formed in 1924. Letter by Consul Stewart, 24 March 1924, RG 84, NA.

29. Traven, *Der Wobbly*, 87.

30. Traven, *Die Baumwollpflücker*, 77.

31. Adam Scharrer, "Traven und sein Erfolg," *Die Linkskurve* 3 (1932). Quoted in Recknagel, *Beiträge*, 211.

32. Ibid., 211.

33. Traven, *Die Baumwollpflücker*, 72.

34. Quoted in Dubofsky, *We Shall Be All*, 46.

35. "The Popular Wobbly," *One Big Union* 2, no. 4 (April 1920): 28.

36. Traven, *Die Baumwollpflücker*, 128.

37. Ibid., 92.

38. Ibid., 23.

39. Traven, *Der Schatz der Sierra Madre*, 9–10.

40. Lief Adleson, "Historia social de los obreros industriales de Tamaulipas, 1909–19" (Ph.D. diss., El Colegio de México, 1982), 327.

41. Traven, *Der Schatz der Sierra Madre*, 9.

42. Adleson, "Historia social," 325.

43. Traven, *Die Baumwollpflücker*, 94–95.

44. Ibid., 93.

45. Adleson, "Historia social," 329.

46. Traven, *Der Schatz der Sierra Madre*, 23.

47. Ibid., 25.

48. Traven, *Die Baumwollpflücker*, 92.

49. Ibid., 70.

50. Traven, *Land des Frühlings*, 204. This entire passage was deleted from the third edition.

51. Personal letter by Juany Olivo Maldonado, who is a friend of Traven's pupil and who made the inquiries on my behalf. In *Land des Frühlings* (pp. 245–46), Traven claimed that he once tried his luck as a tomato farmer but failed when the crop was destroyed by a disease. It is possible that this mishap befell Traven's landlord, the farmer Smith, rather than the author, who was merely a bystander.

52. *Vorwärts*, 21 June 1925, Beilage.

53. Quoted in Wyatt, *The Man Who Was B. Traven*, 26.

54. This photograph is reproduced in Recknagel, *Beiträge*, 164. Traven's correspondence with Ernst Preczang indicates that he had great difficulties coping with a tropical environment. He complained that "writing in these countries when one can't live in a modern hotel, when one has to live in a barrack or a hut, is hell. Not only one's brain, but one's bleeding hands and legs and cheeks, stung through and through by mosquitos and other hellish insects." Quoted in Wyatt, *The Man Who Was B. Traven*, 21. To refer to the house in the photograph as a "barrack or hut" seems unjustified and would only convince someone who had no idea of living conditions in the tropics. What tropical architecture was all about Traven would only understand after his first trip through the Lacandon Forest in Chiapas in 1928.

55. Quoted in Recknagel, *Beiträge*, 26.

56. Unnumbered document, Traven Archives.

57. *Ingeniero* is a title applied in Mexico to university-trained engineers.

58. The Southern Hotel was owned by Germans. All information relating to the Southern Hotel was kindly given to me by Dr. Lief Adleson.

59. Quoted in Wyatt, *The Man Who Was B. Traven*, 19.

60. See Carleton Beals, *Brimstone and Chili* (New York, 1927), esp. chap. 34.

61. Bernadette Scholl, "Die Büchergilde Gutenberg, 1924–1933," *Börsenblatt für den deutschen Buchhandel, Buchhandelsgeschichte* 76 (23 September 1983): B89.

62. This was one of the membership conditions reprinted in every issue of *Die Büchergilde*.

63. That is not to say that Preczang knew any more about Traven than did anyone else. Traven primarily fed his publisher information that was meant to cement the image of a daredevil American living in the Mexican jungle. Whatever *Die Büchergilde* published about the person of Traven had to be approved by the author first. No part of the correspondence between editor and author could be published. Recknagel, *Beiträge*, 22.

64. Scholl, "Die Büchergilde Gutenberg," B100.

65. Quoted in ibid., B90.

66. Quoted in Beck, *Das B. Traven Buch*, 27.

67. *Die Büchergilde* 3 (March 1931): 122.

68. Ibid. 2 (January 1931): 57.

69. Unnumbered document, Traven Archives.

70. Most of these stories are printed in Gabriél Antonio Menéndez, *Doheny el cruel* (Mexico City, 1958), esp. chap. 3. In *Land des Frühlings* (p. 275) Traven indicated that he was familiar with this kind of story.

71. Edward L. Doheny was "the perfect stereotype of the foreign capitalist in Latin America at the end of the nineteenth century; devoid of scruples, it was said, and ready to use any means within his reach to 'get rich quick' with no concern whatsoever for legitimate owners of this natural resource." Lorenzo Meyer, *Mexico and the United States in the Oil Controversy, 1917–1942* (Austin, 1972), 23.

72. Henry C. Smith, *The Roots of Lo Mexicano* (College Station, 1978), 111.

73. Meyer, *Mexico and the United States*, 13.

74. *Frente a Frente: Organo central de la liga de escritores y artistas revolucionarios*, 25 March 1936.

75. Charles R. Humphreys, "B. Traven: An Examination of the Controversy over His Identity with an Analysis of His Major Work and His Place in Literature" (Ph.D. diss., University of Texas, 1965), 118.

76. Traven, *Die weisse Rose*, 21.

77. Ibid., 25.

78. Ibid., 15.

79. Kurt Tucholsky [Peter Panter, pseud.], "B. Traven," *Die Weltbühne* 26 (25 November 1930): 794.

80. Traven, *Die weisse Rose*, 189.

81. Jorge Basurto, *El conflicto internacional en torno al petróleo mexicano* (Mexico City, 1980), 7.

82. See Jesús Silva Herzog, *Petróleo mexicano* (Mexico City, 1940), 68, 71, 76.

83. Traven, *Die weisse Rose*, 200. The CGT of Tampico condemned the de la Huerta Rebellion and the shooting of Governor Felipe Carrillo Puerto of Yucatán. On 4 January 1924, CGT-affiliated workers staged a massive demonstration in the streets of Tampico. María Luisa Serna, "Cronología: Las luchas obreras de 1924," *Historia Obrera* 21 (January 1981): 8.

84. Carr, *El movimiento obrero*, 142.

85. Traven, *Die weisse Rose*, 202.

86. Meyer, *Mexico and the United States*, 283 n.196.

87. Ernest Gruening, *Mexico and Its Heritage* (1928; reprint, New York, 1968), 600.

88. *Científico* (scientist) was the title given to the technocrats and advisers of Porfirio Díaz.

89. Traven, *Die weisse Rose*, 167.

90. Heather Fowler Salamini, "Revolutionary Caudillos in the 1920s: Francisco Múgica and Adalberto Tejeda," in D. A. Brading, ed., *Caudillo and Peasant in the Mexican Revolution* (Cambridge, 1980), 189–90.

91. Traven, *Die weisse Rose*, 128.

Chapter 2

1. André Gunder Frank, *Capitalism and Underdevelopment in Latin America* (1969; reprint, Harmondsworth, 1971).

2. Quoted in Scholl, "Die Büchergilde Gutenberg," B94.

3. Lawrence Hill, publisher, personal letter to author, Westport, CT, 6 January 1987.

4. Enrique Krauze et al., *La reconstrucción económica: Período 1924–1928* (Mexico City, 1977), 21.

5. Quoted in John W. F. Dulles, *Yesterday in Mexico: A Chronicle of the Revolution, 1919–1936* (Austin, 1961), 281.

6. Traven, *Land des Frühlings*, 17.

7. Ibid., 220.

8. Ibid., 42.

9. Ibid., 102.

10. Ibid., 45.

11. Ibid., 361.
12. Gruening, *Mexico and Its Heritage*, 339–40. See also Serna, "Cronologia," 24.
13. Scholl, "Die Büchergilde Gutenberg," B94.
14. Moisés Sáenz, *México íntegro* (1939; reprint, Mexico City, 1982), 93, 95, 96.
15. Traven, *Land des Frühlings*, 25.
16. Frank Tannenbaum, "The Miracle School," *The Century Magazine* (August 1924): 394–423.
17. Traven, *Land des Frühlings*, 211–12.
18. Camile-Nick Buford, "A Biography of Luis N. Morones: Mexican Labor and Political Leader" (Ph.D. diss., Louisiana State University, 1971), 102.
19. Krauze, *La reconstrucción económica*, 24.
20. Traven, *Land des Frühlings*, 419.
21. Ibid., 42.
22. Frank Tannenbaum, *Peace by Revolution: Mexico after 1910* (1933; reprint, New York, 1966), 227.
23. Traven, *Land des Frühlings*, 24.
24. Ibid., 18.
25. Ibid., 346.
26. Ibid., 351.
27. Gruening, *Mexico and Its Heritage*, 550.
28. Alan Knight, *The Mexican Revolution* (Cambridge, 1986), 2: 500.
29. Meyer, *Mexico and the United States*, 30.
30. Traven, *Land des Frühlings*, 415.
31. Krauze, *La reconstrucción económica*, 110.
32. Ibid., 115.
33. Quoted in Hans-Werner Tobler, *Die mexikanische Revolution* (Frankfurt am Main, 1984), 523.
34. Traven, *Land des Frühlings*, 221; Carleton Beals, "Mexico Seeking Central American Leadership," *Current History* (September 1926): 829–44. A Spanish translation of this article can be found in *Boletín del Archivo General de la Nación* 11 (January–March 1980).
35. Traven, *Land des Frühlings*, 222.
36. Ibid., 221.
37. Jean Meyer, *The Cristero Rebellion: The Mexican People Between Church and State, 1926–1929* (Cambridge, 1976), 35.
38. Dulles, *Yesterday in Mexico*, 300.
39. Traven, *Land des Frühlings*, 76–77. See also Alfons Goldschmidt, "Der Kirchenkampf in Mexiko," *Tagebuch* (1926–1927): 1237; and Gruening, *Mexico and Its Heritage*, 281.
40. Dulles, *Yesterday in Mexico*, 306.

41. Traven knew the details of these events and recounted them in his own exaggerated fashion. See *Land des Frühlings*, 38.

42. As in Chamula, where the abandoned church can still be seen at the outskirts of town, the Zinacantán church was abandoned because the saints worshipped in it had failed to "deliver" what they were asked. Their statues were placed at the entrance of the new church and stripped of their elaborate garments. The church of Zinacantán was later repaired.

43. See also Alfons Goldschmidt, *Die dritte Eroberung Amerikas* (Berlin, 1929), 36.

44. Traven, *Land des Frühlings*, 77.

45. The only evidence of such baptisms for the year 1924 is recorded for the city of Torreón in Coahuila where only two proletarian children were baptized. Only one socialist wedding is recorded for 1924. See Serna, "Cronología," 13, 18.

46. Quoted in Meyer, *The Cristero Rebellion*, 44.

47. See Goldschmidt, "Der Kirchenkampf in Mexiko," 1236.

48. Jean Meyer noted that high office in government was only obtainable by Freemasons and that "Mexican anticlericalism, though the work of a minority, was that of a minority in power." Meyer, *The Cristero Rebellion*, 30, 44.

49. Jean Meyer, *La Cristiada* (Mexico City, 1974), 3: 273.

50. *Excélsior*, 1 March 1927.

51. Gruening, *Mexico and Its Heritage*, 279.

52. Traven, *Der Schatz der Sierra Madre*, 94.

53. Traven, *The Treasure of the Sierra Madre* (Cambridge, MA, n.d.), 137. This is a reprint of the 1935 Alfred A. Knopf edition.

54. Tannenbaum, *Peace by Revolution*, 248.

55. Quoted in Anatol Shulgovski, *México en la encrucijada de su historia* (Mexico City, 1968), 46.

56. Traven, *Land des Frühlings*, 153.

57. The expression was coined by Jean Meyer and is quoted in Tobler, *Die mexikanische Revolution*, 487.

58. Quoted in Renate Rott, *Die mexikanische Gewerkschaftsbewegung* (Kronberg/Taunus, 1975), 96.

59. Tobler, *Die mexikanische Revolution*, 491.

60. Carr, *El movimiento obrero*, 163.

61. Traven, *Land des Frühlings*, 93.

62. Ibid., 357.

63. Ibid.

64. Quoted in Robert Freeman Smith, *The United States and Revolutionary Nationalism in Mexico, 1916–1932* (Chicago, 1972), 232.

65. Traven, *Land des Frühlings*, 346.

66. Ibid., 328.

67. Ibid., 207.

Chapter 3

1. Unnumbered document, Traven Archives, Mexico City.

2. Juan Enrique Palacios, *En los confines de la selva lacandona: Exploraciones en el estado de Chiapas* (Mexico City, 1928), 7.

3. Traven, *Land des Frühlings*, 52. Traven also mentioned the government's efforts to fight locust plagues, but he never connected his trip with this issue. See *Land des Frühlings*, 246–47.

4. Gertrude Duby, "The Lacandons," in Evan Z. Vogt, ed., *Handbook of Middle American Indians* (Austin, 1969), 7: 279. Alfred Tozzer, the earliest of these explorers, even lived among the Lacandons for two years.

5. Traven repeated this mistake in *Der Karren*, where Estrellita tells Andreu Ugalde—both Tzeltal Indians of the Mayan race—a story of the birth of the sun that is an Aztec legend.

6. Traven, *Land des Frühlings*, 52.

7. Quoted in Jonah Raskin, *My Search for B. Traven* (New York, 1980), 210.

8. Traven, *Land des Frühlings*, 259. He repeated this point in *Marsch ins Reich der Caoba*, 182.

9. Personal letter by Helvine Hess, daughter of Ewald Hess, to author, dated Guadalajara, 25 October 1985.

10. Traven, *Land des Frühlings*, appendix, 42.

11. Wolfgang Cordan, "Ben Traven-Torsvan," *Die Kultur* (15 October 1958), 9. Personal interview with Adalbert Hotzen, coffee planter from San Carlos, Chiapas, Mexico City, March 1984.

12. Thomas Benjamin, "Passages to Leviathan: Chiapas and the Mexican State, 1891–1947" (Ph.D. diss., Michigan State University, 1981), 188–89.

13. This office opened in 1903 and still existed in the 1930s. Antonio García de León, *Resistencia y utopia* (Mexico City, 1985), 2: 172–73.

14. Wolfgang Cordan, *Mayakreuz und rote Erde* (Zurich, 1960), 78.

15. Traven, *Land des Frühlings*, 102.

16. Ibid., 272. Traven already knew about *tiendas de raya* in Tampico. See *Die Baumwollpflücker*, 126.

17. Ibid., 368.

18. Ibid., 174.

19. The *enganchadores* retained one third of the workers' salary as their commission. Cordan, *Mayakreuz*, 78.

20. Traven, *Land des Frühlings*, 166.

21. Ibid., 84.

22. Frank Tannenbaum, "Agrarismo, indianismo y nacionalismo," *Hispanic American Historical Review* 23 (August 1943): 400.

23. A. Nolden, *Auf Schiffen, Schienen und Pneus: Eine Erzählung* (Selbstverlag, 1928), 92. Nolden professed to have observed this court-

ship ritual on a farm near "San Juan" which, according to the geographical details he supplied, must be San Juan Bautista (Villahermosa) in Tabasco.

24. Traven, *Land des Frühlings*, 157.

25. Ricardo Pozas, *Juan the Chamula: An Ethnological Recreation of the Life of a Mexican Indian* (Berkeley, 1962), 57.

26. Traven, *Land des Frühlings*, 55.

27. Secretaría de la Presidencia, *Chiapas, monografía del estado de Chiapas* (Mexico City, 1975), 120–22.

28. Traven, *Land des Frühlings*, 99.

29. Ibid., 303.

30. Ibid., 323.

31. Victoria Reifler-Bricker, *Ritual Humor in Highland Chiapas* (Austin, 1973), 5.

32. Only in 1931 did Traven finally give up that house and write to his American neighbors that they were free to take from it what they wanted. Unnumbered document, Traven Archives.

33. David Raby, *Educación y revolución en México* (Mexico City, 1974), 29, 26.

34. Plutarco Elías Calles, *Mexico Before the World: Public Documents and Addresses of Plutarco Elías Calles* (New York, 1927), 79.

35. Julian Pitt-Rivers, "Palabras y hechos: Los ladinos," in *Ensayos de antropología en la zona central de Chiapas*, ed. Julian Pitt-Rivers and Norman McQuown (Mexico City, 1970), 26.

36. Traven, *Land des Frühlings*, 43.

37. Angel Corzo, *Historia de Chiapas: Los cuentos del abuelo* (Mexico City, 1943?), 14.

38. Traven, *Land des Frühlings*, 232.

39. Ibid.

40. Ibid., 202.

41. Henri Favre, *Cambio y continuidad entre las mayas de México* (Mexico City, 1973), 337.

42. Edward Weston, *Daybooks*, Nancy Newhall, ed. (New York, 1961), 1:34.

43. Traven, *Land des Frühlings*, 141.

44. Ibid., 294.

45. Ibid., 295.

46. Ibid., 206.

47. Vicente Pineda, *Historia de la sublevaciones indígenas habidas en el estado de Chiapas y gramática de la lengua Tzel-tal* (Chiapas, 1888), 100.

48. Eric Wolf, *Sons of the Shaking Earth* (Chicago, 1959), 218–19. See also Wolfgang Cordan, *Versuch über das Unzerstörbare* (Düsseldorf, 1955), 54.

49. Cordan, *Mayakreuz*, 87–89.

50. Traven, *Land des Frühlings*, 19.

51. The most complete account of the events of 1911 from the Tuxtla Gutiérrez viewpoint is Luis Espinosa, *Rastros de sangre: Historia de la revolución en Chiapas* (Mexico City, 1944), esp. p. 206 concerning *el desorejamiento*.

52. For the history of the ill-fated Chamula leader, see Prudencio Moscoso Pastrana, *Jacinto Pérez "Pajarito": Ultimo líder chamula* (Chiapas, 1977).

53. Traven, *Land des Frühlings*, 428.

54. Ibid., 344.

55. This ending of *Der Schatz der Sierra Madre* seems to have sustained John Huston's interest. When the director made *Under the Volcano* after the novel by Malcolm Lowry, the film ended unlike the novel. Instead, three mean, dirty, and well-armed mestizos in a solitary inn on a deserted road kill the Consul in cold blood. The Mexican cameraman Gabriel Figueroa, a close friend of Traven, collaborated with Huston in the making of both films.

56. Traven, *Land des Frühlings*, 344.

57. Personal letter by Helvine Hess to author, 25 October 1985.

58. Traven, *Land des Frühlings*, 231.

59. Traven, *Die Brücke im Dschungel* (Hamburg, 1980), 40.

60. Traven, *Land des Frühlings*, 413.

61. Traven, *Die Brücke im Dschungel*, 95.

62. Traven, *Die weisse Rose*, 34.

63. Krauze, *La reconstrucción económica*, 27.

64. John Hart, *Anarchism and the Mexican Working Class, 1860–1931* (Austin, 1978), 173–74.

Chapter 4

1. The attendance certificates at the summer school of the Mexican national university in 1927 and 1928 form part of Traven's naturalization file in the Ministry of Foreign Affairs, Mexico City.

2. Unnumbered document, Traven Archives.

3. Diary page, entries for 25, 27, 28 January 1928, Traven Archives.

4. Diary page, entry for 6 February 1928, Traven Archives.

5. Traven, *Der Karren*, 96.

6. Cordan, *Secret of the Forest*, 28, 32.

7. Personal interview with José Hernández Rúiz, timber feller, in Ocosingo, 7 May 1984.

8. Unnumbered document, Traven Archives.

9. Unnumbered document, letter dated 15 November 1929, Traven Archives.

10. Personal interview with Pedro Vega Martínez, Tenosique, Tabasco, 24 April 1984.

11. Benjamin, "Passages to Leviathan," 194.

12. Ibid., 197.

13. Antonio García de León, "Lucha de clases y poder político en Chiapas," *Historia y Sociedad* 22 (1979): 75.

14. Archivo General de la Nación (subsequently given as AGN), Ramo de Trabajo, C692/5, dated 11 January 1928. The *Sindicato de obreros y campesinos de Tuxtla Chica/Chiapas* sent promptly a complaint to the Ministry of Labor in Mexico City, stating that its members were called on "to work six days to preserve the roads and tracks." No reply seems to have been received from Mexico City.

15. Traven commented on this law twice, in *Der Karren*, p. 173, and in *Regierung*, p. 241.

16. Diary pages, entries for 27 December 1929 to 8 January 1930, Traven Archives.

17. Diary pages, entries for 11 to 13 January 1930, Traven Archives.

18. Diary pages, entry for 29 January 1930, Traven Archives.

19. Personal interview with José Toriello Bulnes, former manager of the San Quintín *montería*, Mexico City, 12 May 1984.

20. Traven, *Der Karren*, 107.

21. Cuauhtémoc González Pacheco, *Capital extranjero en la selva de Chiapas, 1863–1982* (Mexico City, 1983), 69.

22. Personal interview with José Hernández Rúiz.

23. Cordan, *Secret of the Forest*, 29.

24. Unnumbered documents, Traven Archives.

25. Personal interview with Rosa Elena Luján, Traven's widow, Mexico City, March and April 1984.

26. Pedro Vega [Pablo Montañez, pseud.], *La Lacandonia* (Mexico City, n.d.), 59.

27. Ibid., 60.

28. Personal interview with Pedro Vega.

29. Medin, *El minimato presidencial*, 24.

30. Lorenzo Meyer et al., *Los inicios de la institucionalización: La política del maximato, período 1928–1934* (Mexico City, 1978), 40.

31. Guillermina Baena Paz, "La Confederación General de Trabajadores, 1921–1931," *Revista Mexicana de Ciencias Políticas y Sociales* 83 (January-March 1976): 123, 132, 135.

32. Ibid., 121.

33. Ibid., 166.

34. Krauze, *La reconstrucción económica*, 211.

35. Quoted in Jean Meyer et al., *Estado y sociedad con Calles: Período 1924–1928* (Mexico City, 1977), 306.

36. John Carroll, *Break-out from the Crystal Palace: The Anarcho-Psychological Critique: Stirner, Nietzsche, Dostoevsky* (London, 1974), 54.

37. Tobler, *Die mexikanische Revolution*, 406. Institutionalization became a magical word for Calles, and it figured predominantly in several of his *informes*. See also Medin, *El minimato presidencial*, 40–41.

38. Quoted in Dulles, *Yesterday in Mexico*, 406.

39. Quoted in Meyer, *Los inicios*, 44.

40. Medin, *El minimato presidencial*, 41.

41. Meyer, *Los inicios*, 100. See also Dulles, *Yesterday in Mexico*, 469.

42. José Vasconcelos, "El vasconcelismo," in Orlando Ortiz, ed., *La violencia en México* (Mexico City, 1971), 298.

43. "Las camisas rojas," in Ortiz, *La violencia*, 310.

44. Robert E. Scott, "Mexican Government in Transition," in James W. Wilkie and Albert L. Michaels, eds., *Revolution in Mexico: Years of Upheaval, 1910–1940* (New York, 1969), 176.

45. Meyer, *Los inicios*, 111.

46. Dulles, *Yesterday in Mexico*, 419.

47. Meyer, *Los inicios*, 85.

48. Medin, *El minimato presidencial*, 182.

49. Hans-Werner Tobler, "Las paradojas del ejército mexicano," *Historia Mexicana* 81 (July-September 1971): 53. Examples of this kind of corruption can be found in nearly every history of the period.

50. Medin, *El minimato presidencial*, 179, 217.

51. *Die Büchergilde* 2 (1931): 260.

52. Diary page, entry for 29 December 1929, Traven Archives. Such incidents of government interference are indeed recorded. See Juan Jaime Maguén E., *La violencia en Chamula* (n.p., n.d.), 17. One of the caciques killed at Chamula was called Salvador Lopez Setjól; another who was kept in his post by soldiers is simply referred to as Agustín.

53. *Frente a Frente*, 25 March 1936.

54. Friedrich Katz, *The Secret War in Mexico: Europe, the United States, and the Mexican Revolution* (Chicago, 1981), 11.

55. Ibid., 14.

56. Knight, *The Mexican Revolution*, 2:88.

57. Alicia Hernández Chávez, "La defensa de los finqueros en Chiapas, 1914–1920," *Historia Mexicana* 3 (1979): 356.

58. Cordan, *Secret of the Forest*, 27.

59. Hernández Chávez, "La defensa," 337, 340.

60. García de León, *Resistencia y utopia*, 2:51.

61. Prudencio Moscoso Pastrana, *El Pinedismo en Chiapas, 1916–1920* (Mexico City, 1960), 29.

62. Karl Kärger, *Landwirtschaft und Kolonisation im spanischen Südamerika* (Leipzig, 1902?), 2:547.

63. Benjamin, "Passages to Leviathan," 141, 144.

64. Ibid., 151.

65. Ibid.

66. García de León, *Resistencia y utopia*, 2:137.

67. Daniela Spenser, "La reforma agraria y la contraofensiva de los finqueros cafetaleros" (typescript, n.d.), 2.

68. Pedro Vega, personal interview. Manuel Bulnes is his uncle.

69. Personal interview with Arturo Trinidad, Ocosingo, 7 May 1984. Arturo Trinidad is the son of Victorino Trinidad.

70. Traven, *Der Karren*, 35.

71. Instituto Nacional Indigenista, *El indigenismo en acción* (Mexico City, 1976), 90.

72. Traven, *Der Karren*, 193.

73. Ibid., 216.

74. See Benjamin, "Passages to Leviathan." See also Spenser, "La reforma agraria," 24–26.

75. Traven, *Der Karren*, 29.

76. Ibid., 108.

77. Benjamin, "Passages to Leviathan," 220.

78. Oliver La Farge and Franz Blom, *Tribes and Temples: A Record of the Expedition to Middle America by the Tulane University of Louisiana* (New Orleans, 1926), 2:325.

79. Friederike Baumann, "B. Traven's Land des Frühlings and the Caoba Cycle as a Source for the Study of Agrarian Society," in Philip Jenkins and Ernst Schürer, eds., *B. Traven: Life and Work* (University Park, 1987), 248.

80. Maguén, *La violencia en Chamula*, 16.

81. AGN, Ramo de Trabajo, 1010/11, Cancúc 1 May 1926.

82. *Más Allá: Revista Católica* (San Cristóbal de las Casas) (13 November 1911): 3. For information concerning electoral fraud in Ocosingo, see also Gral Brigadier Eduardo Paz (Jesús Agustín Castro's predecessor as governor), *La cuestión económica y política local en Chiapas* (Mexico City, 1912), 36–37.

83. *Die Büchergilde* 2 (1931): 260.

84. Traven, *Regierung*, 140.

85. AGN, Ramo de Trabajo, 494/15/10, 5 August 1922.

86. Traven, *Regierung*, 64.

87. Ibid., 81.

88. Ibid., 94.

89. Ibid., 245.

90. John Kenneth Turner's *Barbarous Mexico*, first published in *The American Magazine* in October 1909, caused a furor in the United States as well as in Porfirian Mexico. It was based on the author's experiences during a trip through Mexico in 1908 and 1909, when he discovered

the crassest forms of debt slavery in the Valle Nacional in Oaxaca and on the hemp plantations of Yucatán. The painter José Clemente Orozco honored Turner by including him in his huge mural of forerunners of the 1910 Revolution in the Palacio Nacional in Mexico City. Henry Baerlein, in *Mexico: Land of Unrest* (London, 1912), confirmed Turner's findings about labor conditions on the hemp plantations of Yucatán.

91. "También en México hay 'infiernos,' " *El Universal*, 11 January 1926.

92. Baena Paz, "La Confederación General de Trabajadores," 158.

93. Alan Knight, "Mexican Peonage: What is it and why was it?" *Journal for Latin American Studies* 18 (May 1986): 42.

94. Traven, *Marsch ins Reich der Caoba*, 178.

95. Ibid., 179.

96. Prudencio Moscoso Pastrana, *La tierra lacandona: Sus hombres y sus problemas* (Mexico City, 1986), 104.

97. Personal interview with Pedro Vega.

98. For an account of Pancho Celorio, see Pepe Bulnes, *Personajes tabasqueños* (Mexico City, n.d.), 406.

99. Personal interview with Juan Celorio Hernández, Villahermosa, Tabasco, 25 April 1984. The same story was told by José Toriello Bulnes, in a personal interview, 12 May 1984.

100. Traven, *Marsch ins Reich der Caoba*, 149.

101. Traven, *Regierung*, 172.

102. Golo Mann, *Deutsche Geschichte des 19. und 20. Jahrhunderts* (Frankfurt am Main, 1958), 783.

103. Traven, *Regierung*, 174. Compare with *Der Ziegelbrenner* 16–17 (10 March 1919): 23.

104. See Sebastian Haffner, *Die verratene Republik* (Munich, 1969), esp. 125–47. See also Tankred Dorst, ed., *Die Münchner Räterepublik* (Frankfurt am Main, 1966), esp. 179.

105. Traven, *Marsch ins Reich der Caoba*, 149.

106. *Die Büchergilde* 9 (1931): 122.

107. Traven, *Regierung*, 172.

108. Preczang to Traven, 18 May 1933, quoted in Scholl, "Die Büchergilde Gutenberg," B101.

109. Traven to Preczang, 23 May 1933, ibid.

110. Ibid.

111. See "Gespräch mit Theo Pinkus," in Frederik Hetmann, *Der Mann, der sich verbarg: Nachforschungen über B.Traven* (Stuttgart, 1983), 233.

112. Monika Sperr, "Von Traven lernte ich zweierlei: Mitgefühl und Widerstand," in Beck, *Das B. Traven Buch*, 355.

113. Hansjörg Martin, "Eine Trommel für Traven," in Beck, *Das B. Traven Buch*, 9–10.

114. *Die Büchergilde* (April 1936), quoted in Recknagel, *Beiträge*, 28.

115. August Souchy, "Aus meiner Traven Mappe," in Beck, *Das B. Traven Buch*, 104.

116. Humphreys, "B. Traven: An Examination of the Controversy," 62.

Chapter 5

1. "Exploraciónes del río Usumacinta o de la Pasión, departamento de Ocozingo, Chiapas, año 1822," *Boletín del Archivo General de Chiapas* 3 (August-September 1954): 76.

2. See Juan Ballinas, *El desierto de los Lacandones* (Tuxtla Gutiérrez, 1951).

3. Marcela Tostado Gutiérrez, *El Tabasco Porfiriano* (Villahermosa, 1985), 39.

4. Personal interview with Trinidad Malpica Hernández, journalist and former timber feller, Villahermosa, 23 April 1984.

5. AGN, Ramo de Gobierno, caja 1/carp. 16. Unsigned document entitled "La situación política en Tabasco, 1912."

6. Francisco F. Santamaría, *Bibliografía general de Tabasco* (Mexico City, 1926), 376, 474.

7. Cordan, *Secret of the Forest*, 21. Officially, the Bulnes family "acquired" its land in small lots of not more than 2,500 hectares each, as the law stipulated before the Tierras Baldías Act. Cuauhtémoc González Pacheco notes that the titles for these tracts do not have a purchasing price. It seems that the land was never meant to be paid for. Marcela Tostado Gutiérrez, however, found evidence that the Casa Bulnes paid 50 centavos per hectare in 1881 for 120,000 hectares of forest land in Chiapas.

8. For the operation of the Tierras Baldías Act in the Lacandon Forest, see González Pacheco, *Capital extranjero*, 66, 68, 83. See also Jan de Vos, "Una legislación de graves consecuencias," *Historia Mexicana* 34 (July-September 1984): 76–113.

9. Tostado Gutiérrez, *El Tabasco Porfiriano*, 104.

10. By 1908, Tabasco was desperately short of farmhands, and laborers were, therefore, imported. In that year, *El Eco de Tabasco* reported on a number of occasions that Yaqui Indians from Sonora were being "resettled" in the Romano *monterías*. Ibid., 100.

11. González Pacheco, *Capital extranjero*, 114.

12. Moisés de la Peña, *Chiapas económico* (Tuxtla Gutiérrez, 1951), 1:319. Isolated instances of abuse in the *monterías* persisted. In 1939,

Francisco Bolivar made a representation on behalf of ninety-seven *montería* workers to President Cárdenas stating that the men had not been paid for three years. AGN, Ramo Cárdenas, doc.501.1/236, 24 June 1939. Thomas Benjamin found a similar complaint against the Agua Azul Mahogany Company maintaining that all former abuses continued as before. Thomas Benjamin, "El Trabajo en las monterías de Chiapas y Tabasco, 1870–1946," *Historia Mexicana* 30 (April-June 1981): 521–22.

13. Personal interview with Trinidad Malpica Hernández.

14. Jorge Engerrand and Fernando Urbina, *Informe sobre una excursión geológica a Palenque en el alto Usumacinta y en el estado de Campeche* (Mexico City, 1908), 24.

15. Oficina de Informaciones de Chiapas, *Chiapas: Su estado actual, su riqueza, sus ventajas para los negocios* (Mexico City, 1895), 17.

16. Gustavo López Gutiérrez, *Chiapas y sus epopeyas libertarias* (Tuxtla Gutiérrez, 1932), 2:189.

17. Alberto Correa, *Reseña económica de Tabasco* (Mexico City, 1899), 140.

18. Alfonso Taracena, *Historia de la revolución en Tabasco* (Mexico City, 1981), 1–174.

19. This was confirmed by General Domínguez's secretary, Major Manuel Bolivar Súarez. He made "many copies" of the document for distribution, one of which was shown to Duby in 1946. José Colorado Palma, "Don Luis Felipe Domínguez," *Revista de Tabasco* (27 February 1946): 40.

20. Gertrude Duby and Franz Blom, *La selva lacandona* (Mexico City, 1955), 1:67.

21. See Moscoso Pastrana, *La tierra lacandona*, chap. 5, "Rivalidades entre monteros," 100–102.

22. "México desconocido: Las monterías de Chiapas," *Universidad de México* (February 1931): 326.

23. Moscoso Pastrana, *La tierra lacandona*, 75, 104.

24. "México desconocido," 326–27.

25. Quoted in González Pacheco, *Capital extranjero*, 107.

26. Personal interview with José Toriello Bulnes.

27. Personal interview with Eliecér Mendoza Cambrano, Emiliano Zapata, Tabasco, 19 April 1984.

28. Moscoso Pastrana, *La tierra lacandona*, 20.

29. Quoted in *Más Allá*, 13 November 1910, 3.

30. González Pacheco, *Capital extranjero*, 111.

31. Personal interview with Pedro Vega.

32. Tostado Gutiérrez, *El Tabasco Porfiriano*, 133.

33. Mario Domínguez Vidal, *Las selvas de Tabasco* (Mexico City, 1942), 147.

34. Benjamin, "Passages to Leviathan," 151.
35. González Pacheco, *Capital extranjero*, 109.
36. "También en México hay 'infiernos,' " 326.
37. Quoted in González Pacheco, *Capital extranjero*, 109.
38. "El cáncer de Chiapas," *El País*, 18 April 1911.
39. *Más Allá*, 13 November 1911. See also Duby and Blom, *La selva lacandona*, 1: 281.
40. José Domingo Ramírez Garrido, *La esclavitud en Tabasco* (San Juan Bautista, 1915), 12. See also "México desconocido," 326.
41. Tostado Gutiérrez, *El Tabasco Porfiriano*, 69.
42. Quoted in Ramírez Garrido, *La esclavitud*, 9–12. This publication is comprised of the text of a speech General Ramírez Garrido (cousin of Tomás Garrido Canabal) delivered before his fellow officers during a dinner at San Juan Bautista in September 1914. The purpose of this speech was to convince his fellow revolutionaries of the necessity to pass a law to liberate the serfs of the state.
43. Ibid.
44. Quoted in González Pacheco, *Capital extranjero*, 110.
45. Personal interview with Eliecér Mendoza Cambrano. See also Manuel González Calzada, *42 grados a la sombra* (Mexico City, 1954), 22.
46. González Pacheco, *Capital extranjero*, 110.
47. Ibid.
48. "México desconocido," 326.
49. Traven, *Die Troza*, 64.
50. Pedro Vega [Pablo Montañez, pseud.], *Jataté/Usumacinta* (Mexico City, n.d.), 37.
51. De la Peña, *Chiapas económico*, 2:677.
52. Domínguez Vidal, *Las selvas de Tabasco*, 148–49.
53. Quoted in Duby and Blom, *La selva lacandona*, 1:281.
54. One of these companies was called the Sociedad Agrícola Posada, Romano y Cía de Macuspana. This company exported fresh fruit and received a state subsidy in the form of tax exemption. Tostado Gutiérrez, *El Tabasco Porfiriano*, 95.
55. The Casa Romano employed three hundred Indian peons at San Vicente. González Pacheco, *Capital extranjero*, 111.
56. Quoted in Duby and Blom, *La selva lacandona*, 1:281.
57. "México desconocido," 326.
58. Personal interview with José Rúiz Hernández.
59. Ibid. However, as one observer noted, "*chicleros* were a superstitious lot." Vega, *La Lacandonia*, 79.
60. Tostado Gutiérrez, *El Tabasco Porfiriano*, 124.
61. Ramírez Garrido, *La esclavitud*, 3–4.
62. Tostado Gutiérrez, *El Tabasco Porfiriano*, 132.

63. Duby and Blom, *La selva lacandona*, 1:324. Pedro Vega, who knew Ramírez in his youth, recounted the same story in *Jataté/Usumacinta* at much greater length. Cordan also mentioned this legendary escape. The story today forms part of the surviving *montería* lore.

64. Personal interview with José Toriello Bulnes.

65. Personal interview with Pedro Vega.

66. Vega, *Jataté/Usumacinta*, 35.

67. Vega, *La Lacandonia*, 60.

68. Personal interview with José Toriello Bulnes.

69. "El que no se aclimita, se aclimuere." González Pacheco, *Capital extranjero*, 93.

70. Personal interview with Pedro Vega.

71. Personal interview with José Toriello Bulnes.

72. Moscoso Pastrana, *La tierra lacandona*, 76.

73. Personal interview with Pedro Vega. Many of these rather substantial houses, built or bought by either former oxdrivers or timber fellers, can still be seen in Tenosique and Ocosingo.

74. González Pacheco, *Capital extranjero*, 103.

75. Cristóbal Rendón Trujillo, "La producción de caoba en México y el problema de su exportación" (Ph.D. diss., Escuela Nacional de Agricultura, UNAM, 1945), 31.

76. Traven, *Die Troza*, 91.

77. This information came from José Toriello Bulnes and is cited in González Pacheco, *Capital extranjero*, 107, footnote.

78. Pedro Vega [Pablo Montañez, pseud.], "Los hombres de hierro" (typescript, n.d.), 23.

79. José Coffin, *El General Gutiérrez* (1912; reprint, Mexico City, 1980), 12.

80. Saúl Escobar Toledo, "La acumulación capitalista en el Porfiriato," *Cuadernos de trabajo del departamento de investigaciones históricas INAH* 31 (1980): 19, 24.

81. Coffin, *El General Gutiérrez*, 12–13.

82. Ibid., 13.

83. Personal interview with Juan Celorio Hernández.

84. Traven, *Die Troza*, 23.

85. Cordan, *Secret of the Forest*, 33.

86. Carlos Basauri, *Tojolabales, Tzeltales y Mayas* (Mexico City, 1931), 136.

87. Personal interview with Juan Celorio Hernández.

88. Traven, *Die Troza*, 75.

89. Cordan, *Secret of the Forest*, 115, 152.

90. Ibid., 128.

91. Traven, *Die Troza*, 144.

92. De la Peña, *Chiapas económico*, 2: 677–78.

93. González Pacheco, *Capital extranjero*, 91.

94. Personal interview with Juan Celorio Hernández.

95. Rendón Trujillo, "La producción de caoba," 80.

96. De la Peña, *Chiapas económico*, 2:676. Pedro Vega and José Toriello Bulnes made the same point.

97. Personal interview with Juan Celorio Hernández. This story was also confirmed by José Toriello Bulnes.

98. Basauri, *Tojolabales, Tzeltales y Mayas*, 135.

99. Quoted in González Pacheco, *Capital extranjero*, 146.

100. Ibid., 149. This was also confirmed by Pedro Vega and José Toriello Bulnes.

101. Ibid., 147.

102. Cordan, *Secret of the Forest*, 33.

103. Traven, *Die Rebellion der Gehenkten*, 78.

104. Ibid., 79.

105. Ibid., 183.

106. Ibid., 179.

107. Vega, *Jataté/Usumacinta*, 44.

108. Quoted in Cordan, *Secret of the Forest*, 37.

109. Vega, *La Lacandonia*, 60.

110. Cordan, *Secret of the Forest*, 152.

111. Duby and Blom, *La selva lacandona*, 1:242.

112. Quoted in González Pacheco, *Capital extranjero*, 129.

113. Ibid., 129.

114. Ibid., 130. This information came from José Toriello Bulnes.

115. Personal letter by Pedro Vega to author, 22 September 1988.

116. De la Peña, *Chiapas económico*, 2:677.

117. González Pacheco, *Capital extranjero*, 139.

118. "México desconocido," 326.

119. Traven, *Die Troza*, 119.

120. Ibid., 85.

121. Ibid., 134.

122. Ibid., 147.

123. Personal interview with Trinidad Malpica Hernández.

124. González Pacheco, *Capital extranjero*, 143.

125. Duby and Blom, *La selva lacandona*, 1:276.

126. Traven, *Die Rebellion der Gehenkten*, 99. It was reported from Los Tzendales that men were hanged by their hands, with their feet twenty centimeters above ground, and whipped with a horsewhip. Moscoso Pastrana, *La tierra lacandona*, 122.

127. De la Peña, *Chiapas económico*, 2:671.

128. Personal interview with Pedro Vega.

129. Traven, *Die Troza*, 189, 235.

130. Vega, *Jataté/Usumacinta*, 147. Mijares Escandón was an uncle of Pedro Vega.

131. *Der Ziegelbrenner* 20–22 (6 June 1920). Cited in Recknagel, *Beiträge*, 130.

132. Traven, *Die Rebellion der Gehenkten*, 8–9.

133. Ibid., 131, 125.

134. Humphreys, "An Examination of the Controversy," 120.

135. Benjamin, "El trabajo en las monterías," 515.

136. Taracena, *Historia de la revolución en Tabasco*, 1:174.

137. Traven, *Die Rebellion der Gehenkten*, 53.

138. Ibid., 64.

139. Ibid., 75.

140. Ibid., 72.

141. Ibid., 129.

142. Ibid., 254.

143. Ibid., 255.

144. Ibid., 227.

Chapter 6

1. Manuel Rosado G., *Alto Ahí! Quién vive?* (Mexico City, 1976), 152.

2. *Estado de Tabasco: Actuación política y militar del Señor General de Brigada don Luis Felipe Domínguez* (n.p., n.d.), 7.

3. Ibid., 6.

4. Mario Domínguez Vidal, *El plagio del General de División don José Domingo Ramírez Garrido* (n.p., n.d.), 7. This work responds to José Domingo Ramírez Garrido, *Así fué* (Mexico City, 1943). For details on the smear campaign against General Domínguez, see Taracena, *Historia de la revolución en Tabasco*, 1:296; and Joaquín Rúiz, *La revolución en Tabasco* (Mexico City, 1934), 15–17.

5. Benjamin, "Passages to Leviathan," 132.

6. Traven, *Ein General kommt aus dem Dschungel*, 42.

7. Ibid., 43.

8. Personal interview with Rosa Elena Luján.

9. Cordan, *Secret of the Forest*, 32.

10. Beck, *Das B. Traven Buch*, 45.

11. Allert de Lange was an exiled German publishing house operating from Amsterdam and concentrating on antifascist literature such as Bertolt Brecht's "The Threepenny Opera."

12. Traven, *Ein General kommt aus dem Dschungel*, 31–32.

13. Ibid., 33.

14. Ibid., 29, 31.

15. Ibid., 30, 31.

16. Ibid., 30.

17. Eyler N. Simpson, *The Ejido: Mexico's Way Out* (Chapel Hill, 1937), 216.

18. Ibid., 712. Simpson estimated that an ejidatario earned 44 centavos a day whereas a day laborer earned 80 centavos. The needs of a rural family, however, totaled two pesos per day.

19. Romana Falcón, *El agrarismo en Veracruz: La etapa radical, 1928–1935* (Mexico City, 1977), 13.

20. The ejidal sector's share of the total national food production rose from 11 percent in 1930 to 50.5 percent in 1940. Manfred Mols and Hans-Werner Tobler, *Die institutionalisierte Revolution* (Vienna, 1976), 155.

21. Nora Hamilton, *The Limits of State Autonomy: Post-Revolutionary Mexico* (Princeton, 1982), 134.

22. Traven, *Ein General kommt aus dem Dschungel*, 93. This passage is more than vaguely reminiscent of a scene Max Miller witnessed in Chiapas, when he observed land reform officials staging a theatrical appearance before bamboozled peons of one estate after another. Max Miller, *Mexico Around Me* (New York, 1937), 54–59.

23. Quoted in Hamilton, *The Limits of State Autonomy*, 121.

24. Traven, *Ein General kommt aus dem Dschungel*, 94.

Conclusion

1. This is the profession indicated on Traven's naturalization papers.

2. Alfons Goldschmidt, a Marxist economist, wrote *Tierra y libertad: El desarollo campesino en México* (Mexico City, 1940). Frank Tannenbaum produced *Peace by Revolution: Mexico after 1910*, a discussion of the same developments.

3. Personal interview with Rosa Elena Luján.

4. Quoted in Humphreys, "B. Traven: An Examination of the Controversy," 120.

5. Ibid., 246.

6. Baumann, *B. Traven: An Introduction*, 80, 97.

7. *La puente en la selva*, a 1941 translation of *Die Brücke im Dschungel*, Traven's politically least controversial book, was the first authorized Spanish edition of one of the novels to appear in Mexico. In 1946, *El tesoro de la Sierra Madre* was published, followed by *La carreta* in 1949, *La rebelión de los colgados* and *El barco de la muerte* in 1950, and *Gobierno* and *La rosa blanca* in 1951.

Bibliography

Published Works by B. Traven

Der Ziegelbrenner (The brick burner), written and edited under the name of Ret Marut. Published irregularly between June 1917 and December 1921, mostly in Munich.
"Die Baumwollpflücker" (The cottonpickers), *Vorwärts*, 21 June–2 July 1925.
Das Totenschiff (The death ship) (Berlin: Büchergilde Gutenberg, 1926).
Der Wobbly (The Wobbly) (Leipzig: Buchmeister Verlag, 1926).
Der Schatz der Sierra Madre (The treasure of the Sierra Madre) (Berlin: Büchergilde Gutenberg, 1927).
Land des Frühlings (The land of spring) (Berlin: Büchergilde Gutenberg, 1928).
Der Busch (The bush) (Berlin: Büchergilde Gutenberg, 1928). This is a collection of short stories, all set in Mexico.
Die Baumwollpflücker (Leipzig: Buchmeister Verlag, 1929). This is a revised edition of *Der Wobbly*.
Die Brücke im Dschungel (The bridge in the jungle) (Berlin: Büchergilde Gutenberg, 1929).
Die weisse Rose (The white rose) (Berlin: Büchergilde Gutenberg, 1929).
Der Busch (Berlin: Büchergilde Gutenberg, 1930). This is an expanded collection of short stories.
Der Karren (The cart) (Berlin: Büchergilde Gutenberg, 1931), published in English translation as *The Carreta*.
Regierung (Government) (Berlin: Büchergilde Gutenberg, 1931).
Der Marsch ins Reich der Caoba (The march to the empire of mahogany) (Prague: Büchergilde Gutenberg, 1933), published in English translation as *March to the Montería*.
Die Troza (The trunk) (Prague: Büchergilde Gutenberg, 1936).
Die Rebellion der Gehenkten (The rebellion of the hanged) (Zurich: Büchergilde Gutenberg, 1936).
Die Sonnenschöpfung (The creation of the sun) (Zurich: Büchergilde Gutenberg, 1936). This Aztec legend initially formed part of *Der Karren*.

Djungelgeneralen (Stockholm: Axel Holmström, 1939), published in English translation as *A General from the Jungle*. The German text of the last volume of the Jungle Cycle was published as *Ein General kommt aus dem Dschungel* (A general comes from the jungle) (Amsterdam: Allert de Lange, 1940).

"La tercera guerra mundial" (The third world war), *Estudios Sociales* 11–12 (1945): 9–16.

Macario (Vienna: Büchergilde Gutenberg, 1950).

"Dennoch eine Mutter" (Still a mother), *Neue Illustrierte* 6 (9 May 1951): 25–27, 29–30, 35.

"His Wife's Legs," *Accused Detective Story Magazine* (New York), July 1956.

"An Unexpected Solution," *Short Stories* (New York) (June 1957): 62.

"Ceremony Slightly Delayed," *The Saint* (New York) (October 1957): 88–104.

Aslan Norval (Vienna: Kurt Desch, 1960).

"Der Sarg auf dem Bus: Eine Kurzgeschichte aus Südamerika" (The coffin on the bus: A short story from South America), *Wir Brückenbauer* (Zurich) (10 June 1966): 23.

Archives

Traven Archives, Río Mississippi, Mexico City.

Archivo General de la Nación, Mexico City.

Ethel Duffy Turner Collection, Museo de Antropología, Mexico City.

Archivo General de Chiapas, Tuxtla Gutiérrez.

National Archives, Washington, DC, Tampico Post Records, Record Group 84, "General Corresspondence," 1924. This material was made available to me by Dr. Lief Adleson, Mexico City.

Interviews

Celorio Hernández, Juan. Timber feller. Villahermosa, Tabasco. 25 April 1984.

Luján, Rosa Elena. Widow of B. Traven. Mexico City. March and April 1984.

Malpica Hernández, Trinidad. Journalist and former timber feller. Villahermosa, Tabasco. 23 April 1984.

Mendoza Cambrano, Eliecér. Chronicler of the township of Emiliano Zapata, Tabasco. 19 April 1984.

Mora, Manuel. Former governor of Tabasco. Villahermosa, Tabasco. 12, 17, 19 April 1984.

Moscoso Pastrana, Prudencio. Historian. San Cristóbal de las Casas, Chiapas. 1, 4 May 1984.
Palma de Smith, Sra. Traven's former pupil in Cuauhtémoc, Tamaulipas. Interview conducted by Juany Olivo Maldonado, January 1985.
Ruíz Hernández, José. Timber feller. Ocosingo. 7 May 1984.
Trinidad, Arturo. Son of Traven's friend Victorino Trinidad. Ocosingo. 7 May 1984.
Toriello Bulnes, José. Former manager of the San Quintín logging camp. Mexico City. 12 May 1984.
Vega Martínez, Pedro. Son of the last owner of the San Quintín logging camp. Tenosique, Tabasco. 24 April 1984.

Books

Adleson, Lief. "Coyuntura y conciencia: Factores convergentes en la fundación de los sindicatos petroleros de Tampico durante la década de 1920." In *El trabajo y los trabajadores en la historia de México*, edited by Elsa Cecilia Frost, Michael C. Meyer, Josefina Zoraida Vázquez, and Lilia Díaz. Mexico City, 1979.
Baerlein, Henry. *Mexico: Land of Unrest*. London, 1912.
Ballinas, Juan. *El desierto de los Lacandones*. Tuxtla Gutiérrez, 1951.
Basauri, Carlos. *Tojolabales, Tzeltales y Mayas*. Mexico City, 1931.
Basurto, Jorge. *El conflicto internacional en torno al petróleo mexicano*. Mexico City, 1980.
Baumann, Friederike. "B. Traven's Land des Frühlings and the Caoba Cycle as a Source for the Study of Agrarian Society." In *B. Traven: Life and Work*, edited by Philip Jenkins and Ernst Schürer. University Park, 1987.
Baumann, Michael. *B. Traven: An Introduction*. Albuquerque, 1976.
Beals, Carleton. *Brimstone and Chili*. New York, 1927.
Beck, Johannes, Bergmann, Klaus, and Boehncke, Heiner. *Das B. Traven Buch*. Hamburg, 1976.
Bulnes, Pepe. *Personajes tabasqueños*. Mexico City, n.d.
Calles, Plutarco Elías. *Mexico Before the World: Public Documents and Addresses of Plutarco Elías Calles*. New York, 1927.
Carr, Barry. *El movimiento obrero y la política en México, 1910–1929*. Mexico City, 1981.
Carroll, John. *Break-out from the Crystal Palace: The Anarcho-Psychological Critique: Stirner, Nietzsche, Dostoevsky*. London, 1974.
Coffin, José. *El General Gutiérrez*. 1912. Reprint. Mexico City, 1980.
Cordan, Wolfgang. *Mayakreuz und rote Erde*. Zurich, 1960.
———. *Secret of the Forest: On the Track of the Maya Temples*. London, 1963.

————. *Versuch über das Unzerstörbare.* Düsseldorf, 1955.

Correa, Alberto. *Reseña económica de Tabasco.* Mexico City, 1899.

Corzo, Angel. *Historia de Chiapas: Los cuentos del abuelo.* Mexico City, 1943?

Dominguez Vidal, Mario. *La Brigada Usumacinta.* N.p., n.d.

————. *El plagio del General de División don José Domingo Ramírez Garrido.* N.p., n.d.

————. *Las selvas de Tabasco.* Mexico City, 1942.

Dorst, Tankred, ed. *Die Münchner Räterepublik.* Frankfurt am Main, 1966.

Dubofsky, Melvyn. *We Shall Be All.* New York, 1969.

Duby, Gertrude. "The Lacandons." In *Handbook of Middle American Indians,* edited by Evon Z. Vogt. Austin, 1969.

Duby, Gertrude, and Blom, Franz. *La selva lacandona.* 2 vols. Mexico City, 1955.

Dulles, John W. F. *Yesterday in Mexico: A Chronicle of the Revolution, 1919–1936.* Austin, 1961.

Engerrand, Jorge, and Urbino, Fernando. *Informe sobre una excursión geológica a Palenque en el alto Usumacinta y en el estado de Campeche.* Mexico City, 1908.

Espinosa, Luis. *Rastros de sangre: Historia de la revolución en Chiapas.* Mexico City, 1944.

Estado de Tabasco: Actuación política y militar del señor General de Brigada don Luis Felipe Domínguez. N.p., n.d.

Falcón, Romana. *El agrarismo en Veracruz: La etapa radical, 1928–1935.* Mexico City, 1977.

Favre, Henri. *Cambio y continuidad entre las mayas de México.* Mexico City, 1973.

Frank, André Gunder. *Capitalism and Underdevelopment in Latin America.* 1969. Reprint. Harmondsworth, 1971.

García de León, Antonio. *Resistencia y utopia.* 2 vols. Mexico City, 1985.

Goldschmidt, Alfons. *Auf den Spuren der Azteken: Ein mexikanisches Reisebuch.* Berlin, 1927.

————. *Die dritte Eroberung Amerikas.* Berlin, 1929.

————. *Mexiko.* Berlin, 1925.

————. *Tierra y libertad: El desarollo campesino en México.* Mexico City, 1940.

González Calzada, Manuel. *42 grados a la sombra.* Mexico City, 1954.

González Pacheco, Cuauhtémoc. *Capital extranjero en la selva de Chiapas, 1863–1982.* Mexico City, 1983.

Greene, Graham. *The Lawless Roads.* 1939. Reprint. Harmondsworth, 1979.

Gruening, Ernest. *Mexico and Its Heritage.* 1928. Reprint. New York, 1968.

Guthke, Karl. *B. Traven: Biografie eines Rätsels.* Frankfurt am Main, 1988.

Haffner, Sebastian. *Die verratene Republik.* Munich, 1969.

Hamilton, Nora. *The Limits of State Autonomy: Post-Revolutionary Mexico.* Princeton, 1982.

Hart, John. *Anarchism and the Mexican Working Class, 1860–1931.* Austin, 1978.

Hetmann, Frederik. *Der Mann, der sich verbarg: Nachforschungen über B. Traven.* Stuttgart, 1983.

Instituto Nacional Indigenista. *El indigenismo en acción.* Mexico City, 1976.

Kärger, Karl. *Landwirtschaft und Kolonisation im spanischen Südamerika.* Leipzig, 1902?

Katz, Friedrich. *The Secret War in Mexico: Europe, the United States and the Mexican Revolution.* Chicago, 1981.

Knight, Alan. *The Mexican Revolution.* 2 vols. Cambridge, 1986.

Krauze, Enrique, Meyer, Jean, and Reyes, Cayetano, eds. *La reconstrucción económica: Período 1924–1928.* Volume 10 of *Historia de la revolución mexicana.* Mexico City, 1977.

La Farge, Oliver, and Blom, Franz. *Tribes and Temples: A Record of the Expedition to Middle America by the Tulane University of Louisiana.* 2 vols. New Orleans, 1926.

Lawrence, D. H. *The Plumed Serpent.* 1926. Reprint. Harmondsworth, 1975.

López Gutiérrez, Gustavo. *Chiapas y sus epopeyas libertarias.* 3 vols. Tuxtla Gutiérrez, 1932.

Maguén E., Juan Jaime. *La violencia en Chamula.* N.p., n.d.

Mann, Golo. *Deutsche Geschichte des 19. und 20. Jahrhunderts.* Frankfurt am Main, 1958.

Medin, Tzvi. *El minimato presidencial: Historia política del maximato, 1928–1935.* Mexico City, 1982.

Menéndez, Gabriel Antonio. *Doheny el cruel.* Mexico City, 1958.

Meyer, Jean. *The Cristero Rebellion: The Mexican People Between Church and State, 1926–1929.* Cambridge, 1976.

———. *La Cristiada.* 3 vols. Mexico City, 1974.

Meyer, Jean, Krauze, Enrique, and Reyes, Cayetano, eds. *Estado y sociedad con Calles: Período 1924–1928.* Volume 11 of *Historia de la revolución mexicana.* Mexico City, 1977.

Meyer, Lorenzo. *Mexico and the United States in the Oil Controversy, 1917–1942.* Austin, 1972.

Meyer, Lorenzo, Segovia, Rafael, and Lajous, Alejandro, eds. *Los inicios de la institucionalización: La política del maximato, período 1928–1934.* Volume 12 of *Historia de la revolución mexicana.* Mexico City, 1978.

Miller, Max. *Mexico Around Me.* New York, 1937.

Mols, Manfred, and Tobler, Hans-Werner. *Mexiko: Die institutionalisierte Revolution.* Vienna, 1976.

Moscoso Pastrana, Prudencio. *Jacinto Pérez "Pajarito": Ultimo lider chamula*. Chiapas, 1972.

———. *El Pinedismo en Chiapas, 1916–1920*. Mexico City, 1960.

———. *La tierra lacandona: Sus hombres y sus problemas*. Mexico City, 1986.

Nolden, A. *Auf Schiffen, Schienen und Pneus: Eine Erzählung*. Selbstverlag, 1928.

Oficina de Informaciones de Chiapas. *Chiapas: Su estado actual, su riqueza, sus ventajas para los negocios*. Mexico City, 1895.

Palacios, Juan Enrique. *En los confines de la selva lacandona: Exploraciones en el estado de Chiapas*. Mexico City, 1928.

Paz, Eduardo. *La cuestión económica y política local en Chiapas*. Mexico City, 1912.

Peña, Moisés de la. *Chiapas económico*. 2 vols. Tuxtla Gutiérrez, 1951.

Pineda, Vicente. *Historia de las sublevaciones indígenas habidas en el estado de Chiapas y gramática de la lengua Tzel-Tal*. Chiapas, 1888.

Pitt-Rivers, Julian. "Palabras y hechos: Los ladinos." In *Ensayos de antropología en la zona central de Chiapas*, edited by Julian Pitt-Rivers and Norman McQuown. Mexico City, 1970.

Pozas, Ricardo. *Juan the Chamula: An Ethnological Recreation of the Life of a Mexican Indian*. Berkeley, 1962.

Raby, David. *Educación y revolución en México*. Mexico City, 1974.

Ramírez Garrido, José Domingo. *Así fué*. Mexico City, 1943.

———. *La esclavitud en Tabasco*. San Juan Bautista, 1915.

Raskin, Jonah. *My Search for B. Traven*. New York, 1980.

Recknagel, Rolf. *Beiträge zur Biografie des B. Traven*. Berlin, 1977.

Reifler-Bricker, Victoria. *Ritual Humor in Highland Chiapas*. Austin, 1973.

Rivera Castro, José. *La clase obrera en la historia de México: La presidencia de Plutarco Elías Calles, 1924–1928*. Mexico City, 1983.

Rosado G., Manuel. *Alto ahí! Quién vive?* Mexico City, 1976.

Rott, Renate. *Die mexikanische Gewerkschaftsbewegung*. Kronberg/ Taunus, 1975.

Rúiz, Joaquín. *La revolución en Tabasco*. Mexico City, 1934.

Sáenz, Moisés. *México íntegro*. 1939. Reprint. Mexico City, 1982.

Salamini, Heather Fowler. "Revolutionary Caudillos in the 1920s: Francisco Múgica and Adalberto Tejeda." In *Caudillo and Peasant in the Mexican Revolution*, edited by D. A. Brading. Cambridge, 1980.

Santamaría, Francisco F. *Bibliografía general de Tabasco*. Mexico City, 1926.

Scott, Robert. "Mexican Government in Transition." In *Revolution in Mexico: Years of Upheaval, 1910–1940*, edited by James W. Wilkie and Albert L. Michaels. New York, 1969.

Secretaría de la Presidencia. *Chiapas, monografía del estado de Chiapas*. Mexico City, 1975.

Shulgovski, Ánatol. *México en la encrucijada de su historia*. Mexico City, 1968.

Silva Herzog, Jesús. *Petróleo mexicano*. Mexico City, 1940.
Simpson, Eyler N. *The Ejido: Mexico's Way Out*. Chapel Hill, 1937.
Smith, Henry C. *The Roots of Lo Mexicano*. College Station, 1978.
Smith, Robert Freeman. *The United States and Revolutionary Nationalism in Mexico, 1916–1932*. Chicago, 1972.
Strasser, Charlot. *Vier neue amerikanische Dichter*. Zurich, 1930.
Tannenbaum, Frank. *Peace by Revolution: Mexico after 1910*. 1933. Reprint. New York, 1966.
Taracena, Alfonso. *Historia de la revolución en Tabasco*. 2 vols. Mexico City, 1981.
Tobler, Hans-Werner. *Die mexikanische Revolution*. Frankfurt am Main, 1984.
Tostado Gutiérrez, Marcela. *El Tabasco Porfiriano*. Villahermosa, 1985.
Turner, John Kenneth. *Barbarous Mexico*. 1910. Reprint. Austin, 1969.
Vasconcelos, José. "El vasconcelismo." In *La violencia en México*, edited by Orlando Ortiz. Mexico City, 1971.
Vega, Pedro [Pablo Montañez, pseud.]. *Jataté/Usumacinta*. Mexico City, n.d.
————. *La Lacandonia*. Mexico City, n.d.
Walker, Ronald G. *Infernal Paradise: Mexico and the Modern English Novel*. Berkeley, 1978.
Weston, Edward. *Daybooks*. 2 vols. Edited by Nancy Newhall. New York, 1961.
Wolf, Eric. *Sons of the Shaking Earth*. Chicago, 1959.
Wyatt, Will. *The Man Who Was B. Traven*. London, 1980.

Articles

Baena Paz, Guillermina. "La Confederación General de Trabajadores, 1921–1931." *Revista Mexicana de Ciencias Políticas y Sociales* 83 (January-March 1976): 113–86.
Beals, Carleton. "Mexico Seeking Central American Leadership." *Current History* (September 1926): 829–44.
Benjamin, Thomas. "El trabajo en las monterías de Chiapas y Tabasco, 1870–1946." *Historia Mexicana* 30 (April-June 1981): 506–29.
Colorado Palma, José. "Don Luis Felipe Domínguez." *Revista de Tabasco* (27 February 1946): 30–40.
Cordan, Wolfgang. "Ben Traven-Torsvan." *Die Kultur* (15 October 1958): 9–10.
Escóbar Toledo, Saúl. "La acumulación capitalista en el Porfiriato." *Cuadernos de trabajo del departamento de investigaciones históricas INAH* 31 (1980).

"Exploraciones del río Usumacinta o de la Pasión, departamento de Ocozingo, Chiapas, año 1822." *Boletín del Archivo General de Chiapas* 3 (August-September 1954): 73–103.

García de León, Antonio. "Lucha de clases y poder político en Chiapas." *Historia y Sociedad* 22 (1979): 57–89.

Goldschmidt, Alfons. "Der Kirchenkampf in Mexiko." *Tagebuch* (1926–1927): 1236–38.

Granich, Irwin. "One Big Union in Mexico." *One Big Union* 2 (January 1920): 35–38.

Hart, John M. "The Urban Working Class and the Mexican Revolution: The Case of the Casa del Obrero Mundial." *Hispanic American Historical Review* 58, no.1 (February 1978): 1–21.

Hernández Chávez, Alicia. "La defensa de los finqueros en Chiapas, 1914–1920." *Historia Mexicana* 3 (1979): 325–61.

Jannach, Hubert. "B. Traven: An American or German Author?" *German Quarterly* 36 (1963): 359–468.

Knight, Alan. "Mexican Peonage: What is it and why was it?" *Journal for Latin American Studies* 18 (May 1986): 41–76.

"México desconocido: Las monterías de Chiapas." *Universidad de México* (February 1931): 323–30.

Miller, Charles Henry. "B. Traven: American Author." *The Texas Quarterly* 6 (Winter 1963): 162–68.

"The Popular Wobbly." *One Big Union* 2, no. 4 (April 1920): 28.

Recknagel, Rolf. "Marut-Traven: Ein Stilvergleich." *Die andere Zeitung* (12 July 1962): 13.

———. "Geheimnis und Geschäft: Zu B. Traven." *Neue deutsche Literatur* 9 (February 1961): 86–109; 10 (March 1961): 132–48.

Scharrer, Adam. "Traven und sein Erfolg." *Die Linkskurve* 3 (1932): 29–32.

Scholl, Bernadette. "Die Büchergilde Gutenberg, 1924–1933." *Börsenblatt des deutschen Buchhandels, Buchhandelsgeschichte* 76 (23 September 1983): B89–108.

Serna, María Luisa. "Cronología: Las luchas obreras de 1924." *Historia Obrera* 6 (January 1981): 7–24.

"También en México hay 'infiernos': Monterías en donde no hay protección al trabajador." *El Universal*, 11 January 1926.

Tannenbaum, Frank. "Agrarismo, indianismo y nacionalismo." *Hispanic American Historical Review* 23 (August 1943): 394–423.

———. "The Miracle School." *The Century Magazine* 106 (August 1923): 499–506.

Tobler, Hans-Werner. "Las paradojas del ejército mexicano." *Historia Mexicana* 81 (July-September 1971): 38–79.

Tucholsky, Kurt [Peter Panter, pseud.]. "B. Traven." *Die Weltbühne* 26 (25 November 1930): 793–800.

Vos, Jan de. "Una legislación de graves consecuencias." *Historia Mexicana* 34 (July-September 1984): 76–113.

Woodcock, George. "Mexico and the English Novelist." *Western Review* 21 (Autumn 1956): 22–32.

Unpublished Sources

Adleson, Lief. "Historia social de los obreros industriales de Tamaulipas, 1909–1919." Ph.D. diss., El Colegio de México, 1982.

Benjamin, Thomas. "Passages to Leviathan: Chiapas and the Mexican State, 1891–1947." Ph.D. diss., Michigan State University, 1981.

Buford, Camile-Nick. "A Biography of Luis N. Morones: Mexican Labor and Political Leader." Ph.D. diss., Louisiana State University, 1971.

Humphreys, Charles Robert. "B. Traven: An Examination of the Controversy over His Identity with an Analysis of His Major Work and His Place in Literature." Ph.D. diss., University of Texas, 1965.

Rendón Trujillo, Cristóbal. "La producción de caoba en México y el problema de su exportación." Ph.D. diss., Escuela Nacional de Agricultura, UNAM, 1945.

Spenser, Daniela. "La reforma agraria y la contraofensiva de los finqueros cafetaleros." Typescript, n.d.

Vega, Pedro [Pablo Montañez, pseud.]. "Los hombres de hierro." Typescript, n.d.

Newspapers

Die Büchergilde (Berlin), 1936.

El Eco de Tabasco (Villahermosa), 1911.

El Héraldo de Chiapas (San Cristóbal de las Casas), 1911.

El País (Mexico City), 1910–1912.

El Universal (Mexico City), 1924–1926.

Excélsior (Mexico City), 1926–1927.

Frente a frente: Organo central de la liga de escritores y artistas revolucionarios (Mexico City), 1936.

La Voz de Chiapas (Tuxtla Gutérrez), 1911.

Más Allá: Revista Católica (San Cristóbal de las Casas), 1911.

One Big Union (reprint, New York), 1919–1920.

Vorwärts: Zentralorgan der Sozialdemokratischen Partei Deutschlands (Berlin), 1925.

Index

Chamula Indians, 37, 38, 44, 69,
70, 72, 75, 87, 124, 202; in
1869, 82–83; in 1911, 84–85;
in *monterías*, 168; in Traven's
fiction, 125, 188, 194;
religious practices, 71, 73,
74, 88, 107
Chatto and Windus (London),
132
Chiapa de Corzo, 86, 150
Chiapas: geography, 55, 70, 87,
123, 167, 184, 194, 202;
history, 66, 145, 184, 193–
95, 198; Indians of, 66, 69,
129; logging camps of, xxii,
35, 48, 107, 142, 191; political and social conditions,
46, 67, 68, 94–96, 106, 109–
13, 122, 139; population, 68,
74, 75, 79, 80, 95, 108, 120,
171; reception of Traven's
books in, 98; timber industry of, 43, 67, 93, 97, 100,
136–38, 155, 159, 163 (*see
also* Logging business);
treatment of peons in, 147–
48, 150–52, 166, 177, 181,
205 (*see also* Casa Vega;
Mijares Escandón,
Fernando; San Quintín;
San Roman Tzendales);
Traven's first trip to, 10, 21,
22, 27, 34, 37, 38, 41, 43–46,
57, 66, 81, 88, 94, 209;
Traven's literary treatment
of, 35, 85, 98, 100, 107, 118,
126; Traven's second trip
to, 48, 61, 63, 65, 68, 89, 91,
93, 100; Traven's third trip
to, 93, 95, 97, 100, 102, 111,
135
Chihuahua, 108, 109
Chilón, 67, 68, 117, 119, 141
Ciudad del Carmen, 145, 161
Ciudad Juárez, 7

Coahuila, 108, 206
Coffee Growers' Association
(Chiapas), 69
Coffin, José, 160–63
Collins, Mr. (character), 29–32,
34, 35
Colombia, 16, 89
Columbus (Tamaulipas), 2, 12,
21, 22
Comalcalco, 155
Comitán, 64, 67, 91, 92, 194, 195
Comiteco, 73, 119
Communist Party of Mexico,
101, 207
Communists, 9
Condor Oil Company, 29, 30, 34,
35
Confederación de Trabajadores
Mexicanos (CTM), 102, 207
Confederación General de
Obreros y Campesinos
Mexicanos (CGOCM), 207
Confederación General de
Trabajadores (CGT), 4, 7, 9,
49, 122; decline of, 58–59,
101–2, 106, 207; influence on
Traven, 17, 32, 38, 74; in
Tampico, 8, 10, 14, 38, 48,
89, 104, 129, 189
Confederación Nacional de
Trabajadores (CNT) (Spain),
133
Confederación Regional Obrera
Mexicana (CROM), 4, 7, 9,
54, 56; as instrument of
government, 8, 10, 57–59;
decline of, 101–2, 207; in
Chiapas, 38, 46, 67; in
Tamaulipas, 48
Constitution of 1917, 6, 27, 28,
48, 50, 54, 55, 95
Constitutionalist Army, 66, 108–
11
Constitutionalist government,
185, 198

Contratistas (contractors), 159, 176
Coolidge administration, 33
Cooperatives, 50, 51
Cordan, Wolfgang, 140, 144
Cortés, Hernán, 63
Corzo, Angel, 79
Cristeros, 56, 57
Croves, Hal, xv, xvi, xviii, xix, 125
Cruz, Celso, 193, 194
Cuauhtémoc, 21, 32, 85
Cuernavaca, 95, 101, 104

Debt slavery, 94, 106, 126, 156
Las Delicias, 199
El desorejamiento, 84, 85
Díaz, Felix, 184
Díaz, Porfirio, 136–38; adherents of, 61; dictatorship, 27, 107, 111, 123, 141, 193, 202; overthrow, 66; Traven's literary treatment of, 124
Dobbs, Fred C., xv, 17–19, 22, 23, 86, 87
Döblin, Alfred, 131
Doheny, Edward L., 27, 32–34
Domínguez, General Luis Felipe, 142, 143, 145, 147, 153, 196–98
Domínguez Vidal, Mario, 147, 151, 152
Doux, Señor, 12–14, 16, 17
Dressler, Bruno, 130, 131
Duby, Gertrude, 65, 98, 140, 144, 155
Durango, 86, 206

Ebert, Friedrich, 129
Ein General kommt aus dem Dschungel (Traven), xviii, 83, 155, 191, 200–206, 208; geography of, 199; source for, 194, 196, 198
Eisenstein, Sergei, 200
Eisner, Kurt, 189
Ejidos, 51, 52, 204, 205
Electric Company of Tampico, 5–6, 9, 13, 14
Electricians' union, 9
Emiliano Zapata (Tabasco), 146, 193
Enganchadores (labor contractors), 69, 148, 155, 166, 167, 176, 177
Enganche, 177
Engerrand, Jorge, 141
Erlebnisträger theory, xviii
Escobar Rebellion, 104

Felipe (Traven's *mozo*), 64, 65, 71, 75, 85, 87
Fernández Ruiz, Tiburcio, 66, 67, 96, 109–11
Fiesta de San Juan, 71–74, 80, 87, 188
Flores, Celso, xxii, 97, 121, 168, 180, 186; and group action, 124, 177, 178, 187, 189, 190, 202; second contract, 123, 167
Franco, Francisco, 133
Frank, André Gunder, 37
Frente a frente (journal), 29, 107
Frontera, 94, 145, 161

Gabriel (character), 73, 118, 119, 121, 123, 126, 174, 177, 199
Gale, Gerard, xvii, 22, 23, 34, 85, 87; as Traven's narrator, 2–13, 15, 60; as Wobbly, 16, 17
Gamio, Manuel, 76
Gañanes (oxdrivers' assistants), 160, 162, 163, 170, 178, 181
Garrido Canabal, Tomás, 49, 54, 94, 147
German Printers' Guild, 12, 24
Germany, 13, 69, 133, 183; labor organizations in, 3; Marut in, xxii; Nazi Germany, 43, 126–27, 135, 211; Socialist Party in, 11, 24, 40, 127, 128;

Other Volumes Published in the Latin American Silhouettes Series

William H. Beezley and Judith Ewell, eds., *The Human Tradition in Latin America: The Twentieth Century* (1987). Cloth ISBN 0-8420-2283-X Paper ISBN 0-8420-2284-8

Judith Ewell and William H. Beezley, eds., *The Human Tradition in Latin America: The Nineteenth Century* (1989). Cloth ISBN 0-8420-2331-3 Paper ISBN 0-8420-2332-1

David G. LaFrance, *The Mexican Revolution in Puebla, 1908–1913: The Maderista Movement and the Failure of Liberal Reform* (1989). ISBN 0-8420-2293-7

Mark A. Burkholder, *Politics of a Colonial Career: José Baquíjano and the Audiencia of Lima* (1990). Cloth ISBN 0-8420-2353-4 Paper ISBN 0-8420-2352-6

Kenneth M. Coleman and George C. Herring, eds. (with Foreword by Daniel Oduber), *Understanding the Central American Crisis: Sources of Conflict, U.S. Policy, and Options for Peace* (1991). Cloth ISBN 0-8420-2382-8   Paper ISBN 0-8420-2383-6

Carlos B. Gil, ed., *Hope and Frustration: Interviews with Leaders of Mexico's Political Opposition* (1991). Cloth ISBN 0-8420-2395-X Paper ISBN 0-8420-2396-8

Charles Bergquist, Gonzalo Sánchez, and Ricardo Peñaranda, eds., *Violence in Colombia: The Contemporary Crisis in Historical Perspective* (1991). Cloth ISBN 0-8420-2369-0   Paper ISBN 0-8420-2376-3

Heidi Zogbaum, *B. Traven: A Vision of Mexico* (1992). ISBN 0-8420-2392-5

Jaime E. Rodríguez O., ed., *Patterns of Contention in Mexican History* (1992). ISBN 0-8420-2399-2

Louis A. Pérez, Jr., ed., *Slaves, Sugar, and Colonial Society: Travel Accounts of Cuba, 1801–1899* (1992). Cloth ISBN 0-8420-2354-2 Paper ISBN 0-8420-2415-8